CREATIVITY and PERVERSION

JANINE CHASSEGUET-SMIRGEL

CREATIVITY
and
PERVERSION

Foreword by Otto Kernberg

Free Association Books
London

First published in Great Britain in 1985 by
FREE ASSOCIATION BOOKS
57 Warren Street, London W1P 5PA

First American edition 1984
W.W. Norton & Company, Inc.
500 Fifth Avenue, New York, NY 10110

Reprinted 1988, 1992, 1998

© Janine Chasseguet-Smirgel 1984

A CIP catalogue record for this book is available
from the British Library

ISBN 0 946960 08 9 pbk

Printed and bound by Antony Rowe Ltd, Eastbourne

CONTENTS

	Acknowledgements	vi
	Foreword by Otto Kernberg	vii
1	Perversion and the Universal Law	1
2	Perversion as Exemplified by Three 'Luciferian' Characters	13
3	Narcissism and Perversion	24
4	A Re-reading of 'Little Hans'	35
5	A Re-reading of 'The Wolf Man'	44
6	Narcissism and Group Psychology	55
7	A Psychoanalytic Study of 'Falsehood'	66
8	Reflections on Fetishism	79
9	Aestheticism, Creation and Perversion	89
10	Construction in Analysis and Psychic Construction	101
11	On the Therapeutic Alliance and 'Pervert' Patients	109
12	Some Reflections on the 'Perverse' Way of Thinking	120
13	A Clinical Account: Rrose Sélavy	131
14	A Metapsychological Study of Perversions	146
	Notes on Sources	160
	Bibliography	161
	Index	167

ACKNOWLEDGEMENTS

I wish to express my gratitude to Sir James Lighthill, Provost of University College, London, and to the members of the Board of Management of the Freud Chair, who gave me the marvellous opportunity of teaching and exchanging ideas with the students of the University. I wish also to thank Professor Richard Wollheim, who guided my first steps in this adventure. My thanks go also to Robert Young—my editor, who happened to be a member of my audience—for his confidence in this book, and to his intelligent and lively team. And last but not least, I want to convey my thanks to the patients I speak of in this book for the fascinating things they were generous enough to tell me.

Janine Chasseguet-Smirgel

FOREWORD

This book is a most welcome breakthrough in the language barrier that has separated the original and exciting French contributions of Janine Chasseguet-Smirgel from the English-speaking psychoanalytic community. It also gives the reader a comprehensive view of Chasseguet-Smirgel's theoretical frame, her creative exploration of the intersection of some of the most challenging and complex areas of psychoanalytic inquiry: perversion, narcissism and aggression, particularly as these relate to artistic creativity, group psychology and political ideology.

Creativity and Perversion starts with a re-examination of Freud's concept of perversion. The author develops a subtle yet revolutionary theory of what is implied by the splitting of the Ego in perversion. In the area of denial of reality, Chasseguet-Smirgel expands Freud's concept of the denial of castration into denial of the differences between the sexes and the generations. This understanding of denial facilitates understanding the regressed, sadistically infiltrated fantasy world of the anal structure of perversion and its clinical ramifications, as well as its ramifications in the field of group psychology and political ideology.

Within the Ego segment of recognition of reality in the perverse patient, Chasseguet-Smirgel describes the idealization of derivatives of the anal-sadistic phase that emerge as concerns with aestheticism and may evolve into the idealization of falsity, as in the case of impostors. What remains repressed are the more primitive expressions of direct anal fantasies, fears and conflicts and, on a still deeper level, the Oedipus Complex and its related acknowledgment of sexual and generational differences. Oedipally based, authentic creativity also remains under repression.

Chasseguet-Smirgel questions Freud's theory of phallic monism as the basis of infantile sexuality. In a scholarly re-examination of Freud's writings, particularly a retracing of his clinical cases of Little Hans and the Wolf Man, Chasseguet-Smirgel provides persuasive arguments for an early, possibly innate conception of the vagina as the female sexual organ in parallel with the conception of the penis as the male sexual organ. Behind the image of the phallic mother lurks the image of the mother whose vagina can only be penetrated and filled by the powerful penis of the father. The little boy needs to deny the insufficiency of his small penis in competing with his father's. Castration anxiety becomes condensed with the narcissistic trauma of this recognition and encourages the temptation to regress to an anal world in which faeces become equivalent to the penis, genital and age differences no longer count, and a generalized equalization of all objects signals a perverse transmutation of internal reality. Quantitative elements may influence the balance between (1) the normal developmental striving toward recognition of the differences of sexes and generations, the transformation of the pre-Oedipal Ego Ideal into the Oedipal one and (2) a regressive avoidance of Oedipal conflicts by building up a world of anal fantasies, idealization, and denial. This world goes hand in hand with regressive reinvestment of the maternal Ego Ideal and fantasied refusion between that Ego Ideal and the Ego, leading to the consolidation of narcissistic and perverse psychopathology.

In drawing upon the work of Béla Grunberger on narcissism, Joyce McDougall's analysis of fetishism, Didier Anzieu's work on regression in small groups, and a vast range of both French and English psychoanalytic literature on perversion in the last two decades, Chasseguet-Smirgel presents a rich and evocative picture of the clinical implications of perverse structure, the consequences of these patients' anal-sadistic world for their transference developments and countertransference, and for the formulation of psychoanalytic interventions in these cases. She describes, for example, the countertransference reactions typically induced by patients who cannot tolerate the psychoanalytic situation as a 'transitional space' in Winnicott's sense. These patients' capacity for engaging in fantasy and in emotional exploration of their internal world collapses, and they unconsciously wish to destroy the psychoanalytic situation as a symbolic replica of the Oedipal couple. Their unconscious efforts to sterilize the psychoanalytic situation are the expression of the wishful, fantasied destruction of both parental imagoes in the primal scene and of the potential creation of a new reality—the analytic 'baby'. This example also illustrates the relation between perverse structure and 'perversity' in thinking, as well as Chasseguet-Smirgel's general approach in linking Ego functions, internalized object relations and structuralization of unconscious instinctual fantasies.

Creativity and Perversion reflects contemporary psychoanalytic thinking in France at its best. It presents a free and harmonious integration of Ego psychology, object relations theories, and of new ways of exploring the Oedipal situation as a prototypical intrapsychic structure.

The few Chasseguet-Smirgel papers that have been translated over the years have produced an immediate impact: 'Reflections on the Connections between Perversion and Sadism' in the *International Journal of Psychoanalysis* (1978) and 'Perversion and the Universal Law' in the *International Review of Psychoanalysis* (1983). The book she edited, *Female Sexuality*, was translated into English in 1970 and has become a classic. Indeed, it spearheaded a review of psychoanalytic thinking in this area. Her other books are not yet available in English: *Pour une psychanalyse de l'Art et de la Créativité* (1971), *Les Chemins de l'anti-Oedipe* (1974) and *L'Idéal du Moi: Essai psychanalytique sur la maladie d'Idéalité* (1975). Therefore, to have before us Chasseguet-Smirgel's thinking condensed into this book's lecture format is an exhilarating opportunity for becoming acquainted with her examination of vast areas of clinical, theoretical and applied psychoanalysis.

Chasseguet-Smirgel has much to offer, not only to the psychoanalyst and psychoanalytically oriented psychotherapist, but to all professionals and scholars concerned with the interface between psychoanalysis and the social sciences, psychoanalysis and art, and with the psychoanalytic contributions to studies of group psychology and political ideology. *Creativity and Perversion* provides a refreshing and comprehensive overview of Chasseguet-Smirgel's thinking, and it whets one's appetite for more of her untranslated work.

Otto F. Kernberg, M.D.
Medical Director, The New York Hospital-Cornell Medical Center, Westchester Division
Professor of Psychiatry, Cornell University Medical College
Training and Supervising Analyst, Columbia University Center for Psychoanalytic Training and Research

Chapter 1

Perversion and the Universal Law

Man has always endeavoured to go beyond the narrow limits of his condition. I consider that perversion is one of the essential ways and means he applies in order to push forward the frontiers of what is possible and to unsettle reality. I do not see perversions only as disorders of a sexual nature affecting a relatively small number of people, though their role and importance in the socio-cultural field can never be overestimated. I see perversions more broadly, as a dimension of the human psyche in general, a temptation in the mind common to us all. This is one of the theses I wish to uphold.

My studies and my clinical experience have led me to believe that there is a 'perverse core' latent within each one of us that is capable of being activated under certain circumstances. I hope to give you an insight into what I see as the wider implications of something that, at first sight, is merely a deviation—often a picturesque deviation—of sexual behaviour. We may recall, for example, that perversion and perverse behaviour are particularly present at those times in the history of mankind which precede or accompany major social and political upheavals: the Fall of the Roman Empire, as we know, coincided with a widespread decadence of behaviour.

It has become a banality to connect the advent of Nazism with dissolute sexual behaviour, to the extent that several films show the proliferation of transvestite cabarets, just before Hitler's assumption of power. I am thinking, in particular, of 'Cabaret', 'The Serpent's Egg', and also 'The Damned'. In this last, Visconti imagines that the main character indulges in incest with his mother, dresses up as Marlene Dietrich in 'Blue Angel', and rapes a little girl who, as a result, commits suicide. This is a hint at Matriosha's rape and suicide in 'The Devils' (1873). Dostoievski's Stavroguine belongs to a party of Russian Nihilists. As a matter of fact, Dostoievski was really describing the Netchaiev Group. As for the works of the Marquis de Sade (to which Dostoievski refers, by the way, when Chatov accuses Stavroguine of being a debauchee), they are contemporary with the French Revolution, and the author's life is closely entangled with its significant developments.

A first hypothesis then comes to mind: shouldn't we associate historical ruptures which give an inkling of the advent of a new world, with the confusion between sexes and generations, peculiar to perversion, as if the hope for a new social and political reality went hand in hand with an attempt at destroying sexual reality and truth?

Now, in my opinion, the Oedipal tragedy arises largely from the *chronological time-lag* that exists between the emergence of the boy's desire for his mother and the attainment of his full genital capacity. This time-lag is the result of a kind of prematurity in the human being, who is at birth less fully developed than animals are. It could even be at the root of the universal taboo of incest, where that which is forbidden is substituted for infantile impotence. (I refer here to certain concepts put forward by Béla Grunberger.) The bedrock of reality is created by the difference between the sexes and the difference between generations: the inevitable period of time separating a child from his mother (for whom he is an inadequate sexual partner) and from his father (whose potent adult sexual organ he does not possess). When the child comes to recognize the complementary nature of his parents' genitality, he is reduced to feelings of his own smallness and inadequacy. Recognition of the difference between the sexes is thus bound up with recognition of the difference between the generations.

The perverse temptation leads one to accept pregenital desire and satisfactions (attainable by the small boy) as being equal to or even superior to genital desires and satisfactions (attainable only by the father). Erosion of the double difference between the sexes and the generations is the pervert's objective. He is generally helped to reach it by his mother who, by her seductive attitude towards him and her corresponding rejection of his father, fosters in him the illusion that he has neither to grow up nor to reach maturity, thereby taking his father as a model in order to be her satisfactory partner.

The Anal-Sadistic Universe and Perversion

Regression to the anal-sadistic phase brings about the erosion of the double difference between the sexes and the generations, of all differences in fact, and this regression seems to me to be substantially the same as perversion. In some of my other works I have had occasion to turn to the author best placed to reveal the very essence of anality and sadism, the Marquis de Sade himself. In particular, I have made a study of the Sadian setting but I shall not return to that aspect here. Instead, I should like to examine in some detail the outcome of the process that goes on in the place I have likened to the digestive tract.

Sexual intercourse is naturally the theme present throughout this work. In Sade, it is always a group activity in which protagonists—building up extremely complex positions which are then unmade and transformed—are men and women, children and old people, virgins and whores, nuns and bawds, mothers and sons, fathers and daughters, brothers and sisters, uncles and nephews, noblemen and rabble. 'All will be higgledy-piggledy, all will wallow, on the flagstones, on the earth, and, like animals, will interchange, will mix, will commit incest, adultery and sodomy.' Such is one of the precepts of the 'Code of Laws' of *The 120 Days...* (p. 56).

Sometimes the differences between sexes and ages would be abolished in an obvious way: one of the 'ceremonies' in *The 120 Days...* takes the form of marriages arranged between children: 'Both were extraordinarily arrayed in the most formal dress, but also reversedly, that is to say, the little boy was costumed as a girl, the little girl wore boy's clothes' (p. 148). And likewise: 'That evening, the Bishop, in the guise of a woman, marries Antinoüs, whose role is that of a husband, and then, as a man he weds Celadon, whose role is that of a girl.' Antinoüs and Celadon are both children. Again, Noirceuil says to Juliette:

> For a long time I have been beset by a most extraordinary fantasy, Juliette, and I have been looking forward to your return, as you are the only person in the world with whom I can indulge it. I wish to get married twice in the same day: at ten in the morning I shall dress as a woman and marry a man; at noon, I shall dress as a man and marry a male homosexual in the guise of a woman. And in addition to this... I want a woman to do the same thing: and what woman other than you could indulge this fantasy? You must dress up as a man and marry a female homosexual at the same service in which I, as a woman, will be marrying a man; and then, you as a woman, will marry another female homosexual dressed as a man, while I, having put on clothes befitting my sex, will wed, as a man, a male homosexual dressed up as a girl (*Story of Juliette*, 9, p. 569).

A permutation of the erotogenic zones and their functions also takes place and has the effect of making them interchangeable. 'Mixture' could be considered the heading under which the whole of Sade's fantasy world is placed.

It is clear that, for Sade, incest is in no way connected with assuaging a deep longing for the Oedipal object, but it is linked with the abolition of 'children' as a category and 'parents' as a category. Expressed in more general terms, the pleasure connected with transgression is sustained by the fantasy that—in breaking down the barriers which separate man from woman, child from adult, mother from son, daughter from father, brother from sister, the erotogenic zones from each other, and, in the case of murder, the molecules in the body from each other—it has destroyed reality, thereby creating a new one, that of the anal universe where all differences are abolished.

This, in essence, is the universe of the *sacrilege*. All that is taboo, forbidden or sacred is devoured by the digestive tract, an enormous grinding machine disintegrating the molecules of the mass thus obtained in order to reduce it to excrement. The erotogenic zones and differents parts of the body become interchangeable and are metamorphosed by a kind of diabolical surgery. In *The New Justine* there are, in fact, two sadistic surgeons, Rombeau and Rodin. Rodin will kill his daughter by taking out her womb. This is a demiurgic fantasy, of which I shall have more to say. The Sadian hero puts himself in the position of God, and becomes, through a process of destruction, the creator of a new kind of reality.

I think it appropriate to quote a number of Sadian assertions on murder. At first sight, they would appear to be based on commonplace materialistic arguments. But on giving the matter more thought, we discover they are central to the understanding of Sade, sadism and perversion in general. Rombeau, discussing murder with Rodin, talks of 'these portions of disorganized matter we throw into the crucible of Nature, afford her the pleasure of creating anew, under different forms' (p. 263). Now we have Bressac, talking to Justine:

> The power of destruction is not given to man; the most he can do is to vary the forms, but he hasn't the power to annihilate them. Now all forms are equal in the eyes of Nature; nothing is lost in the gigantic cauldron in which her variations are produced; every piece of matter that falls into it constantly springs forth in other guises. And of what significance is it to her creative hand if this piece of flesh, which today conforms to the shape of a two-legged creature, is tomorrow brought forth as a thousand different insects? (*The New Justine*, 6, p. 202).

Sade endlessly reiterates these ideas, and you can find dozens of examples in his work.

I think this recurring theme of the changing of forms—of man's ability not to annihilate things but to dissolve and metamorphose them after breaking down the molecules—means that all things must revert to chaos, the original chaos that may be identified with excrement. The materialistic reasoning of Sade when he speaks of the equality of man with an oyster, the equality of all human beings, the equality of Good and Evil, the equality of death and life and his denial of the body-soul dualism—ideas inherent in his 'philosophical' arguments—reveals but one basic intention: to reduce the universe to faeces, or rather to annihilate the universe of differences (the genital universe) and put in its place the anal universe in which all particles are equal and interchangeable. The birth of the human as a helpless infant causes the human young to be dependent on the object for survival.

Now this state of helplessness, distress and dependence is openly denied by Sade. Here, for instance, is a fragment of Bressac's conversation with Justine, before he slays his own mother:

...The creature I am destroying is my mother; so it is from this standpoint that we shall examine murder... The child is born; the mother feeds it. In performing this service for the child, we may be sure she (the mother) is directed by a natural feeling that prompts her to get rid of a secretion that might otherwise prove dangerous for her. Thus it is not the mother who is doing the child a service when she feeds him: on the contrary, it is the child who is performing a service for his mother... What! Must I owe a person something for doing me a favour I could perfectly well do without, something that fulfils a need in him alone? So it is clear that, on every occasion in life a child finds himself in a position to dispose of his mother, he should do so without the slightest scruple; he should even do so purposefully, because he cannot but hate such a woman, and revenge is the fruit of hate, and murder, the means of revenge. So let him pitilessly slay this creature to whom he wrongfully imagines he owes so much; let him, without consideration, tear apart this breast that has suckled him (*The New Justine*, pp. 209-10).

We have seen how Sade endlessly repeats the idea that Nature might be a crucible, a melting-pot, that is, the pot in which the chemical fusion of substances takes place. The Sadian hero identifies with her, a cruel and almighty mother, taking over the role of the originator of all creation, that of God himself. For this destruction represents the creation of a new dimension where undifferentiation, confusion and chaos prevail. The Sadian hero actually becomes the grinding machine, the cauldron in which the universe will be dissolved. 'Would that some mechanic might discover a machine that would pulverize the world, he alone would deserve gratitude from Nature, since Nature's hand is impatient to recreate a work... that has failed at the first attempt' (The monk, Clement, to Justine, in *The New Justine*, p. 402). And: 'One day, as I beheld the Etna, whose breast spewed forth flames, I wished I could become this famous volcano. "Mouth of Hell", I cried, as I considered it, "if, like you, I could flood all the towns round about me, what tears I could cause to be shed" ' (Jerome, another monk, in *The New Justine*, p. 45).

Taking over the role of Creator by bringing about the anal universe implies the dethronement of the Creator. Many pages, especially in *Justine* and *Juliette*, are concerned with atheistic professions of faith accompanied by insults and blasphemies towards God: 'God is shallow and ridiculous... We have nothing but contempt for this God you are foolish enough to believe in... He is a creature of the imagination' (in *The New Justine*, p. 130). 'Oh!

Justine, how I loathe and detest this idea of God!' (p. 193). God is an 'idiot', a 'baby's rattle', an 'unworthy phantom', a 'powerless, sterile illusion', a 'bizarre and disgusting idol', a 'bloody fool', a 'deified knave', a 'cunning impostor', a 'fool', a 'base character', etc.

However, following the logic of the principle that requires everything to return to a state of confusion, God himself must undergo a transmutation and become faecal matter. When Bressac tries to convince Justine of 'the deception and stupidity of religion (in *The New Justine*, p. 179), he comes to a point when he tells her:

> ... This great God, the Creator of all we see, will deign to descend 10 or 12 million times every morning in the form of a piece of dough, to be digested by the faithful and soon to be transformed in their intestines into the vilest excrement... and man will eat and defecate his God, because his God is good, and He is omnipotent (p. 190).

For the Sadian hero it is a matter of reaching a state of complete merging, involving the modification of the order of Creation, the suppression of any notion of organization, structure, or division. It implies doing violence to Nature, eradicating the essence of things, and thus instituting the *absolute mixture*. Let us not forget that *The 120 Days...* are considered to be 'a catalogue of perversions', and the fact that perversions are intimately connected with actual sadism, as the need to abolish the (genital) universe of difference and thus subvert reality, means that perversion is inevitably sadistic. The abolition of differences prevents psychic suffering at all levels: feelings of inadequacy, castration, loss, absence and death no longer exist. I should like to show how this universe is contrary in every detail to the one described in that text on which our Judaeo-Christian civilization is based.

The Forbidden Mixture: Hubris and Hybrid

First of all I should like to remind you of some well-known passages from the Bible which, in *The Manual of Instruction in the Israelite Religion*, edited by the Grand Rabbi A. Deutsch (1977), are quoted as examples of the 'forbidden mixture'. Let us take first the famous commandment: 'Thou shalt not seethe a kid in his mother's milk.' This commandment is repeated several times in the *Tora* (Exodus XXIII:19, Exodus XXIV:26, Deuteronomy XIV:21).

Psychoanalysts usually read into this a formulation of the law against incest (the mother and the child being united by the same substance, milk). But an article called 'Prohibitions Against Simultaneous Consumption of Milk and Flesh in Orthodox Jewish Law' by Woolf (1945) goes a step further than this first approximation, and puts forward hypotheses which are, in my opinion, more

Perversion and the Universal Law

complete and more convincing. The author, basing his argument on a series of documents, points out that seething the kid in his mother's milk formed part of the worship of Astarte: '... That seething the kid in his mother's milk means placing the child back in its mother's belly, giving it into the full and undivided possession of the mother. The son belongs to the mother.' The Biblical Commandment would represent an attempt to destroy the matriarchal law. Consequently, the quality of isolation that characterises ritual Jewish eating habits would be the result of the struggle of Jewish monotheism against the paganism all around it, a struggle not only of an external nature, but of an intra-psychic one as well. This hypothesis confronts us with the fact that 'the mixture' (milk and meat) implies the exclusion of the father, in favour of the union between the mother and the child.

In Leviticus XIX:19, the Almighty says: 'Ye shall keep my statutes. Thou shalt not let thy cattle gender with a diverse kind; thou shalt not sow thy field with mingled seed; neither shall a garment mingled of linen and wool come upon thee.' In Leviticus XVIII:6-18, the Almighty lists the commandments more closely connected with incest. However, I should point out that the aim of all these commandments is to prevent the breaking down of the barriers which ensure that the essential nature of things is preserved:

> 6—None of you shall approach anyone that is near of kin to him to uncover their nakedness: I am the Lord.
> 7—The nakedness of thy father, or the nakedness of thy mother, shalt thou not uncover: she is thy mother; thou shalt not uncover her nakedness.
> 8—The nakedness of thy father's wife shalt thou not uncover: it is thy father's nakedness.
> 9—The nakedness of thy sister, the daughter of thy father, or daughter of thy mother, whether she be born at home, or born abroad, even their nakedness thou shalt not uncover.
> 10—The nakedness of thy son's daughter, or of thy daughter's daughter, even their nakedness thou shalt not uncover: for theirs is thine own nakedness.
> 11—The nakedness of thy father's wife's daughter, begotten of thy father, she is thy sister, thou shalt not uncover her nakedness.
> 12—Thou shalt not uncover the nakedness of thy father's sister: she is thy father's near kinswoman.
> 13—Thou shalt not uncover the nakedness of thy mother's sister: for she is thy mother's near kinswoman.
> 14—Thou shalt not uncover the nakedness of thy father's brother, thou shalt not approach his wife: she is thine aunt.
> 15—Thou shalt not uncover the nakedness of thy daughter-in-law; she is thy son's wife; thou shalt not uncover her nakedness.
> 16—Thou shalt not uncover the nakedness of thy brother's wife;

it is thy brother's nakedness.

17—Thou shalt not uncover the nakedness of a woman and her daughter, neither shalt thou take her son's daughter, or her daughter's daughter, to uncover her nakedness; for they are her near kinswomen; it is wickedness.

18—Neither shalt thou take a woman as a rival wife to her sister, to vex her, to uncover her nakedness, beside the other in her life time.

Verses 20-23 forbid adultery, the sacrifice of children to Moloch, homosexuality, intercourse of a man or a woman with an animal. We notice that this catalogue of commandments (a negative catalogue) corresponds almost exactly to the catalogue of transgressions (a positive catalogue) contained in the work of the Marquis de Sade, specifically in *The 120 Days...* Let us take, for example, 'Passion' number 20 of the 3rd part (the 'Passions' are numbered after the fashion of verses in the Bible). We find here the coalescence of several Biblical prohibitions: 'In order to combine incest, adultery, sodomy and sacrilege he embuggers his married daughter with a host.'

We notice that Biblical prohibitions are based on a principle of division and separation. In pathology this quality appears as an isolation mechanism at the root of obsessional neurosis. We know that in this kind of neurosis anal-sadistic regression has replaced genitality, but that anal driving forces are subject to very intense defence techniques. Freud (*Inhibition, Symptoms and Anxiety*, 1926) associates isolation with the taboo of touching and bodily contact, whether it be aggressive or tender, with the object. In passing, I should like to put forward the idea that isolation in obsessional neurosis is a more generalized mechanism that tries to fight off the anal-sadistic desire for muddle and confusion. In this sense, it would take the form of a reaction-formation against the typically perverse ideas of indivisibility and amalgam (the reduction of objects to faeces).

If we turn now to Genesis, we see that it is entirely based on principles of distinction, separation and differentiation: 'In the beginning God created the Heaven and the Earth. And the Earth was without form and void...' God brings order into this original chaos and divides it up:

... And God divided the Light from the Darkness... God said: "Let there be a Firmament in the midst of the waters and let it divide the waters from the waters." And God made the Firmament and divided the waters which were under the Firmament from the waters which were above the Firmament... And God said: "Let the earth bring forth grass, the herb yielding seed and the fruit tree yielding fruit after his kind, whose seed is in itself, upon the earth": and it was so. And the earth brought forth grass and herb yielding seed after his kind, and the tree yielding fruit, whose seed was in itself, after his kind.

In the passage that follows, the adverbial phrase, 'after their kind', is repeated like a leitmotiv. Now in this differentiation between the species we see no intermingling, or more precisely, an absence of hybridization. The commandment not 'to sow thy field with mingled seed' is also translated as 'hybrid seed'. The close connection between the hybridization of seed, materials or animals is clearly defined in Maimonides' explanation of the Jews being forbidden to use lemons from trees that have been grafted. This was to prevent the orgiastic practices that went on when neighbouring people carried out the grafting: during the ritual a couple would have sexual intercourse that was 'against nature' (Mircea Eliade, *Blacksmiths and Alchemists*, 1956-1977, p. 28). The man who does not respect the law of differentiation challenges God. He creates new combinations of new shapes and new kinds. He takes the place of the Creator and becomes a demiurge. Notice that the word 'hybrid' comes from the Greek 'hubris', which means violence, excess, extremeness, outrageousness. 'Hubris' is for the Greeks, we know, the greatest sin. 'And ye shall be as gods', the serpent said to Eve (Genesis III:5).

In Greek, the original meaning of 'nomos', the law, is 'that which is divided up into parts'. Thus we find that the principle of separation is the foundation of the law. This leads to derivations which seem to have only a remote connection with the word: 'musical mode', for example, and 'song'. We can understand the connection better if we take the meaning of 'anomos', 'without laws', which gives us 'without rhythm', and 'a tune that isn't a tune'. A further meaning of 'nomos' (the accent being on the second syllable) is 'division of land', 'province', 'pasture', 'grazing land', i.e., direct applications of the principle of separation (Bailly Dictionary). The noun has much in common with the law, considered as separation, division. It is a part of speech which names a person, place or thing, that is to say, which takes it out of chaos and confusion and gives it definition. In fact, Genesis relates the Story of Creation not merely as a time of separating and dividing, but—and, in my opinion, this comes to the same thing—one of naming. In verse 5, it says: 'God called the light "Day" and the darkness He called "Night".' When He made the firmament (verse 7), 'God called the firmament "Heaven" ' (verse 8), etc. Anomie, on the other hand, implies confusion and lack of differentiation in values.

We know Freud compared obsessional neurosis with a private religion (Compulsive Acts and Religious Exercises, 1907). I would like to put forward the hypothesis here that perversion is the equivalent of Devil religion. Indeed I am borrowing Freud's words on the subject:

I have an idea shaping in my mind that, in the perversions of which hysteria is the negative, we may have before us a residue of a primaeval sexual cult which, in the Semitic East (Moloch, Astarte) was once, perhaps still is, a religion... Perverse actions are always the same—with a meaning and made on some pattern which it will be possible to understand. I dream, therefore, of a primaeval Devil religion, whose rites are carried on secretly, and I understand the severe therapy of the witch's judges (Letter to Fliess, 24 January 1897, p. 243).

The Devil has obvious anal characteristics, but I have dealt with the regressive anal-sadistic element in perversion sufficiently to go on to look at another aspect of the Devil: as the rival of God. The Devil is a fallen angel who revolted against God. He is also called Lucifer—a name that only appeared in the 4th century. Lucifer is a perfect example of Hubris, of man's desire to discredit the power of the Father-Creator, and put himself in His place.

Now it is perfectly clear that the pervert in general, and Sade in particular, sets out, consciously or unconsciously, to make a mockery of the law by turning it 'upside down'. As a consequence teachers, charged with 'bringing up' the child, will be, on the contrary, the means of his intiation into debauchery. The culmination of the deviation of the role of educator comes in 'Philosophy in the Boudoir' with the sub-title 'or Teachers of Immorality—Dialogues for the Education of Young Ladies'. We know what the aim of the work was: the erotic intiation of a young virgin into group love-making, homosexuality, incest and crime.

In *The New Justine*, it is God Himself who is consulted on sexual pleasures. From the mouth of an effigy of God, there fall rolls of paper on which are written injunctions to carry out such and such debauchery. They shout abuse at God: 'Despicable image of the most ludicrous nonentity, you, who are only at home in a bawdy house and useless, except for regulating the pleasures of the ass.' In *The 120 Days...* 'The Code of Laws' lays down the rules of debauchery. The same sort of thing is found in the statutes of 'The Society of the Friends of Crime'.

Subversion of the law, the parody of a religion devoted to the worship of God, seeks to reverse the way leading from indistinctness to separation and demarcation. Here we are very close to the worshippers of Satan and religions of the Devil. A black mass is a parody of the sacrifice of Christ. In it the cross is placed upside down, or facing the wall; the mass is said backwards and the Tetragrammaton is pronounced the wrong way round and is accompanied by sexual orgies. In every case there is a reversal of values leading to a return to primal chaos. In my opinion, this reversal of a system of values is only the first stage in an operation whose end is the destruction of all values.

Down through the ages, philosophies, ideologies, myths and rites have been founded on the belief that we originate from primordial matter from which every other kind of matter will be created. Therefore, the transmutation of one element into another should be possible. This theory is at the centre of the alchemic conception of the world. Here I quote two examples that demonstrate a belief in the possibility of creating a new kind of reality out of original chaos. This belief is linked, sometimes quite openly, with perversion, as in the case of Dionysiac rites involving intersexual disguises. 'Their aim is regression to primordial confusion', writes Mircea Eliade in *Mephistopheles and the Androgyne* (1962, p.141)'...and their goal is the symbolic restoration of "chaos", the state of unity without differentiation that preceded the Creation. This return to confusion manifests itself in a supreme act of regeneration and an enormous increase in power.' The second example is found in the Gospel of Thomas which was popular among the first gnostics. According to it, Christ said: 'When you make two human beings into one, and when you make the inside as the outside, and the outside as the inside and the top as the bottom! And if you make the male and the female into one so that the male is no longer male and the female no longer female, then you will enter into the Kingdom.'

My hypothesis is that perversion represents a similar reconstitution of Chaos, out of which there arises a new kind of reality, that of the anal universe. This will take the place of the psycho-sexual genital dimension, that of the Father. The world of division and separation presupposes a three-dimensional psyche: between mother and son, the Father-Creator (but in fact, reality itself) introduces a barrier, that of incest. Jeremiah describes it in the Bible in a beautiful metaphor: 'Will ye not tremble at my presence, which have placed the sand for the bound of the sea by a perpetual decree, that it cannot pass it? (Jeremiah V:22). This boundary or barrier is the prototype of all 'bounds' or barriers and, consequently, of all differences.

I would like to point out that at a certain level the anal-sadistic universe of confusion and homogenization constitutes an imitation or parody of the genital universe of the father. In fact, one could say that it appears in the history of the development of the individual as a preliminary sketch, a rough draft of genitality. It is only later on in life that it becomes an imitation of it. Freud's article, 'On Transformations of Instinct, as Exemplified in Anal Eroticism' (1917), is quite clear on this subject. In it the anal-sadistic phase appears not as just a specific mode of pregenital organization, but as a sort of protogenitality or pseudo-genitality in which objects, erotogenic sources and pleasures are adapted to the child's potential—contrary to objects, erotogenic zones and gratifications of a genital nature. According to Freud, the faecal mass or 'stick' foreshadows the genital penis, the production of stools becomes a prototype of childbirth (the infantile sexual theory of giving birth through the anus), the daily separation from the faeces is a precursor of castration, and excrement in the rectum anticipates genital coitus. So if, in the course of development, the anal-sadistic phase represents a sort of 'trial gallop' on the part of the child towards adult genitality, to then try to replace genitality by the stage that normally precedes it is to defy reality. It is an attempt to substitute a world of sham and pretence for reality. 'The Planet of the Apes' takes the place of a human world.

It is not my intention to condemn perversion any more than to sing its praises. I simply wish to put it in a more general context than that in which it is usually seen: that of man's attempts to escape from his condition. The pervert is trying to free himself from the paternal universe and the constraints of the law. He wants to create a new kind of reality and to dethrone God the Father: 'Yes, we are gods', says one of the Marquis de Sade's heroes (Saint-Fond). I have also implicitly tried to show that ethics and the conception of reality were based on a common underlying principle.

Chapter 2

Perversion as Exemplified by Three Luciferian Characters

I have already counterposed the universe of perversion — that of mixture — to the Biblical universe, which is both the basis and the expression of our ethic. This world, as distinct from the pervert's, is that of division and separation. By perversion, I had in view a universal human temptation, going beyond the limits of sexual deviation, strictly defined. At the same time, I tried to show that the pervert attempts to take the Father-Creator's place in order to make a new universe from chaos and mixture, a universe where anything becomes possible, and towards which he tends to return. Differences having been abolished, the feelings of helplessness, smallness, inadequacy, as well as absence, castration and death—psychic pain itself—also disappear.

The model of the demiurgic character trying to dethrone the Father God-Creator is Lucifer. I will now take up three 'Luciferian' characters: a historical one, Caligula (in *Suetonius*, 1, 1964); a character in a science-fiction novel by H.G. Wells, Doctor Moreau (1896); and an artist, Hans Bellmer.

Caligula

Caius Caesar was nicknamed 'Caligula' (Little Boot), as a child, by his father's (Germanicus) soldiers. He had been brought up among the troops and used to dress as a soldier. According to Suetonius, as soon as Caligula was in his teens, 'he could not control his natural cruelty and viciousness: he was a most eager witness of the tortures and executions of those who suffered punishment, revelling at night in gluttony and adultery, disguised in a wig and a long robe, passionately devoted besides to the theatrical arts of dancing and singing' (pp. 418-19).

He would have poisoned Tiberius, but, as the latter was still breathing, it is said that he throttled him with his own hands. When he became the master of the Empire, he was regarded as the people's long-awaited prince and was called their 'star', their 'chick', their 'babe', and their 'nursling' (p. 421).

... He soon devised a novel and unheard-of kind of **pageant**; for he bridged the gap between Baiae and the mole at Puteoli, a distance of about thirty-six hundred paces, by bringing together merchant ships from all sides and anchoring them in a double line, after which a mound of earth was heaped upon them and fashioned in the manner of the Appian way. Over this bridge he rode back and forth for two successive days... (p. 431).

In Lyons, he inaugurated 'a contest in Greek and Latin oratory, in which they say, the losers gave prizes to the victors and were forced to compose eulogies upon them' (p. 433). He undertook all kinds of works, planned to build a town at the top of the Alps and to pierce the isthmus of Corinth. 'So much for Caligula as an Emperor, we must now tell his career as a monster' (p. 435), Suetonius continues.

Signs of Caligula's monstrous character, of his hubris are already obvious in his building of a carriageable bridge of ships (a transformation of the intended purpose of things), and the laying down of rules as arbitrary as they were relentless, which placed both victor and vanquished in a monstrous and outrageous relationship. The reversal of values is clearly indicated in the following passage:

> At the plays in the theatre, sowing discord between the commons and the knights, he scattered the gift tickets ahead of time, to induce the rabble to take the seats reserved for the equestrian order. At the gladiatorial show he would sometimes draw back the awnings when the sun was the hottest and give orders that no one be allowed to leave; then removing the usual equipment, he would match worthless and decrepit gladiators against mangy wild beasts, and have sham fights between householders who were of good repute, but conspicuous for some bodily infirmity (p. 447).

Everything happens as if Caligula wanted to modify reality, to transform it to his liking, in the manner of the digestive tract, then the anus, which destroy the differentiated particles in order to amalgamate them in the faecal bolus. Landscapes, rules, bodies are thus ground to bits, then re-moulded. This is even more obvious, in my opinion, through other facts reported by Suetonius: 'Having condemned several Gauls and Greeks to death in a body, he boasted that he had subdued Gallograecia' (p. 451). Thus amalgamating two separate lands, he created solely by his word, a new and chimerical country.

His military expedition is also well-known (his father, Germanicus, was a famous warrior):

> Finally, as if he intended to bring the war to an end, he drew up a line of battle on the shore of the Ocean, arranging his ballistas and other artillery; and when no one knew or could imagine what he was going to do, he suddenly bade them gather shells and fill their helmets and the fold of their gowns, calling them ''Spoils of the Ocean, due to the Capitol and Palatine'' (p. 475).

No matter for my subject whether it is true or not that, according to Suetonius, he wanted to appoint his horse Consul. To ascribe such an action to Caligula reveals a profound intuition of his demiurgic character.

He tried to lower and humiliate the great. He obliged the senators who had exercised the highest magistratures

> to run in their togas for several miles besides his chariot and to wait on him at table, standing napkin in hand either at the head of his couch, or at his feet. Others he secretly put to death, yet continued to send for them as if they were alive, after a few days falsely asserting that they had committed suicide (p. 445).
>
> He assailed mankind of almost every epoch with no less envy and malice than insolence and cruelty. He threw down the statues of famous men, which for lack of room Augustus had moved from the Court of the Capitol to the Campus Martius and so utterly demolished them that they could not be set up again with their entire inscriptions (p. 457).

The spirit of 'hubris' and 'hybridization' may also induce the reversal of roles: 'Once when he stood by the altar dressed as a popa [pagan Roman priest] and a victim was brought up, he raised his mallet on high and slew the culturarius' (p. 455). However, it is the following reflection of Suetonius which best brings out Caligula's actually 'Luciferian' character, his desire to borrow from God (from the gods?) his (or their) creative powers: 'Caring for nothing so much as to do what men said was impossible. So he built moles out into the deep and stormy sea, tunnelled rocks out of the hardest flint, built up plains to the height of mountains and razed mountains to the level of the plain' (p. 463).

To carry out what is supposed to be impossible, to create a new reality, to level all differences, to establish novel relationships between men, to amalgamate objects which are not made to be together, to deviate the purpose of substances, ideas and things, these are the tyrant's passion and aim. Caligula's hubris comes out to the full in his relationship to the gods:

> But on being reminded that he had risen above the elevation both of princes and kings, he began from that time on to lay claim to divine majesty; for after giving orders that such statues of the gods especially famous for their artistic merit, including that of Jupiter of Olympia, should be brought from Greece in order to remove their heads and put his own in their place... and making the temple of Castor and Pollux his vestibule, he often took his place between the divine brethren, and exhibited himself to be worshipped by those who presented themselves. And some hailed him as Jupiter Latians (p. 437).

Flavius Josephus in his *Ancient History of the Jews* (A.D. 66-67), writes that Caligula sent Petronius to Jerusalem (then occupied by the Romans) with an army with the strict order to place his own statues in the Temple, to kill all the Jews who dared oppose it and to subdue the rest of the people. Caligula was killed before he succeeded in carrying out his plan.

Caligula's life of debauchery is well-known. Let me, however, evoke some features which have the same obvious purpose of mixing and twisting reality, as in his actions in general — only apparently dissociated from his sexuality. 'He lived in habitual incest with all his sisters, and at a large banquet he placed each of them in turn below him, while his wife reclined above' (p. 441). He deflowered his sister Drusila; then, when she became a married woman, he abducted her and treated her publicly as his wife. When she died he made a Diva out of her. As for his other sisters, he 'prostituted them to his favourites' (p. 441). He had a mistress, Caesonia, whom he exhibited, naked, to his friends. He fell madly in love with a mime and also with various hostages.

> In his clothing, his shoes, and the rest of his attire, he did not follow the usage of his country and of his fellow-citizens; not always even that of his sex; or in fact, that of an ordinary mortal. He often appeared in public in embroidered cloaks covered with precious stones, with a long-sleeved tunique and bracelets, sometimes in silk and in a woman's robe... But oftentimes he exhibited himself with a golden beard, holding in his hand a thunderbolt, a trident or a caduceus, emblems of the gods, and even in the garb of Venus' (p. 485).

(It is obvious, here, that to become a god and to change one's sex is one and the same manifestation of hubris.)

So cruelty, exactions, depravation, incest, parricide, inverted sexuality, transvestism and murder marked Caligula's short reign (from A.D. 37 to 41). It ended with the assassination of Caligula. The plot was conducted by Cherea. 'For Caius used to taunt him, a man already well on in years, by every form of insult, as being a voluptuous and effeminate man... When Cherea had occasions to thank him for anything, he would hold out his hand to kiss, forming and moving it in an obscene fashion.'

Albert Camus devoted a short play to Caligula. This play written in 1938, was performed in 1945. In his 'Carnets' (in *Albert Camus—Récits, Théâtre, Nouvelles*, 1967), Camus describes the scene between the popa and the culturarius and places these words into Caligula's mouth:

> For once, I wanted to change the course of nature, in order to check what I know: nothing would change. The bystanders were a bit surprised and afraid. As for the rest, the sun set as usual. I inferred there from that changing the course of nature made no

difference. But why wouldn't the sun rise in the West for once?

The dream of Camus' Caligula is to catch the moon. According to Camus, Caligula would have been impassioned for what is impossible:

Caligula: I'm not mad; in fact, I've never felt so lucid. I suddenly felt a desire for the impossible. That's all. (Pauses.) Things as they are, in my opinion, are far from satisfactory... That's why I want the moon, or happiness, or eternal life—something, in fact, that may sound crazy, but which isn't of this world... I'm exploiting the impossible. Or, more accurately, it's a question of making the impossible possible... And what's the use to me of a firm hand, what use is the amazing power that's mine, if I can't have the sun set in the east, if I can't reduce the sum of suffering and make an end of death?
Caesonia (his old mistress): But that's madness, sheer madness. It's wanting to be a god on earth.
Caligula: I want to drown the sky in the sea, to infuse ugliness with beauty, to wring a laugh from pain.
Caesonia: There's good and bad, high and low, justice and injustice. And I swear to you these will never change.
Caligula: And I'm resolved to change them... I shall make this age of ours a kingly gift—the gift of equality. And when all is levelled out, when the impossible has come to earth and the moon is in my hands—then, perhaps, I shall be transfigured and the world renewed; then men will die no more and at last be happy.

In order to reach this levelling out, enabling him to reach the 'impossible', he will confuse and mix both things and beings. He calls old patricians 'my darling' or 'little girl' and obliges them to draw up their wills in the favour of the State. He decides to have them killed according to an arbitrarily established list. He kills Scipio's father and makes the son his lover etc... To Cherea, who says to him, 'Certainly I believe that some actions are—shall I say?—more praiseworthy than others,' he replies, 'And *I* believe that all are on an equal footing.' The hatred of reality, the fury with which he wants to replace it with a new universe, leads the demiurge to the destruction of the real world. 'I live, I kill, I exercise the rapturous power of a destroyer, compared with which the power of a creator is merest child's-play.' And, a short while before being killed by Cherea and the patricians: 'The impossible! I've searched for it at the confines of the world, in the secret places of my heart.'

To Caligula's hubris, reason is counterposed. Cherea tells him why he wants to kill him: 'I'll be no party to your logic.' When Caligula explains to Scipio that a war would have cost more than his extravagancy, the latter replies: 'But at least there'd be *some* sense behind a war; it would be understandable—and to understand

18 *Creativity and Perversion*

makes up for much.' This gives us to understand that there is no perversion without thought disorder. The laws governing the undifferentiated anal-sadistic universe do not coincide with those governing the genital dimension of psycho-sexuality, which is one with the paternal universe, that of logic.

Doctor Moreau

> For a peculiar lizard which was found by the wine-grower of Belvedere, he made wings from skin torn from other lizards and filled them with quick silver, so that they moved and quivered when it walked. Next he made eyes, a beard and horns for it...
> —Vasari quoted by Freud in 'Leonardo da Vinci and a Memory of his Childhood' 1910, p.127

Elsewhere I have shown that the Sadian setting took place inside the digestive tract and ended in the torturer's rectum, with the victim held fast by the sphincter — immobilized, manipulated and eventually destroyed and expelled. *The Island of Doctor Moreau*, H.G. Wells' novel (1896), seems to represent such a setting. An island is such a closed place, without any issue. That of the well-known novel is, moreover, described as follows:

> It was volcanic in its origin, and was now fringed on three sides by coral reefs. Some fumaroles to the northward, and a hot spring, were the only vestiges of the forces that had long since originated it. Now and then a faint quiver of earthquake would be sensible, and sometimes the ascent of the spire of smoke would be rendered tumultuous by gusts of steam (pp. 120-21).

The place where the Creatures made by Moreau are huddled together and where they learn the Law (that of Moreau) is thus described by the hero:

> It was extremely dark, this passage after the blinding sunlight reflected by the sulphurous ground. Its walls grew steep, and approached one another... I stood in a floor of a chasm which was at first absolutely dark to me... I became aware of a disagreeable odour like that of a monkey's cage ill-cleaned (p. 103).
> The place was a narrow passage between high walls of lava, a crack in its knotted flow and on either side interwoven heaps of sea-mat, palm fans and reeds leaning against the rock, formed rough and impenetrably dark dens. The winding way up the ravine between these, was scarcely three yards wide, and was disfigured by lumps of decaying fruit pulp and other refuse which accounted for the disagreeable stench of the place. (p. 104).

What is going on in that landscape? You remember Doctor

Moreau's horrible activities. He explains:

> You forget all that a skilled vivisector can do with living things... Surgery can do better things than that. It is building up as well as breaking down and changing... A flap of skin is cut from the forehead, turned down on the nose, and heals in the new position. This is a kind of grafting in a new position a part of an animal upon itself (p. 22).
> Grafting of a freshly obtained material from another animal is also possible... Hunter's cockspur—possibly you have heard of that—flourished on the bull's neck. And the rhinoceros rats of the Algerian Zouaves are also to be thought of—monsters manufactured by transferring a slip from the tail of an ordinary rat to its snout, and allowing it to heal in that position... These creatures you have seen are animals carved and wrought into new shapes... To that—to the study of the plasticity of living form—my life has been devoted (p. 113).
> You begin to see that it is a possible thing to transplant tissue from one part of an animal to another or from one animal to another, to alter its chemical reactions and methods of growth, to modify the articulations of its limbs, and indeed to change it in its most intimate structure? (p. 114)

'I wanted—it was the only thing I wanted— to find out the extreme limit of plasticity in a living shape' (p. 116), says Moreau, once again.

I should like to emphasize this neo-creation, that of new forms, of hybrid beings, which takes place in this anus-island. The hero continues: 'In each animal Moreau had blended this animal with that one; one perhaps was ursine chiefly, another feline chiefly, another bovine chiefly; but each was tainted with other creatures—a kind of generalized animalism appeared through specific dispositions' (p. 151). At the bottom of the stinking ravine the hero observes a strange ceremony:

> And then began the insanest ceremony. The voice in the dark began intoning a mad litany, line by line, and I and the rest to repeat it...
> "Not to go on all-fours; *that* is the Law. Are we not Men?"
> "Not to suck up Drink; *that* is the Law. Are we not Men?"...
> We ran through a long list of prohibitions, and then the chant swung round to a new formula:
> "*His* is the House of Pain."
> "*His* is the Hand that makes."
> "*His* is the Hand that wounds."
> "*His* is the Hand that heals... "
> A horrible fancy came into my head that Moreau, after animalizing these men, had infected their dwarfed brains with a kind of deification of himself (p. 105).

When Moreau dies, the hero, in order to prevent the monsters' rebellion, that of the 'Ape-Man', the 'Leopard-Man', the 'Swine-Man', the 'Horse-Rhinoceros', the 'Dog-Man', the 'Bull-Man', the 'Bear-Man', the 'Hyena-Swine' and of a 'particularly hateful (and evil smelling) old Woman made of Vixen and Bear' (p. 122) declares: 'Children of the Law, he is *not* dead... He has changed his shape—he has changed his body... For a time you will not see him. He is... there—I pointed upward ... he can see you' (p. 136). Moreau said to the hero, 'I maybe fancy that I have seen more of the ways of this World's Maker than you—for I have sought his laws in my way, all my life' (p. 115). It is again, like Scipio and Cherea before Caligula, to reason that the hero appeals, a reason waning before 'a blind fate, a vast pitiless mechanism, (which) seemed to cut and shape the fabric of existence. I must confess I lost faith in the sanity of the world when I saw it, suffering the painful disorder of this island' (p. 131).

If Caligula's hubris is openly associated with perverse sexuality, Moreau's is not obviously sexualized. Without exhaustively discussing this problem, we may suppose that from the demiurge's instinct of mastery originates a sexual excitation linked to the intensity of hubris, to the excess, to the outrageousness. (I am not speaking of sadism because it would suppose that the problem of sexualization had already been solved.) This involves a necessary phenomenon of sexual excitation which turns the instinct of mastery into sadism (Freud, *Three Essays...*, 1905, p. 105).

Hans Bellmer

> Has not another time a diabolical anatomist put me into pieces as an articulated doll destined to be used for all kinds of hellish experiences, wanting to see, for example, what impression would be made if one of my feet were planted in the middle of my neck, or my right arm fixed along my left leg?'
> —Hoffman, 'The Magnetizer'

It is in Germany in 1933 that Hans Bellmer created 'The Doll'. Constantin Jelinski, writing on it, says: 'It is a fetish, an idol' and calls its maker a 'demiurge': 'Disarticulated, placed in a doorway, its limbs scattered over a bed, or reduced to a pair of legs, set off with lace, The Doll, embodied fancy, seems as Olympia to escape the will of its demiurge' (*Les dessins de Hans Bellmer*, 1966).

Jean Brun had the intuition that the Doll is a product whose aim is to dethrone the father and his (genital) begetting capacities. Brun writes:

> The engineer's tool (Hans Bellmer's father was an engineer), so familiar that it made the son sick, is then used in an irremediably

compromising way. The father is vanquished. He sees his son holding a hand-drill, securing a dolly's head between his brother's knees, and telling him: "Hold on to her for me, I've got to pierce her nostrils." Pallid, the father goes out, while the son eyes this daughter, now breathing as it is forbidden to do' (p. 7).

'To adjust the hinges', writes Hans Bellmer (in 'La poupée' 1934),

> to extract from the spheres and their radii the image of children's attitudes, to gently follow the valley-contours, to relish the curves and to shed—not without resentment—the acrid taste of deformation. And finally to refrain from standing still before the inner mechanism, to peel away the little girls' secret thoughts, and make visible, preferably through the navel, the very bottom of these thoughts: a panorama disclosed in the depths of the belly by means of multicoloured electric lighting. Isn't that the solution? (*Obliques*, 1975).

In 1937 Bellmer builds a second Doll, 'challenging nature: around the central sphere, two pelvises could be hinged, two pairs of legs, whereas the pelvis itself, being reversible may evoke at will, the upper part of the thighs or the breasts, crowned or not by a head.' 'At that moment, I had materialized what is impossible' (Constantin Jelenski). In 1957, Hans Bellmer wrote 'L'anatomie de l'image' ('The Anatomy of the Image'). He explained in a letter to a friend that, in assembling doll's parts, or more or less complete ones, he experienced 'the unleashing of a matchless pleasure, eventually comparable with that felt by he who finds the treasure he had feverishly pursued for twenty or thirty years' (*Obliques*). In the *Anatomy of the Image*, Bellmer writes this sentence, often quoted:

> According to our intact memory of a photographic document, a man, so as to transform his victim, had securely tied up her thighs, shoulders, and breast with a taut wire that was haphazardly criss-crossed, thus producing the flesh to swell into irregular spherical triangles, lengthening puckers, dirty lips, multiplying outrageous breasts in unavowable places (quoted by C. Jelenski, p. 19).

In 'Post-scriptum à Oracles et spectacles' ('Postscript to Oracles and Shows' written by Unica Zürn, 1965), Hans Bellmer writes this famous sentence: 'The body can be compared to a sentence inviting one to disarticulate it for its true elements to be recombined in a series of endless anagrams' (*Obliques*, p. 109).

Concerning the body as an anagram, Bellmer says: 'The displacements, the metamorphoses, the impossible permutations. To obtain by mere permutation the sentence: "O rire sous le couteau" (To laugh beneath the knife), starting from the phrase:

"Roses au coeur violet" (Violet-hearted roses) is a miracle!' (*Les dessins de Hans Bellmer*). Hans Bellmer composes the following anagram: Leib (body), Lieb (love), Beil (axe). 'We are seized by the prodigy which carries us away on a broomstick.'

The sadism of these anagrams is striking. But it is also a question of prodigies, miracles, witchcraft. Bellmer's exultation is that of he who has at last found a magical technique to violate stubborn reality, and found the solution, as he himself says of the Doll. This work is fascinating and frightening at the same time. It enables us to understand a more general problem. Why some rigidly cling to order and want 'order at all costs', an attitude which sometimes ends with the return of the repressed, terror and chaos.

The distrust of technique, science and all that is new is sometimes due to a confusion between *magic*, which wants to circumvent reality and create a new one, and *knowledge*, which enables man to actually probe the secrets of 'creation' without intending to deviate its order. Social intolerance towards sexual aberrations has the same origin, whereas we know that a perverse symptom is not sufficient to delimit a whole perverse organization. As such, a perverse sexuality, as long as it does not wrong other people, of course, can be practised freely and is part of individual rights. The affects awakened by perversion may also help us to understand why certain people praise what is new without worrying whether it is beautiful, good, or true, why they long for 'disorder as such', and for anomie, which, think they, will conjure up a new reality.

I find it important that one of our 'Luciferian' characters is a scientist in conflict with another scientist, the hero, and Wells' spokesman, Wells himself being a scientist. When, in 'The Two Principles of Mental Functioning' (1911), Freud studies the substitution of the reality principle for the pleasure principle, he considers the process within the framework of religion, science, education and art. According to him, science is nearest to the triumph of the reality principle over the pleasure principle. The ultimate aim of the scientist suffering from hubris would not be to reach truth (according to the reality principle), but to place his discoveries (and, therefore, reality and truth) in the service of the pleasure principle. For Moreau, it is not a question of penetrating the secrets of nature, as an end in itself and, eventually, to derive from it applications for re-establishing its order ('reparation' would justify the practice of vivisection, for instance). Rather it is a question of subverting the order of nature to create a new reality. Here also, the use of the instinct of mastery goes with a sexualization of the excitations (Moreau speaks of 'strange delights'). We can ask if such a diversion of the scientific process is effectual, which is questionable. The faulty identification with the father—the subject wanting to become God—involves faulty sublimation. This is perfectly obvious in the Nazi physicians' experiments on the persons deported to concentration camps: they did not lead to any valid scientific result.

Nowadays, genetic manipulations fall under suspicion, as they can *actually* give man the Creator's power. Let me put forward the hypothesis that, beyond the undeniable dangers of these new fields of experimentation, it is the very idea that man would thus be able to change the order of nature (the divine order?) that arouses terror. An investigation into what is at stake in a given scientific process enables us to distinguish between hubris and the quest for truth, between a diversion of thought and creative audacity.

On returning to civilization, the hero of *The Island of Doctor Moreau* still felt his reason vacillating. He tried to cling to 'the vast and eternal laws of matter', to the laws of Creation, as we would say, and to science which enables us to lay hands upon the Father's powers in our wishing to identify to him, slow as the process may be, and not to circumvent his prerogatives by substituting a new reality to his. The last words of Wells' hero, after his adventure in the kingdom of hubris, are: 'My days I devote to reading and to chemistry, and I spend many of the clear nights in the study of astronomy. There is, though I do not know how, and where, a sense of infinite peace and protection in the glittering hosts of heaven' (p. 156). Such a sentence is highly reminiscent of Kant's 'Starry Vault Above', the counterpart of the moral law within. This tie between ethics and reality is something which I have already highlighted in Chapter 1.

Chapter 3

Narcissism and Perversion

My approach to perversion embraces the more general problem of its relation to reality and hence to truth. In this chapter I shall not go into all the details of the loss of reality in perversion. This will be the topic of another chapter. I intend, now, to pursue my topic further by concentrating on the way in which the pervert gets around the inescapable nature of human destiny. To this end I shall examine the connection between perversion and narcissism.

I feel it is important to bring out into the open, and to come to an understanding of, the processes used by the pervert in his relation to reality. As I have already stated, all of us are open to the perverse solution which constitutes a balm for our wounded narcissism and a means of dissipating our feelings of smallness and inadequacy. This temptation can lead to our losing the love for truth and replacing it with a taste for sham.

We know that very early in his works Freud studied the relation of the psychotic to reality. In his article 'Formulations on the Two Principles of Mental Functioning' (1911), what interests him, however, is the relation of man in general to reality. '...We are now confronted with the task of investigating the development of the relation of neurotics and of mankind in general to reality.' In this text he enlarges on the idea expressed in *The Interpretation of Dreams* (1900), according to which there could be a first stage of satisfaction during which

> Whatever was thought of (wished for) was presented in a hallucinatory manner... It was only the non-occurrence of the expected satisfaction, the disappointment experienced, that led to the abandonment of this attempt at satisfaction by means of hallucination... A new principle of mental functioning was thus introduced; what was presented in the mind was no longer what was agreeable but what was real, even if it happened to be disagreeable. This setting up of the *reality principle* proved to be a momentous step.

Further on Freud explains that, upon the setting up of the reality principle, 'The place of repression, which excluded from cathexis as productive of unpleasure, some of the emerging ideas, was taken by an *impartial passing of judgement* which had to decide whether a given idea was true or false, that is, whether it was in agreement with reality or not...' He thus confirms the equivalence between truth and reality. Let me now jump over many years in order to enter into Freud's conceptions concerning the specific relation of the pervert to reality. (Once again, I shall not go into this question in great detail now.) I refer to his incomplete article on 'The Splitting of the Ego in the Process of Defence' (1938). Let me quote a lengthy passage from it as each word is, I feel, of great importance for my subject:

> Let us suppose, then, that a child's Ego is under the sway of a powerful instinctual demand which it is accustomed to satisfy and that it is suddenly frightened by an experience which teaches it that the continuance of this satisfaction will result in an almost intolerable real danger. It must now decide either to recognize the real danger, give way to it and renounce the instinctual satisfaction, or to disavow reality and make itself believe that there is no reason for fear, so that it may be able to regain the satisfaction. Thus there is a conflict between the demand by the instinct and the prohibition by reality. But in fact the child takes neither course, or rather he takes both simultaneously, which comes to the same thing. He replies to the conflict with two contrary reactions, both of which are valid and effective. On the one hand, with the help of certain mechanisms he rejects reality and refuses to accept any prohibition; on the other hand, in the same breath he recognizes the danger of reality, takes over the fear of the danger as a pathological symptom and tries subsequently to divest himself of the fear. It must be confessed that this is a very ingenious solution of the difficulty. Both of the parties to the dispute obtain their share: the instinct is allowed to retain its satisfaction and proper respect is paid to reality. But everything has to be paid for in one way or another, and this success is achieved at the price of a rift in the Ego which never heals but which increases as time goes on. The two contrary reactions to the conflict persist as the centre point of a splitting of the Ego. The whole process seems so strange to us because we take for granted the synthetic nature of the processes of the Ego. But we are clearly at fault in this. The synthetic function of the Ego, though it is of such extraordinary importance, is subject to particular conditions and is liable to a whole number of disturbances.

The example Freud gives of this 'ingenious solution' is, precisely, a case of perversion. It is that of a boy who, between the ages of 3 and 4, was seduced by an older girl and given the opportunity to observe her genitals. When this relationship came to an end he began to practise masturbation so as to continue the sexual stimulation previously obtained. Then came a threat of castration proffered by a governess but to be carried out, 'as usual' Freud says, by the father. The little boy is consequently horrified. The perception of the little girl's genitals which, at the time, had been harmless, acquires now a new meaning: the threat of castration may be put into effect for there are human beings with no penis, i.e., 'castrated'. I shall not dwell here on this pattern of the castration complex as needing two consecutive incidents in order to take on its full meaning.

What does seem important for the development of my own hypotheses, however, is the next part of Freud's clinical account. He says that in the case of a 'normal' or neurotic person the masturbational activity usually ceases, this activity being connected with unconscious incestuous fantasies taking the mother as object. The child renounces the instinctual satisfaction in order to preserve his penis, internalizes the incest prohibition and prohibitions in general, and establishes a seat of morality within himself, namely the Superego. The young boy in Freud's example found another way out. He created a fetish which, according to Freud, is a substitute for the mother's missing penis. This allows him to disavow the reality of castration. Thus he saves his penis *and* preserves his instinctual satisfaction at the same time. The masturbational activity does not cease.

Leaving aside the significance Freud attributes to the fetish, let me emphasize that perversion—fetishism, in this case—constitutes a means of eluding the fatal character of the Oedipus Complex. The alternative of either losing one's penis or renouncing the incestuous wish is skipped, conjured away, so to speak, by the 'ingenious solution' that constitutes the perversion. At the price, it is true, of turning himself away from reality and of splitting his own Ego, the pervert succeeds in escaping human destiny since he preserves his genitals and, at the same time, their sexual function. In 'The Splitting of the Ego in the Process of Defence', perversion appears as a rebellion against the universal law of the Oedipus Complex. Speaking of this process in the same article, Freud says: 'This way of dealing with reality... almost deserves to be described as artful.' (In German Freud speaks of 'Kniffige Behandlung der Realität'.)

The importance of narcissism for the subject we are dealing with cannot be overestimated. (Here I summarize some of the ideas from my book on *The Ego Ideal*, 1973.) In 1914, in his article entitled 'On Narcissism: an Introduction', Freud introduces this concept, although he had previously made mention of it several times, particularly in reference to perversions.

In 1914, he introduces the Ego Ideal in association with narcissism and develops a statement he had made in his article, 'Creative Writers and Day-Dreaming' (1908): '...Whoever understands the human mind knows that hardly anything is harder for a man than to give up a pleasure he has once experienced. Actually we can never give anything up; we only exchange one thing for another.' In 1914 the Ego Ideal appears as one of the essential outcomes of narcissism.

As always when the libido is concerned, man has here again shown himself incapable of giving up a satisfaction he has once enjoyed. He is not willing to forgo the narcissistic perfection of his childhood... he seeks to recover it in the new form of an Ego Ideal. What he projects before him as his ideal is the substitute for the lost narcissism of his childhood in which he was his own ideal.

Owing to its original helplessness, the narcissistic monad, which supposedly composes the human being in the beginning, breaks and opens out onto the external world (*Project for a Scientific Psychology*, 1895-1950). Its state of distress is such that survival depends on the intervention of another's care ('Instincts and their Vicissitudes', 1915, *Inhibitions, Symptoms and Anxiety*, 1926).

Thus narcissism, which is the stage of development in which the Ego furnishes itself with its own ideal, gives way to the object relation. The Ego is led to break with a part of its narcissism by projecting this form of an Ego Ideal. From this point onwards, there will be a gap, a rift between the Ego and its Ideal. The Ego will aim at stitching the two gaping sides of the wound which is henceforth its characteristic. Union with the first object in which the lost narcissistic perfection has been vested will become one way by which to retrieve its initial narcissism. As may be supposed, and clinical experience confirms this to some extent, the narcissistic state is fantasized as identical in nature to the fusion between the infant and its mother on the model of the intra-uterine situation (which Freud supposes is a primal phantasy).

Ferenczi considers that the basic human wish is to return to the mother's womb (in 'Thalassa—A Theory of Genitality', 1924). Genital coitus, which is the apex of sexual development, contains and is an expression of the wish to return to the mother's womb, where, Ferenczi says, the rift between the Ego and the environment has not as yet taken place. According to him, this would explain the nuclear presence and role of the Oedipal wish, namely to have intercourse with one's mother, and furnish its biological basis. I prefer to speak of the narcissistic basis of the Oedipus Complex.

If the incestuous wish rests not only on a sexual drive but also on the desire to retrieve lost narcissistic unity, we can understand that in the course of his development the boy reaches a point at which he cathects the father's image with his Ego Ideal. He places his narcissism in his father who thus becomes his model, that is to say, his aim for identification.

The incestuous fixation which expresses itself through the Oedipus Complex would undoubtedly be easy to overcome if it were caused solely by the sexual drive. There is, in fact, no such thing as an 'Oedipal drive'. According to the Libido theory, only sexual drives exist. The tenacity of the bond welding the (sexual) drive to the object at the moment of the Oedipus Complex would result from the deep narcissistic roots of the incestuous love. What pushes the boy ahead, towards the Oedipus Complex and genitality, would be nostalgia for his glorious past when he himself was his own ideal.

The Ego Ideal as it is conceived by Freud (1914) in 'On Narcissism: An Introduction' acts as a point of contact between infantile omnipotence and the object relationship, between the pleasure principle and the reality principle. As a matter of fact, the Ego Ideal is a stage in the development of the Ego: 'The development of the Ego consists in a departure from primary narcissism and gives rise to a vigorous attempt to recover this state. This departure is brought about by means of displacement of libido on to an Ego Ideal... and satisfaction is brought about by fulfilling this ideal.'

Projection of infantile narcissism onto the parents, which results in the Ego Ideal, is a step towards the conquest of reality and object love, since primary megalomania is discarded in favour of the object. The formation of the Ego Ideal is also in conformity with the reality principle, since it does not choose the shortest path of discharge in order to obtain satisfaction (this being characteristic of the pleasure principle). The Ego Ideal implies that there is a 'plan', 'hope' and 'promise'.

'Promise', 'hope' and a 'plan' imply postponement, detours, and entrance into a temporal order, all of which are characteristic of mental functioning in accordance with the reality principle, whereas the pleasure principle is characterized by the immediacy of the discharge. The idea of 'development' and 'evolution' are implicit throughout. In fact, the mother's responsibility—at least in the early stages of life—is to bring the child to project his Ego Ideal onto successive and ever more advanced models. Frustrations and gratifications, correctly applied, should encourage the child to renounce certain satisfactions which go with the acquisition of specific functions and a specific way of being, so that he may acquire new ones. Each phase of development must bring with it gratification enough to counteract any desire to turn back, and frustration enough to urge him onwards rather than halt his evolution through fixation. In short, the expectations which will help the child move forward have to be maintained. Thus, the child is guided by his mother who induces him to project his Ego Ideal ahead of him by stimulating its instigating role, sustaining in this manner its aspect of 'promise'.

Now, it can happen that the mother, instead, leads the child's Ego Ideal astray, through an insufficiency of narcissistic and object gratification, or through an excess of satisfaction. For my purposes I shall consider only the latter hypothesis.

Freud emphasizes more than once in his works the fact that over and above all the child wishes to be grown-up. For example, in 'Creative Writers and Day-Dreaming' (1908) he writes: 'A child's play is determined by wishes: in point of fact by a single wish—one that helps his upbringing—the wish to be big and grown up. He is always playing at being "grown up", and in his games he imitates what he knows about the lives of his elders.' We may consider the wish 'to be big' as a basic content of the Ego Ideal. As a matter of fact, all feelings of admiration push towards identification. The mother's attitude of seduction may, however, destroy in her child this wish to be big and grown up and prevent him from experiencing this admiration for his father who becomes his model for identification, the bearer of the child's Ego Ideal.

Then, it is as if the mother had pushed her child into a trap, making him believe that, with his infantile sexuality and his prepubescent penis, he is a perfect partner for her, and consequently, that he has nothing to envy his father for—halting, in this manner, the child's evolution. The child's Ego Ideal remains attached to a pregenital model, instead of cathecting the genital father and his attributes. As a matter of fact, the pervert, helped more often than not by his mother, lives under the illusion that pregenitality is equal or even superior to genitality. The father and his attributes come to be disqualified.

I believe that the incestuous wish rests upon narcissistic motivations: the desire to re-experience that time when the Ego and the Non-Ego were merged. If so, the future pervert will be under the illusion that it is not necessary to wait for the height of sexual development in order to reinstate the fusion with the mother. In normal cases, as we have seen, nostalgia for primary narcissism when the child himself constituted his own Ideal, pushes the subject to project his narcissism ahead of him onto the Oedipal father.

He projects his penis in a phantasy of genital fulfillment containing the promise of a return to the original state of blessing. Nostalgia for primary narcissism may, however, lead the future pervert to avoid the whole process. Forward projection of narcissism by the subject in the form of the Ego Ideal is, as I said before, in conformity with the reality principle which leads to maturation and development. In contrast, the perverse illusion exerts itself in favour of the choice of the short path: merging with the mother is going to take place here and now, without the need for evolution and growing up. Thus the long path which leads the subject to the Oedipus Complex and genitality must be seen as opposed to the short path which maintains the subject fixed in pregenitality. These two paths define two different forms of Ego Ideal.

For a better understanding of these two forms of Ego Ideal, I am going to study examination dreams, 'typical dreams' according to Freud. I shall give you my personal interpretation of them and compare the examination dream of the neurotic with that of the pervert.

Freud devotes two pages to the study of examination dreams in

The Interpretation of Dreams (1900).

> Everyone who has passed the matriculation examination at the end of his school studies complains of the obstinacy with which he is pursued by anxiety dreams of having failed or of being obliged to take the examination again, etc. In the case of those who have obtained a university degree, this typical dream is replaced by another one which represents them as having failed in their university finals; and it is in vain that they object, even while they are still asleep, that for years they have been practicing medicine or working as university lecturers or heads of offices... After we have ceased to be schoolchildren, our punishments are no longer inflicted on us by our parents or by those who brought us up or later by our schoolmasters. The relentless causal chains of real life take charge of our further education, and now we dream of matriculation or finals (and who has not trembled on these occasions, even if he was well-prepared for the examination?) whenever, having done something wrong or failed to do something properly...

Freud defines matriculation and finals, which are the privileged themes of examination dreams, as 'two crucial points in our studies'. The interpretation given by Freud to these typical dreams is said to result from the remark of 'an inexperienced colleague' who had noted that only persons who had in fact passed their matriculation dreamed these dreams (though in my experience there are exceptions to this rule). Freud comes to conclude as follows:

> It would seem, then, that anxious examination dreams which, as has been confirmed over and over again, appear when the dreamer has some responsible activity ahead of him next day and is afraid there may be a fiasco, searches for some occasion in the past in which great anxiety has turned out to be unjustified and has been contradicted by the event... What is regarded as an indignant protest against the dream: "But I'm a doctor, etc. already", would in reality be the consolation put forward by the dream, and would accordingly run: "Don't be afraid of tomorrow! Just think how anxious you were before your matriculation, and yet nothing happened to you. You're a doctor, etc. already." And the anxiety which is attributed to the dream would really have arisen from the day's residue.

That may be so, but wouldn't it be simpler, and more in line with the dreamer's desires, to dream of succeeding in his enterprise? Why does he need this complicated twist? Examination dreams constitute a problem within the theory of dreams wherein a dream is the fulfillment of a wish. Here the anxiety is not provoked by any immanent satisfaction of a drive, nor is it a dream of punishment in the true sense of the word. (Which infantile wish would it be punishing?)

In my opinion, it is the Ego Ideal which manifests itself here. It expresses strong demands regarding the way our Ego is constituted; it rejects short-circuits and make-belief in its maturation. Examinations mark out the child's life, that of the adolescent and often the young adult. They ratify, so to speak, the successive phases of maturation and are the symbols of the integration of these phases. The wish which is fulfilled in the examination dreams is, in my opinion, ruled by Ego Ideal—the non-avoidance of difficulties, integration of conflicts, the different stages of evolution that supply the Ego with the completeness necessary to reach the state where genitality and narcissism reign together.

I think that something of my hypothesis is discernible in the following fragment of the interpretation of the examination dreams by Freud:

> The interpretation of examination dreams is faced by the difficulty which I have already referred to as characteristic of the majority of typical dreams. It is but rarely that the material with which the dreamer provides us in associations is sufficient to interpret the dream... Not long ago I came to the conclusion that the objection, "You're a doctor, etc. already", does not merely conceal a consolation, but also signifies a reproach. This would have run: "You're quite old now, quite far advanced in life, and yet you go on doing these stupid, childish things."

Thus, the emphasis is put on the gap between the true age (the examination that has been passed) and the infantile character of the Ego (the 'childish things'). I believe, therefore, that examination dreams express the wish of the Ego Ideal to bring into line these two elements, namely the examination which supposes maturity, and the 'childish things' which do, indeed, exist, so that the true Ego and the apparent Ego will coincide with one another.

The motivation of the examination dream is, in my opinion, a wish ruled by the Ego Ideal (to bring the Ego close again to the Ideal). This wish aims at filling in the gaps in maturation by restructuring the defective process. This wish which mobilizes one or several drives, once again, comes up against barriers which have not yet been broken down and causes anxiety.

It is noteworthy that the examination which Freud, in *The Interpretation of Dreams*, reports as having occurred the most frequently in his own dreams, was an examination whose success was linked to the memory of a minor act of cheating (i.e., the camouflage of a shortcoming).

> In my dreams of school examinations, I am invariably examined in History, in which I did brilliantly—though only, it is true, because (in the oral examination) my kindly master (the one-eyed benefactor of another dream) did not fail to notice that on the

paper of questions which I handed him back, I had run my fingernail through the middle one of the three questions included, to warn him not to insist upon that particular one.

The minor act of cheating involved in the successful passing of the examination is not accepted by the Ego Ideal, not because of guilt, but because it symbolizes a maturity which is only make-believe.

A very short play written by Ionesco (1965) shows a member of the French Academy, decorated with medals 'down to his belt', the holder of several degrees, President of the Board of Examiners for Admission to Professorship, President of the Matriculation Examination Board, of the Ministry of Education, Doctor 'Honoris Causa' of the University of Amsterdam, and the secret university colleges of the Dukedom of Luxembourg, holder of the Nobel Prize on three occasions, etc., who is informed that he has failed his matriculation examination. His wife's words are:
'You should not have sat for it...'
And the Academy Member's reply: 'Something is missing.'
His wife: 'Nobody would have known.'
The Academy Member: 'I knew... Others could have found out...'
The play is called: 'Something is Missing' ('La lacune', 1965).

One of my patients dreams that she fails her matriculation exam. She associates as follows:

> Whenever I feel stress I dream the same dream. I fail my matriculation exam, and I say to myself: "But I finished the Arts School, therefore it is a trifling matter." At the same time I have the idea that my studies at the Arts School are not valid, because I have not matriculated, something is missing.
> I really did fail my matriculation exam, despite the fact that I was a very good pupil. The nuns were always telling me about the sacrifice my parents had made so that I could study. I was only admitted to university ten years later, when a decree made university entrance possible by special examination.

The 'stress' she speaks of, as being at the origin of her dream, is linked to the approach, through the transference, of her relationship with her mother. Here we are confronted with a dream which, contrary to those Freud speaks of, centres around an examination in which the dreamer actually failed. The patient seems to have come up against certain unresolved rivalry problems (her elder sisters had not carried their studies very far). Later on, she was presented with the possibility of sitting for a 'special' examination, which she passed and which, apparently (objectively), made up for the previous failure but which did not by any means camouflage the actual gap symbolized by the matriculation she failed. This gap had to do with her own Ego, that is, her lack of integration of her rivalry with regard to her elder sisters. The dreamer's wish seems to consist in not being satisfied with a makeshift which would hide the gap.

She wants actually to fill in the gap and to face her conflicts. She has the same dream at times of stress in her life because she faces the same dilemma each time, that is to say, whether to go back to the roots of her problem, or to short-circuit and elude it by means of the 'special examination'. The Ego Ideal prefers absolute solutions.

I will now consider the propensity of a perverse patient to adopt the alternative solution; his Ego Ideal adapts to the short path and all the sham involved. The focus of the following clinical material is also an examination dream.

Jean-Jacques, twenty-eight years of age, is the youngest son and the fifth child in a very Catholic family of six children. He was born with a congenital defect which was corrected soon after his birth. When he was young his mother used to have him in bed with her because of this handicap and the surgery he had undergone. She repeatedly concealed from the father certain of the child's 'follies'. This young man, who is now married and a father, masturbates in his mother-in-law's pyjamas, with accompanying overtly sadomasochistic fantasies. He has sexual relations with his wife, whom he binds with ropes. As an adolescent, he had a homosexual relationship with a one-legged man (who was older than he) in whom his father placed 'complete trust'. This man, who was looked on with respect by the city authorities, especially by the police, protected my patient from prosecution when he had a car accident, driving without a licence in the presence of this man.

In the course of his analysis, my patient dreamed he failed his matriculation examination. The failure worried and angered him. One of his teachers drew him aside to tell him: 'They (the board of examiners) are a bunch of fools. I'm going to fix it!' At that moment he associated to his mother, who used to take him to bed when he was a small child and conceal his 'follies' from his father, and then to the one-legged man. The teacher who singled him out in the dream seemed to make sexual advances toward him. The teacher thus plays the role of the mother who, as an accomplice, helps him avoid his Oedipal conflict (with the examination board) and fraternal rivalry (with the other candidates). Through the teacher he obtains his matriculation without having had to integrate or resolve conflicts, just as his mother, by allowing him to share her bed, had led him to believe that he had no need to mature in order to take his father's place. Similarly, the one-legged man helps him deceive the authorities (both his father, 'who had complete trust in him', and the police). He can drive without a licence (without an examination), therefore without acquiring the necessary ability (maturity), thanks to the complicity of his friend, a substitute for his mother. (I intentionally leave aside other aspects of this relationship with the one-legged man.)

At the very beginning of his analysis, he found a job in the following manner. An ex-classmate had told him he was going to apply for a job which was vacant in an institution managed by a woman. My patient, without a word to his friend, went to see the woman and got the job. This acting-out was a clear indication of the manner in which the treatment was going to proceed. Later on, after he had missed a session, he told me he had used the time he should have been at the session to visit his mistress and be unfaithful to his wife, who believed he was with his analyst. After all, so long as he paid for the lost session, he could spend the time as he pleased.

It became obvious that he wished me to take up the role of the teacher in his dream as well as that of the one-legged man, i.e., his mother's role. He did this in order to help him cheat the examiners, i.e., the father, and, during the affair with his mistress, his wife, too. Both the father and the wife represent a discredited Superego as well as a devalorized Ego Ideal. (The castrated father, unworthy of becoming his Ego Ideal, says: 'They are a bunch of fools.')

It seems to me that this material shows how the pervert seeks to obtain matriculation without having to pass the exam, contrary to the neurotic who, in my experience, seeks to sit the examination again for fear of having obtained the diploma without deserving it. The neurotic attempts conciliation of his being with his seeming, whereas the pervert contents himself with make-believe.

Time, as a dimension of life, is rejected by the pervert. Freud's paper, 'Analysis Terminable and Interminable' (1937), begins with criticism of all attempts to shorten psychoanalytic treatment. Throughout this article, Freud shows how the analysis comes up against obstacles whose nature he tries to elucidate, whilst recognizing how fruitless it is to imagine that they can be short-circuited. It is also in this article that he makes the following statement: 'We must not forget that the analytic relationship is based on a love of truth—that is, a recognition of reality—and that it precludes any kind of sham or deceit.'

Recognition of obstacles, temporality and reality are one and the same thing.

> How poor are they that have no patience!
> What wound did ever heal but by degree?
> Thou know'st we work by wit and not by witchcraft
> And wit depends on dilatory time.
> —'Othello', Act II, Scene III

The pervert rejects 'dilatory time', this absence of witchcraft. However, the opposition between him and the neurotic, between him and ourselves, is not always clearly delimited. We are all, in differing degrees, tempted to live in a world of lies and illusion.

Chapter 4

A Re-reading of 'Little Hans'

My argument about perversion demands that we radically reconsider the infantile sexual theory of phallic monism. I would now like to put this theory to the test by re-reading 'Little Hans'. At the same time, I would like to end up casting light on the boy's wishes to castrate his father, whereas we remember that Freud puts the emphasis on the boy's fear of castration without taking into account that this fear could follow, at least in part, from the fear of retaliation. At the same time, a re-reading will give us the opportunity to compare Little Hans — a charming little neurotic — with the pervert.

To start with, it seems necessary to recall some of Freud's statements which aim at showing that the male child has no desire to penetrate his mother. In the *Three Essays* (1905), Freud begins the fifth and last chapter of the Third Essay, 'Transformations of Puberty', with this sentence which is, to say the least, a very curious one: 'The processes at puberty thus establish the primacy of genital zones; and, in a man, the penis, *which has now become capable of erection* (italics mine), presses forward insistently towards the new sexual aim — penetration into a cavity in the body which excites his genital zone. Simultaneously on the psychic side the process of finding an object, for which preparations have been made from earliest childhood, is completed' (p. 222).

Now, it is banal to point out that erections exist in infants. It is precisely their precociousness which led Jones, in his criticism of 'The Phallic Phase' (1933), to emphasize the link between erection and pressure forward, and, consequently, the search for a cavity. He thence concluded that it is impossible to cast doubt on the existence of boys' wishes to penetrate, long before puberty, and on the search for a complementary organ. The knowledge of the vagina would then be repressed because of psychic conflicts at work. For Freud, the penis is indeed involved in the incestuous fantasies. The castration threat is applied to the very seat of excitation. But the aim of the sexual impulse linked to the Oedipus Complex remains ill-defined, vague, 'obscure', 'imprecise', 'of some sort'. Thus, when Freud examines the third typical sexual theory — the sadistic view of coitus (in 'On the Sexual Theories of Children', 1908), he writes:

... They have interpreted the act of love as an act of violence. But

this view of it itself gives an impression of being a return of the obscure impulse towards cruel behaviour which becomes attached to the excitations of the child's penis when he first began to think about the problem of where babies come from (p. 221).
The possibility, too, cannot be excluded that this premature sadistic impulse, which might so nearly have led to the discovery of coitus, itself first emerged under the influence of extremely obscure memories of parental intercourse, for which the child has obtained the material—though at the same time he made no use of it—while he was still in his first years and was sharing his parents' bedroom.

Freud refers here to a previous exposition in the same article:

If children could follow the hints given by the excitation of their penis they would get a little nearer to the solution of their problem. That the baby grows inside the mother's body is obviously not a sufficient explanation. How does it get inside? What starts its development? That the father has something to do with it seems likely; he says that the baby is *his* baby as well. Again the penis certainly has a share, too, in these mysterious happenings; the excitation in it which accompanies all these activities of the child's thoughts bears witness to this. Attached to this excitation are impulses which the child cannot account for—obscure urges to do something violent, to press in, to knock to pieces, to tear open a hole somewhere. But when the child thus seems to be well on the way to postulating the existence of the vagina and to concluding that an incursion of this kind by his father's penis into his mother is the act by means of which the baby is created in his mother's body, at this juncture his enquiry is broken off in helpless perplexity. For standing in its way in his theory that his mother possesses a penis, just as a man does, and the existence of the cavity which receives the penis remains undiscovered by him.

We can question the child's ignorance of this cavity and wonder which is primary: the idea of the universality of the possession of a penis (which would prevent knowledge of the cavity), or the knowledge of the cavity (i.e., the vagina) for which the theory would be a substitute, owing to certain motives which have to be determined? Furthermore is not the child's passion to penetrate a secret, to see through a riddle, the equivalent, at the level of mental work, of a sexual penetration (for lack of something better)? Freud ceaselessly insists on the impassioned character of children's curiosity.

The instinct to know, and its backing by the instinct to see as well as that to master, is undoubtedly related to the wishes to penetrate. A look may also be 'piercing' or 'penetrating'. A patient once said to me, with regard to his curiosity as a child towards female genitals, 'My eyes *darted* women's groins.' In 'The Dissolution of the Oedipus Complex' (1924), Freud writes again: 'The child may have had only very vague notions as to what constitutes a satisfying erotic intercourse; but certainly the penis must play a part in it, for the sensations in his own organ were evidence of that' (p. 176). In *An Outline of Psycho-Analysis* (1938-1940), Freud says once more: 'The boy enters the Oedipus phase; he begins to manipulate his penis and simultaneously has phantasies of carrying out some sort of activity with it in relation to his mother...' (p. 155).

We shall now turn to 'Little Hans', 'Analysis of a Phobia in a Five-Year-Old Boy' (1909), in order to examine whether the clinical material supports the theory of phallic monism. We remember that Hans' father, in the letter he sent to Freud to inform him of the outburst of a phobia in his little boy, had written: 'He is afraid a *horse will bite him in the street*, and this fear seems somehow to be connected with his having been frightened by a large penis' (p. 22). This big penis will be referred to throughout the narrative as the one Hans ascribed to his mother. However, in spite of the possible overdeterminations, a large number of clues show—at least in my opinion—that the penis at issue *belongs to the father*.

In his investigation to find out the origin of Hans' phobia, his father comes to the episode with Fritzl, the little boy's playmate at Gmunden. As Fritzl was pretending to be the horse, 'he hit his foot on a stone and bled' (p. 58). Hans thinks, 'That was how I got the nonsense.' Hans has already said that 'there's a white horse at Gmuden that bites. If you hold your fingers to it it bites.' His father was struck by his saying 'fingers' instead of 'hand'.

The episode with Fritzl recurs as follows:

> Afternoon, in front of the house, Hans suddenly ran indoors as a carriage with two horses came along... I... asked him what was wrong. "The horses are so proud", he said, "that I am afraid they'll fall down." (The coachman was reining the horses in tight, so that they were trotting with short steps and holding their heads high. In fact their action *was* proud.) I asked him who it really was that was so proud:
> He: "You are, when I come to bed with Mummy."
> I: "So you want me to fall down?"
> He: "Yes. You've got to be naked (meaning 'barefoot' as Fritzl had been) and knock up against a stone and bleed, and then I'll be able to be alone with Mummy for a little bit at all events..."
> I: "Can you remember who it was that knocked up against the stone?"
> He: "Yes, Fritzl."
> I: "When Fritzl fell down, what did you think?"
> He: "That *you* should hit the stone and tumble down" (p. 82).

The fallen horses, the object of Hans' phobia, may be considered as symbols of the father (or of his penis); 'fallen' is equivalent to castrated, and is the opposite of 'erected'. This is particularly clear concerning 'proud' horses 'holding their heads high'. This pride (of the horses) is directly associated by Hans with his father's 'pride' when Hans is in bed with Mummy. It is to be understood, according to me, as referring to the father's genital capacities, to the erection of his big penis, capable of satisfying his mother. Father's proud charger has to become less arrogant! He has to subdue his pride; he must roll in the dust and bleed!

As for Hans, he does not possess this desirable organ. Just before the outburst of his phobia, he had to come into his mother's bed and said, in order to attract her: 'Do you know what Aunt M. said? She said: "He *has* got a dear little thingummy." ' Yes, indeed, a dear thingummy, but a *little* one. Not a big one, like the horses', of which he is particularly afraid. Thence forward he developed a theme referring to the comparison between his little penis and the animal's big one which he envies. It is this envy which, in my opinion, causes his fear that horses might bite his fingers. It also arouses a more diffused fear of animals with obvious phallic characteristics: the giraffe (because of its neck), the elephant (because of its trunk), the pelican (because of its beak).

According to Freud, Hans' remark, 'My widdler will get bigger as I get bigger,' has to be understood as follows: 'We may infer from his self-consolatory words... that during his observations he had constantly been making comparisons, and that he had remained extremely dissatisfied with the size of his own widdler' (p. 34). Indeed, we are entitled to think that his phobia is partly due to his wish to pull off the horses' and other phallic animals' big widdlers which, in turn, threaten him. We may notice that Hans has not chosen the 'short path'. He is really a neurotic, not a pervert. He thinks that his wish—of getting a big widdler—will be satisfied in the future.

His father and Freud himself come to the conclusion that Hans is afraid 'that his mother did not like him, because his widdler was not comparable to his father's' (p. 40). The accomplishment of his wish to get a big penis will happen through his phantasy of a plumber coming to give him a big widdler. This phantasy takes place when his phobia is practically cured: *'The plumber came; and first he took away my behind with a pair of pincers, and then gave me another, and then the same with my widdler. He said: "Let me see your behind!"* and I had to turn round, and he took it away; and then he said: "Let me see your widdler!" (p. 98). His father grasps the very meaning of this phantasy, and does not doubt for an instant as to how to interpret it:

I: "He gave you a *bigger* widdler and a *bigger* behind?"
Hans: "Yes."
I: "Like Daddy's; because you'd like to be Daddy" (p.98).

Here we see Hans' obvious wish to be like his father and to obtain his virile attributes.

Freud associates the phantasy about the plumber to a previous one referring to the same plumber: '*I was in the bath and the plumber came and unscrewed it. Then he took a big borer and stuck it into my stomach*' (p. 65). While Freud retrospectively interprets this first phantasy as prefiguring the second one, I think that these two phantasies are complementary. For Freud, the bath represents Hans' behind, and the borer the big widdler thus given to him. For me, the first phantasy shows *how* Hans will get his father's—the plumber's—big penis.

It is indeed striking that these sado-masochistic phantasies do not arouse any kind of anxiety in Hans. On the contrary, they seem to please him. It seems to me that the appropriation of his father's penis by Hans is accomplished here under the cover of a sham attack supposed to have been performed by the father or his substitute, the plumber. The borer struck into Hans' stomach is a symbolic presentation of a passive homosexual coitus. This passivity features again in the second phantasy where the plumber manipulates Hans with pincers accomplishing the castration of his behind and widdler. Thanks to that apparent submission, Hans finally succeeds in taking possession of the paternal attributes—without guilt and, therefore, without any fear of retaliation.

We may see here how homosexuality plays a determining part in the process of identification with the father and in the introjection of his virility. We may speak of 'anal introjection', anality being presented not only through Hans' behind but through the very personage of the plumber and the sado-masochistic relationship—active and passive—predominating both phantasies. We may suppose that Hans has worked through his fears concerning his father enough to be able to give way, under the cover of a masochistic camouflage, to his wish of taking possession of his father's penis. Béla Grunberger, in his article 'An Essay on a Psycho-Dynamic Theory of Masochism' (1954), describes a decisive masochistic mechanism necessary to achieve paternal identification. This mechanism is, at the same time, a method of softening one's Superego. The subject tries to prove that he is the one who has been castrated. Thus cleared from any charge, he may perform with impunity the introjection of his father's penis.

The wish to castrate the father seems to be easy to follow throughout Hans' material: he seeks to catch father's penis in order to deprive him of what makes him the object of mother's desire, to attack the bond between the parents and, thus, to destroy the primal scene, to seduce the mother through becoming the owner of the big and 'proud' paternal penis. Such are the ends that Hans pursues. But why such a need of a big penis, like his father's, in order to please his mother if Hans does not know his mother possesses an organ which his 'dear little thingummy' is unable to fill and fulfil? This knowledge of the vagina appears very clearly in two other phantasies he relates to his father: 'I was with you at Schönbrunn where the sheep are; and then we crawled through under the ropes, and then we told the policeman at the end of the garden, and he grabbed hold of us' (p. 40).

The second phantasy is the following: 'I went with you in the train, and we smashed a window and the policeman took us off with him' (p. 41). The idea that his penis is too small for his mother's vagina appears once more, we may infer, in his fear that his mother should let him fall in the big bath. That this fear may have been overdetermined by his wish for his mother to let Anna fall in the big bath does not invalidate this hypothesis. It is with him as with the child Freud mentions who said, referring to his little sister: 'The stork must take her back!' Hans may want to send Anna back where she came from: the vagina-bath. Afterwards, Hans will speak of the big box (the mother's tummy): 'Really Daddy. Do believe me. We got a big box and it was full of babies; they sat in the bath' (p. 69). Just before, as he was walking, he knocked on the pavement with his stick, and asked his father if there was not a man beneath, i.e., the father or his penis inside the mother (p. 69). We can but acknowledge, in Hans' phantasies and in his phobia, an Oedipal desire involving the genital possession of his mother and the giving to her of a baby thanks to a penis stolen from his father. Now, it is striking that Freud sees this; in fact, the material cannot be understood otherwise. In spite of that, he maintains the theory of phallic monism and of the correlative ignorance of the vagina. He says:

> Some kind of vague notion was struggling in the child's mind of something that he might do with his mother by means of which his taking possession or her would be consummated; for this elusive thought he found certain pictorial representations, which had in common the qualities of being violent and forbidden, and the content of which strikes us as fitting in most remarkably well with the hidden truth. We can only say that they were symbolic phantasies of intercourse... (pp. 122-23).

And, later on: 'But this father, whom he could not help hating as a rival, was the same father he had always loved and was bound to go on loving, who had been his model... ' (p. 134). We have here the major difference between the neurotic and the pervert.

> ... But his father not only knew where children came from, he actually performed it—the thing that Hans could only obscurely divine. The widdler must have something to do with it, for his own grew excited whenever he thought of these things—and it must be a big widdler too, bigger than Hans' own. If he listened to

these premonitory sensations, he could only suppose that it was a question of some act of violence performed upon his mother, of smashing something, of making an opening into something, of forcing a way into an enclosed space—such were the impulses that he felt stirring within him (pp. 134-35).

Here, we think that Freud is very close to acknowledging the existence of the vagina in Hans' mind, at least on a preconscious level. Then comes this strange conclusion: 'But although the sensations of his penis had put him on the road to postulating a vagina, yet he could not solve the problem, for within his experience no such thing existed as his widdler required. On the contrary, his conviction that his mother possessed a penis just as he did stood in the way of any solution' (pp. 134-35).

Freud expresses here a succession of conjectural and even contradictory opinions: first, contrary to what he had said in *Three Essays* (1905), and to what he continued to assert in his subsequent studies, the boy's wish to penetrate does exist long before puberty as well as the 'obscure' and 'premonitory' idea of the vagina. Even if Hans imagined his mother as having genitals like his own, this idea may quite easily be superimposed on that of the vagina. We might then wonder if 'standing in the way of any solution', as Freud says, it would not play a defensive role, purely and simply. Indeed, we can guess Freud's answer: the castration fear induces the little boy into wanting to see a penis where it does not exist. But we know that, according to Freud, castration fear is all the stronger as the child ignores the vagina. What he imagines then is not genitals different from his own but—to his horror—a lack of genitals.

The way Freud suggests that Hans' father should undertake the little boy's sexual enlightenment is precisely in line with a description of female genitals as that of 'default', a lack, i.e., confirming purely and simply the phantasy of the so-called feminine castration:

> I further suggested to his father that he should begin giving Hans some enlightenment in the matter of sex knowledge. The child's past behaviour justified us in assuming that his libido was attached to a wish to see his mother's widdler; so I proposed to his father that he should take away this aim from Hans by informing him that his mother and all other female beings (as he could see from Hanna) had no widdler at all (p. 28).

As for the question: 'Where do children come from?' Hans seems to be much better prepared to give an answer than Freud supposes and as the clinical material itself shows. Particularly, birth is properly associated by Hans with his mother's genitals: when Hans was 3½ years old, his little sister, Hanna, was born. That day, his father wrote in his agenda: 'At five in the morning labour began and Hans' bed was moved into the next room. He woke up there at seven, and, hearing his mother groaning, asked: "Why's Mummy coughing?" Then, after a pause, "The stork's coming to-day for certain" (p. 10). Later on he was taken into the kitchen. He saw the doctor's bag in the front hall and asked: 'What's that?' 'A bag', was the reply. Upon which he declared with conviction: 'The stork's coming to-day' (p. 10). After the delivery, 'he was called to the bedroom. He did not look at his mother, however, but at the basins and other vessels, filled with blood and water, that were still standing about the room. Pointing to the blood-stained bed-pan he observed in a surprised voice: "But blood does not come out of *my* widdler." '

This passage shows quite well that Hans knows that delivery is painful, since he associates his mother's groans with the stork's coming. For certain reasons, such as his being overwhelmed by excitations linked with aggressiveness against his unfaithful mother and his consequent guilt, he prefers, however, to transform the groans into coughs, which are less disturbing. At the same time, he associates the doctor's bag with the coming of the stork. He knows very well that all will occur inside his mother's body. Moreover, without having attended the delivery, he understands that the child came out of his mother's genitals, since he associates blood with his widdler.

Therefore, I think that the interpretation of Hans' phobia has to take into account the castration wish of which the father is the object. These wishes may only be understood if we link them to a knowledge— if not a conscious one, at least a repressed one—of the parents' genital complementarity, and, consequently, of the mother's vagina. The horse, as the father's substitute (or as the father's penis substitute), is not only the object onto which Hans had displaced his castration fears, but also the object onto which he had projected his wishes to castrate his father. It is through the two mechanisms—of displacement and of projection—that the horse has become a source of anxiety.

Hostility against the father is indeed pointed out by Freud as essential for the symptom formation, but as a death wish. For instance he says: 'Hans really was a little Oedipus who wanted to have his father "out of the way", to get rid of him, so that he might be alone with his beautiful mother and sleep with her... But subsequently... the wish had taken the form that his father should be *permanently* away—that he should be dead' (pp. 111-12). Also, in connection with the fallen horses, a theme which I have understood as expressing a strong wish for castration, Freud writes: 'His father pointed out to him that when he saw the horse fall down he must have thought of him, his father, and have wished that he might fall down in the same way and be dead' (p. 125). As we see, there is no mention of the wish of castrating the father. Even when Freud resumes the study of Little Hans in *Inhibitions, Symptoms and Anxiety* (1926), he mentions only the death wish. By emphasizing the links between the knowledge of the vagina, of the genital primal scene and the wish to identify with one's father, and to introject his attributes, I have attempted to contribute to the differentiation between the normal or neurotic process of development and the perverse one.

Before finishing this presentation, I would like to quote one of Freud's notes in 'Little Hans' added in 1923. It is not essential to this chapter but it will be important for the one on fetishism:

> Since this was written, the study of castration complex has been further developed in contributions to the subject by Lou Andreas-Salome (1916), A. Stärcke (1910), F. Alexander (1922), and others. It has been urged that every time his mother's breast is withdrawn from a baby he is bound to feel it as a castration (that is to say, as a loss of what he regards as an important part of his own body); that, further, he cannot fail to be similarly affected by the regular loss of his faeces; and, finally, that the act of birth itself (consisting as it does in the separation of the child from his mother, with whom he has hitherto been united) is the prototype of all castration. While recognizing all these roots of the complex, I have nevertheless put forward the view that the term "castration complex" ought to be confined to those excitations and consequences which are bound up with the loss of the *penis*. Anyone who, in analysing adults, has become convinced of the invariable presence of the castration complex, will of course find difficulty in ascribing its origin to a chance threat—of a kind which is not, after all, of such universal occurrence; he will be driven to assume that children construct this danger for themselves out of the slightest hints, which will never be wanting (p. 8).

For my chapter on fetishism, the first part of this note, dealing with prefigurations of castration, has to be kept in mind.

Chapter 5

A Re-reading of 'The Wolf-Man'

Here, through a reading of 'The Wolf-Man' (1918), I continue with my attempt to question the infantile sexual theory of phallic monism in Freud's clinical accounts. I would like, at the same time, to introduce an *economic* theory of the building up of the imago of the phallic mother. The purpose of this theory is not to replace the already existing ones (Freud's and Klein's), but to be added to them.

If Little Hans' phobia was focused upon the positive side of the Oedipus Complex, the 'infantile neurosis' of the Wolf-Man was focused on the negative one, on the desire 'to be copulated with by his father', to take the mother's place in the primal scene. We know that, when he was 1½ years old, the child would have witnessed his parents having intercourse *a tergo* (from behind) and that he dreamt the wolf-dream when he was 4. Now, according to Freud, 'The activation of the primal scene in the dream now brought him back to the genital organization. He discovered the vagina and the biological significance of masculine and feminine' (p. 47). Here we see a contradiction with the theory of the discovery of the vagina at the time of puberty. In a rather curious way, Freud asserts that the observation of the coitus *a tergo* brought the Wolf-Man to the conviction of the reality of castration.

Now, not only is the fore-part of the female body, in this position, wholly hidden (to Freud's 'realistic' arguments one is tempted to answer in the same 'realistic' way), but we find here an ambiguity as regards the role that knowledge of the vagina plays in masculine castration complex. Here, this knowledge is considered as being chiefly accountable for the Wolf-Man's castration fears; the vagina would be, precisely, the wound resulting from castration by the father. According to Freud, the child would have repressed his knowledge of the female organ in order to preserve his old theory of anal intercourse:

> But now came the new event that occurred when he was four years old. What he had learnt in the meantime, the allusions which he had heard to castration, awoke and cast a doubt on the "cloacal theory"; they brought to his notice the difference between the sexes and the sexual part played by women. In this contingency, he behaved as children in general behave when they are given an unwished for piece of information, whether sexual or of any

other kind. He rejected what was new (in our case, from motives connected with his fear of castration) and clung fast to what was old. He decided in favour of the intestine and against the vagina... He rejected the new information, and clung fast to what was the old one (p. 79).

Here again we find an assessment which is inconsistent with other formulations by Freud. In 'Analysis Terminable and Interminable' (1937), he shows that passivity towards a man, whatever its nature, may be felt as a castration, and an actual penetration is not a prerequisite for arousing fears of losing one's penis. Anal penetration, *a fortiori*, would not prevent a man from fearing castration. The fear of passivity forms the bed-rock of male patients' analysis.

At no other point in one's analytic work does one suffer more from an oppressive feeling that one's repeated efforts have been in vain, and from a suspicion that one has been "preaching to the winds", than... when one is seeking to convince a man that a passive attitude to men does not always signify castration and that it is indispensable in many relationships in life (p. 252).

That leads to the idea that there exists in every man, so to speak, a normal 'paranoiac core' with a very largely spread sexualization of social feelings. Furthermore, it is striking that the wishes for penetration by the father's penis were active in the Wolf-Man's case when observing parental coitus at the age of 1½, and revived in his dream at the age of 4, yet the same wish for penetration arises in the girl's case only in puberty! The Wolf-Man, like President Schreber, wishes to have a child by his father, an instinctual wish bound up with his feminine identification, while the girl's wish is only a substitute for, an ersatz version of, her penis envy. The man's feminine wishes to be penetrated would therefore be more direct than the woman's. Moreover, how can we think that the boy, in the negative (or inverted) side of his Oedipus Complex, could have wishes to be penetrated (like his mother), and that he would not have *active* wishes to penetrate his mother as bound up with the positive side of his Oedipus Complex?

Indeed, the Wolf-Man's material is really puzzling. Our perplexity is possibly tied to the very nature of the trouble the patient suffers from. For to state that they are focused on the inverted form of Oedipus Complex, on the feminine, passive relationship to the father, and on the fears of castration which are thus aroused, is undoubtedly an over-simplification. When Freud resumes the study of the case in *Inhibitions, Symptoms and Anxiety* (1926), he is of course informed of the subsequent destiny of the Wolf-Man's so-called neurosis—which is to be understood when Freud questions the possibility of a libidinal instinctual regression in the 'Russian' when fearing to be *devoured* by the wolf. He thought: 'The case history of the Russian Wolf-Man gives very definite support to the second, more serious view' (p. 105).

However, he uses the case of 'the Russian' as well as Hans', with their symptoms focused on anxiety-inducing animals, as models of phobias, entirely generated by castration anxiety. This position is the more striking as, in this work, the castration complex is clearly a part of a spectrum of which it is not the end (the latter is the anxiety before the Superego). Now, when comparing Hans with the Wolf-Man, he writes: 'This force was the same in both of them. It was the fear of impending castration... It was from fear of being castrated... that the little Russian relinquished his wish to be loved by his father, for he thought that a relation of that sort presupposed a sacrifice of his genitals—of the organ which distinguished him from a female' (pp. 107-8).

Although he focuses his reflections on castration anxiety in the Wolf-Man's case, Freud provides a very fruitful hypothesis, in order to support his rejection of the Adlerian theory:

> ...A juster appreciation of the process of repression in our present case would lead us to deny that narcissistic masculinity was the sole motive force. The homosexual attitude which came into being during the dream was of such overwhelming intensity that the little boy's Ego found itself unable to cope with it and so defended itself against it by the process of repression. The narcissistic masculinity, which attached to his genital being opposed to the homosexual attitude, was drawn in, in order to assist the Ego in carrying out the task ('The Wolf-Man', pp. 110-11).

We may understand this description as being that of a traumatic situation; for Freud, the primal scene dream is to be considered as a trauma. According to the description given by Freud of the traumatic situation later on in *Inhibition, Symptoms and Anxiety* (1926), there the Ego is in a state of helplessness, because of its immaturity and inability to master the excitations overwhelming it. It is then the seat of automatic anxiety. Repression is then of a primary kind. Castration is perhaps not the ultimate threat. This we may suppose to concern the Ego's actual foundations. The subject would try, in this way, to pass *from the sphere of catastrophe to that of castration*. The question is the following: why a homosexual attitude of 'such overwhelming intensity'? After all, there are certainly many children who observe their parents' intercourse without being overwhelmed by their desires of feminine, passive identification.

I do not claim to solve the problem, and I shall approach only those aspects which seem to be related to my purpose: to test the validity of the theory of phallic monism. This theory stipulates the attribution, by the boy, of a penis to all human beings, women included. At least, until the dissolution of the Oedipus Complex, it would fundamentally contradict the wish to castrate women. In connection with Freud's 'Leonardo da Vinci', I have elsewhere sketched out a different idea. I supposed that maternal seduction intruding upon the child, and, in fact, every situation in which the Ego is overwhelmed by excitations (and, therefore, every traumatic situation), end in the building up of a maternal phallic imago. Now, it seems that the Wolf-Man suffered from several kinds of trauma: to begin with, he had been severely ill as an infant, after which he had been seduced and had witnessed his parents' intercourse. These traumas seem to me to favour the building up of such a particularly dangerous imago.

Freud considers that 'the sexual development of the case that we are now examining has a great disadvantage from the point of view of research, for it was by no means undisturbed. It was first decisively influenced by seduction, and was then diverted by the scene of observation of the coitus, which in its deferred action operated like a second seduction' (p. 47).

If we stick to my hypothesis of a building up of a maternal phallic imago in the case of cumulative traumas, I may imagine that the penis thus ascribed to the mother is linked to the lack of psychic working through of the events experienced by the subject, which broke into him, and which remain in him as a foreign body. Because of the threats of being overwhelmed weighing heavily upon it and its very existence, the Ego may be led into attempting to transform the nature of the danger. At the beginning, it was of a merely economic kind, but, owing to the call to narcissistic masculinity, it would change into the dynamic kind bound up with a conflict.

The precocious mobilization of the conflict in order to master the overwhelming of the Ego is, in fact, added to the effects of the first trauma. The impulses and defences are activated and break into the Ego. If the subsequent projection onto the maternal imago of the 'foreign body' under the form of a penis obeys the principle of constancy, at the same time it acquires a persecutory value, since the release of the instinctual excitations and the working through of the conflict by the Ego have not been performed. This part of the Ego which is projected onto the mother will attempt to return to the subject's Ego; for that reason, it will persecute him. In my opinion, it is the mother who is the object of that projection; for, at the time of these traumatic experiences, when the Ego was immature, they were inevitably ascribed to the mother. (I am thinking, here, of the Wolf-Man's early illnesses, as well as of the two seductions. We should notice that we have no information about the Wolf-Man's relationship to his mother.)

Having read 'Little Hans', Abraham asked Freud if he thought that the father is always preponderant, and added that in his own cases it was often the mother (Letter 7 April 1910, in *Letters of Sigmund Freud and Karl Abraham*, 1965). Whereas the mother is to some extent present in Little Hans, she is almost absent in the Wolf-Man.

The influx of internal excitations which surges in the dream or during the observation of parental intercourse when the child was 18 months old induces us to question the nature of the instincts thus activated, and of their object. For Freud, homosexual instincts are undoubtedly involved. Their object is the father, according to the inverted Oedipus Complex. However, in my opinion, the question remains. What gives this instinctual impulse its overwhelming intensity, and makes its passive and submissive nature so attractive, and, at the same time, so dangerous, would be linked to the threatening persecutory maternal imago, underlying the father, and whose instrusion into the Ego is, at once, dreaded and inexorable. For economic reasons bound up with projection, the Ego can never get rid of itself. But it never stops attempting to do so. This brings us back to the problem of the wish to castrate women as seducers.

Freud confers a decisive importance to the (active) seduction by the sister. However, children's sexual games do not always have such an important negative effect. But what the account does show is the stifling, close and oppressive atmosphere of this childhood as well as the possibly psychotic character of this sister, a precocious, sensual and gifted child who was to commit suicide as an adolescent.

Chapter III begins with two screen-memories related to the English governess. She is supposed to have said on one occasion: 'Do look at my little tail.' On another occasion, her hat flew off 'to the two children's great satisfaction' (p. 19). At once Freud links these memories to a threat of castration uttered by the governess. (Notice that it is a construction.) The Wolf-Man then has dreams of aggression against his sister and the governess: 'It was as though... after her bath... he had tried... to undress his sister... to tear off her coverings... or veils, and so on.' In fact, we are informed that this sister had seduced him. These aggressive fantasies would have been an attempt at playing the active part in the seduction. He would have developed an aversion to his sister as a result of his being seduced.

Now, this theme—the hat which flies off, the torn off veils... —is not only a series of aggressive fantasies, but also of castration fantasies. The sister would have 'oppressed him by her merciless display of superiority' (p. 22); afterwards, the Wolf-Man fell in love with

> servants whose education and intelligence were necessarily far inferior to his own. If all of these objects of his love were substitutes for the figure of the sister whom he had to forego, then it could not be denied that an intention of debasing his sister and of putting an end to her intellectual superiority, which he had formerly found so oppressive, had obtained the decisive control over his object choice (p. 22).

How is it possible to deny here an obvious wish of castration? So, when he begins to catch flies, and pull off their wings, to crush beetles, to imagine that he beats horses, we may think that all these doings are equivalent to castration of a woman's penis.

Later on, concerning Grouscha, he will dream that a man pulls off an Espe's wings. Freud will question him, and discover that, in fact, he is speaking of a Wespe (a wasp). 'The Espe, Freud said, was of course a mutilated Wespe'. Freud comments: 'The dream said clearly that he was avenging himself on Grouscha for the threat of castration' (p. 94). If we suppose that Grouscha had actually threatened him (another construction), the punishment is mutilation, i.e., the castration of an insect which possesses a sting.

We could, of course, wonder why the trauma—a foreign body—is projected in the form of a sexual organ (a penis). In my opinion, the trauma represents a situation liable to arouse a sexual excitation. Remember that Freud said in the *Three Essays* (1905) that nothing important happens in the organism without immediately arousing a sexual excitation. We may, therefore, think that the projected foreign body will be sexualized at once.

We must now come back to the hypothesis according to which the homosexual instincts and the subsequent fear of castration would derive their intensity from the imago of the phallic mother in the background. It would be its persecutory nature which would imbue the relationship to the father, and would give it its threatening character. We may even suppose that the homosexual submission to the father constitutes an attempt at escaping submission to the maternal imago. This is a fruitless attempt indeed, since the primary relationship with the mother filters through to the relationship with the father, but this attempt is all the more desperately pursued.

The inverted Oedipus is part of the 'normal' Oedipus. Usually boys achieve its integration on the quiet, so to speak, as in Little Hans' case. Indeed, his plumber phantasy can be seen as one of the aspects of his inverted Oedipus Complex enabling him to identify with his father without losing his penis, but rather getting it, and thus securing a future masculine identity just like his father's ('His father was his model'). If the case of the little Russian is not the same, if he is stopped by the difficulty of his task, if his castration fears are so strong, is it not in relation to this maternal phallic imago which simultaneously pushes him towards his father, and sets its seal on the relationship to him? Castration anxiety would then be the heir of the previous persecutory relationship, a resort against the disintegrating influx of excitations. (Here, I am following Freud's ideas.) The anxiety-inducing animal would remain marked by the ambiguity of the paternal figure concealing the maternal one. This would account for the fact that if the horse's biting is only a way of expressing, in oral language, the fear of castration, the wolf which would devour the little Russian would represent an instinctual (libidinal) regression to the oral stage: 'This stage, while only hinted at in "Little Hans's" fear of being bitten, was blatantly exhibited in the Wolf-Man's terror of being devoured' (*Inhibitions, Symptoms and Anxiety*, 1926, p. 106).

These hypotheses would enable us to understand the wishes to castrate women, as presented by the Wolf-Man. His castration fears would no longer need to be ascribed to the (hypothetical) perception of his mother's genitals, a perception which, as we have noticed, led Freud to contradictory statements—the knowledge of the vagina becoming an additional motive of anxiety, the anal relationship with his father being supposed to reassure him, and so on...

If we agreed that there exists an innate knowledge of the vagina and of sexuality as a whole, including genitality, it would save us all these troubles. In fact, the Freudian theory of sexuality oscillates between two poles. One is the ontogenetic pole, the other, the phylogenetic one. As we know, it is in the Wolf-Man that Freud unfolds this second aspect of his ideas.

Thus he supports the thesis according to which the castration threat, even if uttered by women, is finally ascribed to the father:

> There is no doubt whatever at that time his father was turning into the terrifying figure that threatened him with castration... At this point the boy had to fit into a phylogenetic pattern, and he did so, although his personal experiences may not have agreed with it. Although the threats or hints of castration which came his way had emanated from women, this could not hold up the final result for long. In spite of everything it was his father from whom in the end he came to fear castration. In this respect heredity triumphed over accidental experience; in man's prehistory it was unquestionably the father who practised castration as a punishment (Wolf-Man, p. 86).

Freud is referring here to the 'scientific myth' of the primal horde (*Totem and Taboo*, 1912-13).

At the end of his study on the Wolf-Man, Freud goes back to his theory of inherited phylogenetic schemata and unfolds it:

> I have come to an end of what I had to say about this case. There remain two problems, of the many that it raises, which seem to me to deserve special emphasis. The first relates to the phylogenetically inherited schemata, which, like the categories of philosophy, are concerned with the business of "placing" the impressions derived from actual experience. I am inclined to take the view that they are precipitates from the history of human civilization. The Oedipus Complex, which comprises a child's relation to his parents, is one of them—is, in fact, the best known member of the class. Wherever experiences fail to fit in with the hereditary schema, they become remodelled in imagination—a process which might profitably be followed out in detail. It is precisely

such cases that are calculated to convince us of the independent existence of the schema. We are often able to see the schema triumphing over the experience of the individual, as when, in our present case, the boy's father became the castrator and the menace of his infantile sexuality in spite of what was in other respects an inverted Oedipus Complex. A similar process is at work where a nurse comes to play the mother's part or where the two become fused together. The contradictions between experience and the schema seem to supply the conflicts of childhood with an abundance of material (pp. 119-20).

Freud has, therefore, a conception of psycho-sexual development which might by called 'orthogenetic', an orthogenesis which is possibly disturbed by the various events in the personal story. An example would be seduction; according to Freud, it disrupts the normal succession of the different libidinal stages, as in the Wolf-Man case. The necessity of classifying the impressions, and of forcing them into the schema, is positively fundamental; it enables the subject to emerge from confusion and chaos.

If we leave aside the question of phylogenesis, while agreeing with the existence of schemata and of the classification, it allows us or, rather, it orders us to understand that the Wolf-Man had indeed desperately tried to transpose the conflict with his primary imago onto his father. He had also felt the necessity to fight in order to differentiate his imagos, and had subsequently failed, giving way to psychosis. But Freud continues:

> The second problem is not far removed from the first, but it is incomparably more important. If one considers the behaviour of the four-year-old child towards the re-activated primal scene, or even if one thinks of the far simpler reactions of the one-and-a-half-year-old child when the scene was actually experienced, it is hard to dismiss the view that some sort of hardly definable knowledge, something, as it were, preparatory to an understanding, was at work in the child at the time. We can form no conception of what this may have consisted of; we have nothing at our disposal but the single analogy—and it is an excellent one—of the far-reaching *instinctive* knowledge of animals.
> If human beings too possessed an instinctive endowment such as it is, it would not be surprising that it should be very particularly concerned with the processes of sexual life, even though it could not be by any means confined to them. This instinctive factor would then be the nucleus of the unconscious, a primitive kind of mental activity, which would later be dethroned and overlaid by human reason, when the faculty came to be acquired, but which in some people, perhaps in every one, would retain the power of drawing down to it the higher mental processes (p. 120).

It is striking to see how much the idea of an *instinctive* knowledge—the nucleus of the unconscious—is, at first sight, opposed to the idea of a progressive libidinal development, to the absence of a preformed sexual instinct with its determined aim and object, this latter idea being a fundamental one in Freud's theory. In the same line, he asserts that there is no such thing as an instinctual attraction between the sexes. (The infantile theory of phallic monism results from that.) However, we see that Eros, in the last Instinct Theory, runs counter to this idea, for, as a principle of binding, it is based on the model of the fusion of the germinal cells.

Perhaps we could try to get rid of these contradictions between 'innate knowledge' and 'ignorance of the vagina', between an instinct of reproduction and the phallic phase, if we turn to Freud's writings where he describes the dissolution of the Oedipus Complex as associated with the gap between the child's desires and his ability to satisfy them. To begin with, remember Freud's dark picture of the Oedipal child in *Beyond the Pleasure Principle* (1920):

> The early efflorescence of infantile sexual life is doomed to extinction because its wishes are incompatible with reality and with the inadequate stage of development which the child has reached. That efflorescence comes to an end in the most distressing consequences and to the accompaniment of the most painful feelings. Loss of love and failure leave behind them a permanent injury to self-regard in the form of a narcissistic scar, which in my opinion, as well as in Marcinowski's (1918), contributes more than anything to the "sense of inferiority" which is so common in neurotics. The child's sexual researches, on which limits are imposed by his physical development, lead to no satisfactory conclusion; hence such later compaints as 'I can't accomplish anything; I can't succeed in anything.' The tie of affection, which binds the child as a rule to the parent of the opposite sex, succumbs to disappointment, to a vain expectation of satisfaction or to jealousy over the birth of a new baby—unmistakable proof of the infidelity of the object of the child's affections. His own attempt to make a baby himself, carried out with tragic seriousness, fails shamefully. The lessening amount of affection he receives, the increasing demands of education, hard words and an occasional punishment, these show him at last the full extent to which he has been scorned (pp. 20-21).

The relinquishing of the Oedipal object seems, in this context, tied to the child's painful recognition of his smallness and inadequacy. This is the tragedy of lost illusions. In 'The Dissolution of the Oedipus Complex' (1924), Freud, at the beginning of his article, examines the motives of the dissolution of the Oedipus Complex after having been prominent. He comes back to the same conclusions: 'In this way the Oedipus Complex would go to its destruction from its lack of success, from the effects of its internal possibilities.' (Of course, for Freud, this 'lack of success' is one of the motives of the dissolution of the Oedipus Complex. To it, he adds the idea of an innate 'programme': 'Time has come for its disintegration,' and, above all, the castration complex.)

Béla Grunberger, in 'Narcissism and the Oedipus Complex' (1966), lays stress on the narcissistic injury of the Oedipal child who is hampered by his (physiological) incapacity to act out his incestuous wish. He points out the consequences of the chronological gap existing between the manifestation of the Oedipal wishes in the child and the ability to satisfy them. The establishment of the barrier against incest aims at preserving the narcissism of the child: he substitutes a prohibition for an internal inability. The author ascribes to the premature birth of human beings this chronological lag between the desire and the ability to satisfy it.

We may recall that this idea of a lack of achievement and its ensuing helplessness (Hilflösigkeit) plays an important part in Freud's work. Let me just quote the following studies: in 'The Project' (1895), he refers morals to the child's dependency on adults for his survival. '... The initial helplessness of human beings is the primal source of all moral motives' (p. 138).

We may remember that the long dependency of the child and the castration complex are put side by side in *The Ego and the Id* (1923) as motives of the setting up of the Super-Ego. In *Inhibitions, Symptoms and Anxiety* (1926), he ascribes to human primary helplessness—which he calls 'the biological factor'—a major part in the causation of neuroses:

> The biological factor is the long period of time during which the young of the human species is in a condition of helplessness and dependence; its intra-uterine existence seems to be short in comparison with that of most animals, and it is sent into the world in a less finished state. As a result, the influence of the real external world upon it is intensified and an early differentiation between the Ego and the Id is promoted. Moreover, the dangers of the external world have a greater importance for it, so that the value of the object which can alone protect it against them and take the place of its former intra-uterine life is enormously enhanced. The biological factor, then, establishes the earliest situations of danger and creates the need to be loved which will accompany the child through the rest of its life (pp. 154-55).

As I have emphasized many times, the theory of phallic monism is a means of healing a part of the narcissistic injury, common to human beings, resulting from the child's helplessness. We may suppose that it is precisely this primary helplessness which makes the innate, animal-like knowledge of man vanish into oblivion and leave way for a slow and painful maturation. It is the noncoincidence between the incestuous wish and the aptitude to satisfy it which gives its importance to infantile sexuality, to pregenitality, to fantasy life, to symbol-formation and to infantile sexual theories: the latter are children's creations whose purpose is not only to penetrate the secrets of adult life, but also to distort the sexual truth in order to make it tolerable.

We may here use a metaphor: the totality of human sexual potentials would be present from birth, as a rolled up tape, which development and maturation would progressively unroll. Because of human helplessness, sexuality changes into psycho-sexuality, and the impossibility for man to achieve immediately his incestuous wish, 'presses (him) ever forward unsubdued' (*Beyond the Pleasure Principle*, 1920, p. 42, from Faust: 'Ungebändigt immer vorwärts dringt').

Chapter 6

Narcissism and Group Psychology

To start with, I would like to relate a movie. It was shown in Paris in the early 1970s and was not on for long. However, in my opinion it is a work of genius, called 'The Corpse Incinerator'; the director is a Czechoslovak named J. Herz. The main character is played by an outstanding actor, whose name is Hrusinsky. The story is that of a criminal pervert, a necrophile, who disguises the anal-sadistic character of his occupation (he works in a crematorium) by idealizing it. He explains to an apprentice that cremation enables the soul to free itself from the body (clearly likened to a blemish that he helps it to get rid of), how beautiful and useful a thing death is, that it shortens suffering, etc. He himself will become the murderer of his wife and children, for they have 'impure' blood in them.

He loves 'beautiful' music and buys 'beautiful' paintings—in fact, 'kitsch', whose anality he does not succeed in entirely concealing. He is in the habit of walking around 'pretty' churchyards whose statues he admires. His wife is supposed to be an 'angel'; his marriage provided him with an 'angelic life'. He is wont to stroke the faces of young dead women, to comb their hair, and then to comb his own hair; the comb may be considered here as a fetish. At the same time, he is a mystic, fascinated by Buddhism. (Compare here metempsychosis with Sade's ideas that annihilation does not exist but that all things and beings only change their forms.) He imagines a huge collective crematorium where, at least, souls will be quickly delivered, more quickly than in an ordinary crematorium. He will offer his service to the Nazis and will end in believing he is the Dalailama.

We see clearly that here he uses mysticism to magnify his own anal-sadistic activity, to remove all its 'faecal' character, to transform excrement into gold, and to transform digestion—which is combustion, just like incineration—into a marvellous alchemy, freeing the soul from the body, which is nothing but mere refuse. Béla Grunberger (1959) speaks of digestion as a 'fragmentation of ingested food and its degradation into less and less differentiated elements, which progressively lose their former peculiarities, and forming finally a homogeneous mass, the faecal bolus', a fact he associates (among others) with the Auschwitz gauleiter's words by calling his camp 'the anus of the world'. Now, the hero of the film notices that the ashes resulting from the process of cremation are perfectly homogeneous, 'all entirely identical', he says.

In this movie, we see clearly how a pervert may find, in a collective movement, a possibility for acting-out, through crime, all his phantasies to their utmost conclusions. The necrophile's occupation did not enable him to go that far, and the satisfactions he derived from it were incomplete. Thanks to the Nazis' arrival, his perversion is put into the service of Good. For we must never forget that all ideologies always present themselves as being associated with Good. Even if we see Nazism as a repugnant doctrine, we must not forget that it prided itself on creating a new and pure man. Who is not in favour of purity? It is a value which, at first sight, has a strongly positive connotation. I shall later mention ideologies in so far as they are relevant to the topic.

But I would like to take the direction opposite to that of the movie I have just described. The people I shall consider are not perverts, but ordinary people, perhaps you and me—who are possibly inveigled into doing... anything. I do not mean that everybody, under certain circumstances, may become an S.S. stormtrooper or a terrorist. For that, something more than the pervert core, common to us all, and of which I have spoken, is necessary. But I have only to glance at contemporary history to find immediate support for my claim that everybody—or nearly everybody—may become a Nazi or a member of any extremist movement.

I would like to try to make use of psychoanalysis to endeavour to give an explanation of this phenomenon, which is undoubtedly one of the most disturbing of our day and age, although it is not the exclusive privilege of our time. I hope that, once this attempt has been brought to its conclusion, it will be *more* difficult for us to understand how and why certain people offer resistance to great collective movements—why they do not become 'rhinoceroses' (Ionesco's metaphor in his play devoted to totalitarian temptation)—than to understand why and how great human masses join in against their better judgement.

We should notice at once that there is, at a certain level, a fundamental difference between the Ego Ideal as the heir of narcissism, and the Superego as the heir both of the Oedipus Complex and of the castration complex which, according to Freud, are intrinsically bound up together. The former (the Ego Ideal)—at least at the beginning—constitutes an attempt at recovering the lost omnipotence. The latter (the Superego), according to Freud, results from the internalization of the barrier against incest, a process ruled by the fear of castration. The former aims at reinstalling illusion, the latter instauring reality. The Superego breaks the ties between child and mother; the Ego Ideal, as I have emphasized, prompts him to merging with his mother.

The wish to be their own Ideal, as at the very beginning of life, seems never to be given up by most human beings. To different degrees it persists unchanged, despite the vicissitudes it undergoes, at another level, parallel to the Ego's evolution. The Freudian Superego is the latest agency of the psychic apparatus. When Freud introduces the Superego in the structural theory, we know that he identifies it with the Ego Ideal. Thus he says (in *The Ego and the Id*, 1923):

> The Superego is, however, not simply a residue of the earliest object-choices of the Id; it also represents an energetic reaction-formation against those choices. Its relation to the Ego is not exhausted by the precept: "You *ought to be* like this (like your father)". It also comprises the prohibition: "You *may not be* like this (like your father)"—that is, you may not do all that he does; some things are his prerogative (p. 34).

In our perspective, as we continue to differentiate the Ego Ideal from the Superego, we may say that the positive injunction originates from the heir of narcissism (i.e., the Ego-Ideal) and the negative one from the heir of the Oedipus Complex (i.e., the Superego). Remember also that, according to Freud, many adults never reach a real 'moral conscience', resulting from internalized prohibitions. They feel no real 'guilt feelings' but only 'social anxiety'; in short, they have no actual Superego and are only prevented from doing evil by the fear of being discovered (*Civilization and its Discontents*, 1929). This idea had been previously expressed through similar remarks, in particular in 'On Narcissism: an Introduction' (1914), and in the chapter on Identification, in *Group Psychology and the Analysis of the Ego* (1921); at that moment, Freud had not yet introduced the structural theory.

In 1933, studying the different agencies of the psychic apparatus (in 'The Dissection of the Psychic Personality', in *New Introductory Lectures*), he was yet more radical:

> Following a well-known pronouncement of Kant's which couples the conscience within us with the starry Heavens above, a pious man might well be tempted to honour these two things, as the masterpieces of creation. The stars are indeed magnificent, but as regards conscience, God has done an uneven and careless piece of work, for a large majority of men have brought along with them only a modest amount of it or scarcely enough to be mentioned.

It seems to me that, reading psychoanalytical literature, this Freudian proposition has not been taken very seriously; on the contrary, the emphasis is on the universal cruelty of the Superego. There is sometimes a lack of differentiation between various factors which are indistinctly ascribed to the heir of the Oedipus Complex.

In fact, certain circumstances even favour the sweeping away of this recently fixed, sometimes almost non-existent, and, in any case fragile agency. This sweeping away happens when the old wish for union of the Ego with the Ego Ideal is suddenly reactivated. For example, it was one of Alexander's patients who told him that the Superego was soluble in alcohol. It is, indeed, a feeling of narcissistic elation, the encounter of the Ego with the Ego Ideal that dissolves the Superego.

Collective phenomena seem to be particularly suited to instigating the dissolution of the Superego. Freud had already noticed this in *Group Psychology and the Analysis of the Ego* (1921):

> For us it would be enough to say that in a group the individual is brought under conditions which allow him to throw off the repressions of his unconscious instinctual impulses. The apparently new characteristics which he then displays are in fact the manifestations of this unconscious, in which all that is evil in the human mind is contained as a predisposition. We can find no difficulty in understanding the disappearance of conscience or of a sense of responsibility in these circumstances. It has long been our contention that "social anxiety" is the essence of what is called "conscience" (pp. 74-75).
>
> In obedience to the new authority [that of the group] he may put his former "conscience" out of action, and so surrender to the attraction of the increased pleasure that is certainly obtained from the removal of inhibitions. On the whole, therefore, it is not remarkable that we should see an individual in a group doing or approving things which he would have avoided in normal conditions of life... (p. 85).

Freud says yet again: '...We should have to admit that in any collection of people the tendency to form a psychological group may very easily come to the fore' (p. 100). As we know, Freud considers the group 'as a revival of the primal horde' (p. 123) which was made up of 'an individual of superior strength among a troop of equal companions' (p. 122). 'The primal father is the group ideal, which governs the Ego in the place of the Ego Ideal' (p. 127), whereas the members of the group, after having put one and the same object in the place of their Ego Ideal, identify themselves with one another in their Ego. The cohesiveness of the group depends first of all on its relationship with the leader which prompts the component members to lose their individuality.

Thus each member of the group likens himself to the others: 'If an individual gives up his distinctiveness in a group and lets its other members influence him by suggestion, it gives one the impression that he does it because he feels the need of being in harmony with them rather than in opposition to them—so that perhaps after all he does it 'ihnen zu Liebe' [for love of them] (p. 92). 'So long as a group formation persists or so far as it extends, individuals in the group behave as though they were uniform' (p. 102). And also:

> We thus have an impression of a state in which an individual's private emotional impulses and intellectual acts are too weak to come to anything by themselves and are entirely dependent for this on being reinforced by being repeated in a similar way in the other members of the group. We are reminded of how many of these phenomena of dependence are part of the normal constitution of human society, of how little originality and personal courage are to be found in it, of how much every individual is ruled by those attitudes of the group-mind which exhibit themselves in such forms as racial characteristics, class prejudices, public opinion, etc.

This erasing of individual characteristics comes about as the members of the group identify with each other after having built up a common Ego Ideal by projecting it onto the same object—that is, the leader. This erasing seems therefore all the more absolute as the individual characters present a greater intrinsic weakness. In the primal horde

> the will of the individual was too weak; he did not venture upon action. No impulses whatever came into existence except collective ones; there was only a common will, there were no single ones. An idea did not dare to turn itself into an act of will unless it felt itself reinforced by a perception of its general diffusion (note, pp. 122-23).

Moreover, there would exist a will to make the members of the group uniform; this will would originate from sibling rivalry:

> If one cannot be the favourite oneself, at all events nobody else shall be the favourite... What appears later in the shape of Gemeingeist, esprit de corps, "group spirit", etc... does not belie its derivation from what was originally envy. No one must want to put himself forward, everyone must be the same and have the same. Social justice means that we deny ourselves many things so that others may have to do without them as well, or, what is the same thing, may not be able to ask for them (pp. 120-21).

Discussing the herd instinct, Freud stated that what is demanded by the members of a group is that 'all the members must be equal to one another, but they all want to be ruled by one person. Many equals who can identify themselves with one another, and a single person superior to them all' (p. 121); consequently Freud prefers to assert that man is, rather than a herd animal, a horde animal, that is, 'an individual creature in a horde led by a chief' (p. 121).

If we put these propositions together we are led by Freud to a situation relating to the father-complex (one of Freud's expressions for the Oedipus Complex which stresses the relations with the father), the leader being a father substitute, and the individuals composing the group being likened to a brotherhood. It seems to me that all human gatherings, and particularly groups, do not correspond to this schema, which refers to a relatively advanced kind of situation.

An illuminating article by Didier Anzieu, 'L'illusion groupale' (1971), corroborates the thesis I shall try to present here. The author establishes an analogy between the group and the dream. All group situations would be felt as an imaginary accomplishment of a wish. He points out that 'under thousands of various disguises, in the course of history, the group has been imagined as this fabulous place where all wishes can be satisfied... Thomas More's Utopia, Rabelais' Abbey of Theleme, Fourier's phalanstery, Jules Romain's chums...'

According to the author, in the group as in the dream, the mental apparatus undergoes a threefold regression. In the temporal one, the group tends to regress to primary narcissism. In the topographical one, the Ego and the Superego have to give up their control. There the Id takes possession of the mental apparatus together with the Ego Ideal which 'tends to achieve fusion with the almighty mother and to re-establish, by means of introjection, the first lost love object. The group becomes, for its members, the substitute of this lost object'. As for the formal regression, it reveals itself through the recourse to ways of expression infiltrated by primary processes, similar to the first verbal exchanges between mother and child. Didier Anzieu thus shows that a group which functions by itself—without any organ of control in charge of reality testing—'functions, by nature, in the register of illusion'.

Anzieu describes three successive observations of groups which will let certain themes constituting 'the group illusion' come to the fore. It is a question of setting up an egalitarian theory: 'Bumps and hollows have to be smoothed out, the heads have to be levelled even, each one reduced to the common denominator.' This statement is interpreted by the author as the negation of the difference between the sexes, and, more comprehensively, that of primary phantasies. The egalitarian ideology is a defence against castration anxiety. A denial of the primal scene appears as well. The group is supposed to be self-engendered. It represents the almighty mother. It is not a question of organizing around a central figure (the monitor), but around the group itself. 'The group illusion' would therefore be the accomplishment of the wish to 'heal one's narcissistic injuries', and to identify with the good breast (or with the almighty mother).

It seems to me that Didier Anzieu's study helps one to account better for certain group phenomena. In fact, what he describes is exactly the accomplishment of the wish of fusion between the Ego and the Ego Ideal by the most regressive means. Those means which characterize the pleasure principle take the shorter path and abolish all the acquisitions obtained through development.

In fact, the paternal figure is expelled and excluded from the group as well as the Superego. All this happens as if the group formation itself should constitute the brotherhood's hallucinatory accomplishment of possessing the mother in the regressive manner of primary fusion. However, the leader may exist (we have only to think of the Nazi crowds). In my opinion, he must not be confused with the father: the leader is he who activates the ancient wish of union of the Ego with the Ego Ideal. He is the one who promotes illusion, the one who lures men away by dangling it before their wonder-struck eyes, the one by whom it will be achieved.

Time will be fulfilled, D-Day or the extremists' great Day of Revolution will come about, we will behold, all starry-eyed, the Celestial Jerusalem, our needs will be satisfied, the Aryans will conquer the world, the sun will rise, the forthcoming days will resound with song, etc. Groups thirst less after a leader than after illusions. And they choose as their master he who promises the union of the Ego with the Ideal. The leader is Cagliostro. There is no absolute chief without an ideology. In fact, he is a mediator between the group and ideological illusion, and behind ideology there always lies the narcissistic fantasy of omnipotence.

We may notice that Freud, following Gustave Le Bon, says that the leader 'must himself be held in fascination by a strong faith (an idea) in order to awaken the group's faith' (p. 81), but there he leaves the idea. We may also notice that Freud says that 'the notion of impossibility disappears for the individual in a group'; this point is closely linked with ideologies themselves. They make us believe that the impossible is possible. From that point of view the leader—as he who promises the union between the Ego and the Ego Ideal—may be compared to the pervert's mother who makes her son believe that there is no need to wait and to grow up in order to take the father's role and possess his mother. As Freud says, the group 'cannot tolerate any delay between its desire and the fulfilment of what it desires' (p. 77).

I have already described the chronological time-lag between the appearance of the Oedipal wish and the activity to satisfy it. I associate it with the sexual theory of phallic monism and its role in perversions. In fact, I believe this theory to be the prototype of ideologies. We may recall that all of them rest on the promise of a possible abolition of obstacles and efforts, in short, abolition of evolution and development. Thus considered, the leader is not the father's substitute; on the contrary, he is the man who implicitly promises the coming of a world without any father and a correlative union with the almighty mother, the one before the breaking up of primary fusion, even with the one before birth. Not long after May 1968 (the so-called 'student revolution' in France), a song which made a hit was entitled: 'All of Us Will Go to Heaven'.

Nazism has often been compared to a religion, the Nuremberg meetings to a Roman Catholic Mass, and Hitler to a High-Priest. However, the cult thus celebrated has a Mother-Goddess (Blut und Boden, or blood and earth)—rather than the father—as its object. In such groups, what we see is an actual eradication of the father and paternal universe as well as of all the Oedipus Complex derivatives. In the case of Nazism, the return to Nature, to the old Germanic mythology, expresses a yearning after the fusion with the almighty mother.

From this standpoint we understand better that the Superego can be so violently and positively swept away, as well as the Ego Ideal in its developed form, each time the illusion has been activated within a human gathering. If the Ego and the Ego Ideal can be reunited, all that has been acquired through development is useless and even cumbersome, for it has been acquired progressively, precisely because of the gap between the Ego and the Ego Ideal. Joseph Sandler, in his paper 'On the Concept of Superego' (1960), points out that

> ...situations do exist in which the Ego can and will totally disregard the standards and the precepts of the Superego, if it can gain a sufficient quantity of narcissistic support elsewhere. We see this impressive phenomenon in the striking changes in ideals, character, and morality which may result from the donning of a uniform and the feeling of identity with a group. If narcissistic support is available in sufficient quantity from an identification with the ideals of a group or with the ideals of a leader, then the Superego may be completely disregarded, and its functions taken over by the group ideals, precepts and behaviour. If these group ideals permit a direct gratification of instinctual wishes, then a complete character transformation may occur... and the extent to which the Superego can be abandoned in this way is evident in the appalling atrocities committed by the Nazis before and during the last war' (pp. 156-57).

I can only agree with J. Sandler, since I stress the narcissistic reconquest which serves as a project to groups based on ideology. On the other hand, it seems to me that the capability of performing atrocities (as instinctual satisfactions) is not only due to the adoption of the group's moral criteria (taking over the personal Superego), but is the necessary consequence of the group's ideology. Everything likely to hamper the success of the illusion must disappear.

Now, the aim of illusion is the idealization of the Ego (the fusion of the Ideal into the Ego), and there is no idealization of the Ego without projection, so those upholding the projection have to be harassed and ruthlessly annihilated. I think it is not enough to say that murder is then perpetrated in the name of the Superego, and thus becomes lawful; I think it is perpetrated, above all, in the name of the Ideal, as the Infidels were murdered by the Crusaders on the way to Jerusalem. Each reactivation of illusion is thus inexorably followed by a bloodbath if the group possesses external means equal to its internal violence.

It is important to underline the fact that the group members I am speaking of are not necessarily assembled in the same place. It is not only a question of actual groups or crowds but also of individuals (potential group members) united by the same political, mystical, mystico-political or philosophico-mystical convictions: a religion in the etymological sense of the word. This is true even when they do not get together. The regression which takes place in these groups is not induced simply by certain precise, tangible conditions (being in a closed place, cut off from the external world, as described by D. Anzieu), though these conditions favour it. On the contrary, regression seems to depend vitally on the illusion whose advent the leader promises. This promise activates the desire of union between Ego and Ego Ideal through regression, and induces the Ego to merge into the almighty primary object, to absorb the whole universe (Federn's 'egocosmic' Ego).

We may then understand that, in a general way, the propensity to lose Ego boundaries renders the individual particularly liable to identifying himself, not only with each member of the group, but with the gathering as a body. Thus his megalomania is satisfied, each individual's Ego embracing the whole group. The members of the group lose their individualities and start resembling ants or termites; this loss of personal characteristics is all the more necessary as it contributes to homogenizing the whole group. Thus, each member need not feel like a tiny indistinguishable particle in a huge gathering, but, on the contrary, can identify with the aggregate.

Such an operation gives to each an omnipotent Ego, a gigantic body. The sportive youth demonstrations in totalitarian countries, where an aggregate draws huge slogans or colossal portraits with streamers or on coloured boards, materializes this merging of individual Egos into the group. But, whereas an outside observer can suppose that a narcissistic weakening accompanies the fact of being thus reduced to a tiny fragment in a monumental graph, the exaltation of the participants (together with the crowd of bystanders partaking in the same illusion) shows that unconsciously the psychic Ego of each component has spread to the whole mass. The Ego, having thus extended to the whole group, enables its component individuals to anticipate the pleasure of the Ego being reunited with the Ego Ideal—or rather, to satisfy this wish in a quasi-hallucinatory manner. The group is at once the Ego, the primary object and the Ego Ideal all finally merged.

In *Group Psychology and the Analysis of the Ego* (1921), Freud ascribes the reality testing to the Ego Ideal. In *The Ego and the Id* (1923), he attributes it to the Ego. However, it seems that, in the group situation, this reality testing may be lodged with the Ego Ideal represented by the group and the leader whose role is to promote and maintain the illusion. The individual Ego, merged into the group, gives up its prerogatives to the group. What becomes right and just is only what the whole group decrees as such. He who does not think as the group does is excluded, harassed, killed or declared insane.

In 'The Corpse Incinerator', of which I have previously spoken, an agitated woman, accompanied by her husband who vainly tries to prevent her from creating a stir, makes episodic appearances. One of the sequences—an allegorical representation of the concentration camps—shows a fair where wax figures mime bloody historical scenes, as at Madame Tussaud's. One of the characters holds a knife and, jerkily as though actuated by machinery, he drives it into another wax figure's back. At this very moment, the woman begins to scream: 'But it is blood, real blood, I told you so!' Her husband tries to quieten her and promptly takes her away, telling the bystanders: 'She is completely mad.' It goes without saying that the wax figures represent the deportees, who have been deprived of their human dimension. Only the woman sees them as beings of flesh and blood. She represents the isolated individual whose Ego has not handed over to the group its reality testing function. But reality, at that moment, has become that of the group, representing the Ego Ideal; and whoever has not given up his reality testing function to the group is considered insane. As the film proceeds, the woman's appearances become rarer and rarer; towards the end she disappears, with her husband desperately looking for her. This indicates that the group has entirely taken over reality testing. Everybody has become a rhinoceros. And the group will only set the seal of reality on what is in line with the illusion.

Indeed, it is impossible for a gathering, based on ideology, to refrain from proselytism. It cannot but destroy not only its enemies, not only the people (mentioned above) who are the objects of projection, but also all those who remain outside the group. As they do not play into the hands of those supporting the illusion, they question it, *ipso facto* ('They who are not with us are against us,' said Lenin). Therefore, it is vital to reduce the indifferent and the sceptics, to oblige them to surrender the function of reality testing to the 'believers' ('Der Führer hat immer recht'; 'The Party is always right').

From that point of view, we can understand that it is both dangerous and stressing not to yield to the law of the group, to be a wet blanket. If you do not always risk your life in it, at least your sources of narcissistic supplies will dry up. You become a Pariah condemned to solitude, no longer entitled to your fellow men's love.

However, there is always someone who says: 'Eppur si muove!', or 'Ca n'empêche pas d'exister!' (It does not prevent things from existing!). We may think not only that this person has a better-rooted Oedipal Superego, but that his Ego Ideal has cathected maturation itself, and that he finds—in spite of the sufferings that the lack of love inflicts on each one of us—a narcissistic satisfaction in the very fact that he has not yielded to the seduction of illusion.

Chapter 7

A Psychoanalytical Study of 'Falsehood'

In my chapter on 'Aestheticism, Creation and Perversion', I shall approach the question of the pervert's relation to Art and his *compulsion to idealize*, subsequent to his vital need—vital for the maintenance of his self-esteem—to disguise his pregenital Ego and to conceal its anal character. Indeed, I did not begin my investigations into the difficulties of the creative process with the study of the pervert. I began the other way round, by wondering about what falsehood is. I happen to live in a country, in a town and at a time where false values—aesthetic and intellectual as well as ethical—seem to be gratified with admiration and success at the expense of 'true' values. Maybe you are already wondering what allows me to decide that this is 'true' and that is 'false'. It is, indeed, a difficult question; I am hoping that, to a certain extent, this exploration will help me to find an answer!

So, while I was first interested in what differentiates the 'true' from the 'false', and why the false is so popular, I soon came to the conclusion that the pervert was the 'prototype' of those who go in for falsity. For this reason I became interested in perversions and in perverts, those beings who have the quite enviable faculty of creating an artful universe.

Here, I would like to tell you of my first research, which gave rise to an article entitled 'The Emperor of China's Nightingale—A Psychoanalytical Essay on Falsehood' (1968). I would like to speak of the ideas I then put forward. Of course, they will be interspersed with more recent reflections, some of which will be expounded in my lecture on aestheticism. First I shall summarize the well-known story by Hans Christian Andersen on 'The Nightingale'.

Beyond the limits of the Emperor of China's garden, there was a lovely forest with lofty trees and deep lakes. The forest sloped down to the sea, so that great ships sailed under the shadow of its branches. In these branches lived a nightingale whose exquisite singing enchanted the poor fisherman. The nightingale was soon famous throughout the country. Travellers from every country in the world came to the city in order to admire the palace and the Emperor's garden. But when they returned home they were convinced the nightingale was the best of all the Emperor's wonders.

The Emperor got wind of the nightingale's existence from the books that the wonder-struck travellers had devoted to it.

He called his lord-in-waiting, a man so distinguished that, if anyone of rank inferior to his spoke to him or asked him a question, he would answer: 'Pooh', which means nothing. The Emperor ordered him to bring him the bird, failing which the whole court would be trampled upon after supper. A poor girl in the kitchen was the only person at the court who knew of the nightingale. She led the lord-in-waiting to the nightingale, but he was disappointed to see a little grey bird in the branches and thought it looked ordinary. Nevertheless he invited it to the palace to sing before the Emperor. The nightingale sang so sweetly that tears came into the Emperor's eyes. He gave the bird his golden slipper to wear round its neck but the nightingale declined the offer, having been sufficiently rewarded already by the tears it had seen in the Emperor's eyes. It was now to remain at the court, to have its own cage and was free to go out night and day. The whole city spoke of it. Eleven children were named after it, even though not one of them could sing a note.

One day the Emperor received a large parcel on which was written 'The Nightingale'. It was a work of art contained in a casket, a mechanical nightingale supposed to look like a living one, but it was covered all over with diamonds, rubies and sapphires. As soon as the artificial bird had been wound up, it could sing like the real one, and could move its tail, which sparkled with silver and gold, up and down. It was a present from the Emperor of Japan to the Emperor of China. Very soon after its arrival, the whole court enthused over the mechanical nightingale, which was so beautiful to behold and which could sing thirty times over the same tune at a tempo the real nightingale could not sustain. No one noticed when the real nightingale flew out of the window, back to its green woods. The music-master asserted that the mechanical bird was better than the real one, not only in its glittering dress but also in itself. Everybody agreed in this opinion except the poor fisherman, who said that there seemed something wanting, though he could not say what.

The real nightingale was banished from the Empire and the artificial bird occupied the seat of honour, close to the Emperor. The music-master wrote a work in 25 volumes about the artificial bird, and a very learned work it was, full of the most difficult Chinese words; yet all the people said they had read it and understood it, for fear of being thought stupid and being beaten on their stomachs. But one day the mechanism of the bird got jammed. The delicate wheels were worn. It was allowed to sing only once a year.

Five years went by and the Emperor became severely ill. He could scarcely breathe because Death was sitting on his chest. He implored the artificial bird to sing for him. But the bird remained silent, for there was no one to wind it up, so it could not sing. Death continued to stare at the Emperor with its hollow eyes, when suddenly a sweet song came through the window. It was the living nightingale who, answering its Emperor's call, had flown back to sing him the song of Hope. Death, then, slowly withdrew. When the servants came in expecting to see the dead Emperor, he was standing dressed in full uniform and pressing his golden sword to his heart. He said: 'Good morning!'

This fable is said to have been written in honour of Jenny Lind, called 'the Swedish nightingale', whose success had been overshadowed for a while by the more precise technique of some Italian singers; their technique, in fact hid a lack of real talent. We may think, however, that Andersen wanted to approach a wider problem, that of artistic creation and the public's reactions. More broadly speaking, this tale seems to pose the problem of 'falsehood' in general.

Indeed, we are able to observe the existence of a propensity to prefer what is false to what is true. This propensity is more or less strong, according to each person, as I pointed out in examination dreams. Such a propensity may be that of the creator himself or that of one who appreciates a false creation over-enthusiastically. This alacrity seems to originate from a specific factor whose nature remains to be brought to light. In other words, the question is to know who is prompted to create an artificial bird, and why, and who will be fascinated by this bird at the expense of the real one and why. But, first of all, how is it possible to define what is 'true' and what is 'false'?

In the case of Andersen's tale, the distinction seems easy to draw. The 'false' is identified with the inanimate and the 'true' with the living. We know that in most cases this distinction is not a sufficient one and, above all, is not so easy to assert. The inanimate or living characteristics of an aesthetic or intellectual creation do not force themselves upon the mind in such an obvious way.

However, we may follow the Danish story-teller's intuition and thus anticipate my further conclusions. For my own reflection is placed in a similar light to his: the 'true', indeed, is likened to the living, for it is always engendered by its natural causes, in conformity with its essence, and in turn it engenders according to the same law, whereas the 'false' is situated beyond any natural continuity, though it tries to make us believe that it is an organic link in a chain. In other words, it pretends to obey the principle of filiation. This definition is off-hand, both too broad and too particular, and can only be temporary. I hope the rest of my argument will be more precise and enlightening.

Once more, we must emphasize the *anal* factor in these creations as well as the fact that it is always a question for the producer of the 'false', and for his incense-bearer, of making a presentation of the *phallus* for worship. Here again, Andersen's intuition serves us as a guide since he invites us to decide between the merits of two birds. It seems to me that the pervert's creations represent the prototype of these creations of an anal phallus, a factitious penis whose kinship with the fetish is undeniable. Certainly the pervert does not have the monopoly of these factitious creations, but the process involved is similar to his. On the other hand, many perverts are able to accomplish genuine creations. Indeed, it seems to me that we do not emphasize enough the great quantities of libido used for sublimation in every human being, even those who are not creators. The pervert may have at his disposal a certain quantity of libido to be sublimated, even if a large part of it is directly discharged.

Idealization may be found in Andersen's tale where the artificial nightingale is covered with an abundance of dazzling jewels, whereas the real nightingale is a plain grey bird. The true nightingale has nothing to hide, whereas the artificial one must make people forget that it is nothing but a collection of wheels.

I have tried to point out the effects of maternal seduction on the Ego Ideal stopped in its progression. I have stressed the fact that, contrary to the neurotic or to the 'normal' subject, the future pervert does not project his Ego Ideal onto his father. This is entirely in line with Freud's ideas about 'normal' development. 'A little boy will exhibit a special interest in his father; he would like to grow like him and be like him, and take his place everywhere. We may say simply that he takes his father as his ideal' (*Group Psychology and the Analysis of the Ego*', 1921, p. 105). And also: 'We can only see that identification endeavours to mould a person's Ego after the fashion of the one that has been taken as a model' (p. 127).

When in *The Ego and the Id* (1923) Freud studies the Superego—from now on it has become one with the Ego Ideal— he lays stress on the identification with a *loved and admired* father, a fact which contributes to this new agency:

> As a substitute for a longing for the father, it contains the germ from which all religions have evolved. The self-judgement which declares that the Ego falls short of its ideal produces the religious sense of humility to which the believer appeals in his longing. As a child grows up, the role of the father is carried on by teachers and others in authority; their injunctions and prohibitions remain powerful in the Ego Ideal and continue in the form of conscience, to exercise the moral censorship' (*The Ego and the Id*, 1923, p. 37).

As he wants to give an answer to those who assert that there exists 'a higher nature in man', Freud says: '... here we have higher nature, in this Ego Ideal or Superego, the representative of our relations to our parents. When we were little children we knew these higher natures, we admired them and feared them; and later we took them into ourselves' (p. 36).

I have proposed the following guideline: Those who have not

been able to project their Ego Ideal onto their father and his penis and, who subsequently have gaps in their identifications, will feel the necessity, for obvious narcissistic motives, to grant to themselves their missing identity by different means, creation being one among others. The work thus created will symbolize the phallus, the gap in the identity being likened to castration. Despite being unable to identify with his father, the subject will be led to create; yet, instead of begetting his work, he will fabricate it. This work does not obey the principle of filiation, as he himself does not. As the introjection of paternal capacities and attributes has not been accomplished, and as the desires linked to that process have been repressed and counter-cathected, the subject will not have at his disposal the desexualized (sublimated) libido necessary to achieve his work. Its originator will be the Ego Ideal but the raw material employed will not have been basically modified. As he is 'The Son of Nobody' (the title of a play by Henri de Montherlant), the creator I am describing will find it difficult to be the father of a genuine work. The identity he bestows upon himself is necessarily usurped, since it is based on the negation of himself as being a link in the chain of the generations.

The work thus created will often represent a phallus superior to his father's genital penis. Indeed, it can only be a make-believe because of the faulty introjection of the paternal attributes. It is a question of making the Ego and the Ego Ideal coincide by circumventing the process of sublimation which, as we shall see, implies the identification with the father. At the same time, it is a question of avoiding conflicts associated with introjection which reinforces castration anxiety, for introjection of the paternal penis is felt as castrating the father and arouses fears of retaliation.

The pervert attempts to project his Ego Ideal onto pregenital instincts and objects instead of projecting them onto his begetter in order to identify with him. Yet, despite his attempt, the pervert is not entirely blind to the fact that his father possesses prerogatives and capacities of which he is devoid. Thus, in order to maintain his illusion, he will be obliged to pass off his little pregenital infertile penis *as a penis as valid as his father's* by idealizing it. In my opinion the pervert's creation represents his own magnified phallus which, for lack of an adequate identification with the father, can only be factitious. Indeed, this process may also be detected elsewhere than in perversions, whenever we come across any sizeable failure in identification on both sides of the Oedipus Complex. Such a process involves a projection of the Ego Ideal onto archaic pregenital imagos, as well as a want of an evolutive kind of Ego-Ideal (for precise historical reasons), which prompt the subject to choose the maintenance of illusion—of the make-believe—rather than to fill in the gaps which the neurotic (or the 'normal') subject aspires to fill. Though it is legitimate, at a certain level, to differentiate between perverse organization as such and other failures of identification, it may be interesting to try and delimit the common core of various disorders ranging from perversion to certain character formations, psychopathy and even toxicomania.

To extend the list, an example is given in the story of a swindler of genius, a subject who, like the pervert, avoids his identification process. Samuel Fuller's film, 'The Baron of Arizona' (1950), shows a man who, faking various documents, claims that a little girl—whose interests he manages—descends from the Kings of Spain. (These had formerly colonized Arizona.) And, as such, she is to take possession of this state. At the story's end, the forgery is brought to light. Three times he is told: 'Your affair is a bad cigar wrapped in a rich Spanish leaf.' The superficial character of idealization—and the anal phallus (the cigar) which is concealed—are made obvious here. We may compare this intuition of the character of idealization, as a mask concealing anality, to Napoleon's opinion of Talleyrand: 'Shit in a silk stocking.'

The subjects considered here use particular solutions to their problems. If we examine them carefully, we find that *acting-out* is always present and that the creation itself may be considered as an acting-out aiming at miraculously filling in the gap between water and wine, the prepubescent penis and the genital one, the child and its father.

In her article, 'Delictious Acts as Perversions and Fetishes' (1956), Melitta Schmideberg expresses a point of view similar to my own attempt at grasping the common core of a range of disturbances which do not belong to the neurotic or psychotic field. She thinks that certain delinquent acts may be classified among perversions or be considered as equivalent to fetishes (p. 422). The work of art achieved by subjects presenting such a structural core, however cut off it may be from its paternal roots—indeed, for this very reason—and however original it claims to be, is nevertheless nothing but an imitation, a copy of the genital penis. This imitation is linked to the intrinsic nature of the archaic identifications involved here, and to the lack of evolved identifications, of an Oedipal and post-Oedipal kind.

The often-noticeable studies of certain authors help me to strengthen my hypothesis. In her already classical study on 'Some Forms of Emotional Disturbances and their Relationship to Schizophrenia' (1942), and on the 'as if' structure, Helen Deutsch described a relationship to life which involved a lack of authenticity which, from the outside, seems 'as if' it were complete. The first clinical case she speaks of is that of a young girl gifted at drawing who enters, during the analysis, a school of Fine Arts. The analyst (it was long ago) receives a report from her teacher who declares himself impressed by the speed with which the young girl has taken up his technique and 'manner'; but he had found something undefinable in her which left him reticent and puzzled. He added that the young girl, having changed teachers, had immediately taken up with the greatest ease her new teacher's technical and theoretical conceptions.

This facility at changing identifications would be seen in the 'as if' patients in their enthusiastic adhesion to a philosophy which can be rapidly and entirely replaced by another perfectly contradictory one, without the slightest trace of any internal modification. The author lays stress on the fact that the apparently normal relationship of the 'as if' subjects corresponds to the child's capacity to imitate, and is only a mimicry. Common to all these cases is a profound disturbance of the sublimation process which follows altogether from the failure in the synthesis of the different infantile identifications into a unique and integrated personality and from the faulty, lopsided, purely intellectual sublimation of the instincts. According to H. Deutsch, the aetiology of this state of affairs is, above all, linked to the devaluation of the object used by the child as a model for its personality. As for the Superego, it would be insufficiently internalized, and the 'as if' personalities would adopt the moral criteria of their objects for the time being, for lack of internal independent criteria.

In a more recent study, 'The Impostor—A Contribution to the Ego Psychology of a Type of Psychopath' (1955), the same author studies the case of the impostor. In all his undertakings his patient played a role: dressing in a certain way, dying his hair and eyebrows when he was supposed to be a 'gentleman farmer', playing the intellectual when he had a literary salon, etc. Sometimes the imposture became obvious: he changed his name in order to make it almost the same as that of a well-known personality. He was constantly in search of his identity. The denial of his own identity seems to be, according to the author, the main motive of his actions, as it is in other cases of imposture. Studying well-known impostors, the author shows that, in certain cases, they could have acquired prestige under their own names, but that they always chose another one, that of men they wanted to look like. (As the name is what establishes filiation, it seems to me that changing one's name is equivalent to disavowing one's origin, that is, one's father.) The author claims that, because of his incapacity for sublimation, her patient was only able to fulfil his phantasies of greatness by a naive acting-out, pretending that he was really in agreement with his Ego Ideal. Now, some of the patient's undertakings were creations. He began to write, then to go in for scientific research and inventions.

For Phyllis Greenacre, 'The Impostor' (1958) whom she studies presents three main characteristics:
1) He has to act out his family romance.
2) Both his identity and sense of reality are distorted.
3) His Superego presents a malformation, from the viewpoint of

moral conscience as from that of ideals.

Now, we know that one of the meanings of the family romance is the rejection of the family generation ties and an attempt to give oneself a new (and false) identity.

Samuel Novey, in 'Some Philosophical Speculations about the Concept of the Genital Character' (1955), gives a definition of the family romance as an attempt at establishing one's uniqueness. He considers it as a central instance of man's escape from the idea of an existence bound to its biological determinism. As for the impostor's family, its description by Phyllis Greenacre brings it close to that of the pervert: the mother is very attached to her child, as if he were a part of herself. The father is non-existent: the child is placed in a position of definite superiority to the father. Moreover, Phyllis Greenacre writes: 'I have elsewhere indicated that if, under these conditions, the child has been exposed to the sight of the genitals of an adult male, it may produce in fantasy an illusory enlargement of its own phallus which becomes indeed a kind of local imposture involving the organ and contributes to the already forming tendency to general imposture' (1958, p. 369). The impostors quoted by Phyllis Greenacre are often creators. The sexuality of the clinical cases quoted by the author is often of a perverted kind and mixed with toxicomania. In my opinion, we must understand that the imposture is generally an answer to the infantile need existing in certain individuals to pass off their little infertile penis for the genital penis.

Abraham's impostor ('The History of an Impostor in the Light of Psycho-analytic Knowledge', 1925), instead of acquiring a penis through progressive identification with his father, immediately gets a symbolic phallus by disavowing his origins. As he longs for a gaudy pen-box or for a pencil of a particular colour, he enters a bookshop passing himself off as the son of a general who lived in the neighbourhood. He is immediately given the objects he longed for. Abraham says that he had no possibility of elevating his father up to the rank of an ideal figure; on the contrary, very early he had wanted another father.

In three very important papers, 'Narcissistic Object Choice in Women' (1953), 'Early Identifications as Archaic Elements in the Superego' (1954), and 'Pathologic Forms of Self-Esteem Regulation' (1960), Annie Reich describes disturbances in identification and their relationship to Ego Ideal and sublimation. She speaks of the 'magic identification' with the idealized parent which takes the place of the (more mature) wish to become like him: 'The formation of the Superego is based upon acceptance of reality; in fact it represents the most powerful attempt to adjust to reality. The Ego Ideal, on the other hand, is based upon the desire to cling in some form or another to a denial of the Ego's... limitations' (pp. 188-89).

In the normal development, the Ego Ideal is modified, becomes more realistic and fuses with the Superego. The cases Annie Reich considers present not real identifications but superficial imitations. The author gives an example which allows us to differentiate between imitation and identification. Imitation (or magic identification) is that of the child who holds the newspaper as his father does. Identification comes when the child is learning to read. In imitation, the question is to *be* the envied parent, and not necessarily to *become* like him. This is the sphere of magical achievement.

> In many respects the child cannot be fully like the adults. There normally develops a faculty for self-evaluation on reality appreciation, which enables the child to recognize certain aspects of parental images as something he has not yet reached but wishes to become. Here we see a type of Ego Ideal; we might call it the normal one... In... pathological cases... instead of solid identifications being formed, there develops the wish to be like the object... But... there is not even an impulse to translate these fantasies into reality (pp. 213-14).

Sublimation is often faulty. The Ego's aggrandizement has the value of a magic denial of castration.

In her article, 'The Self and the Object World' (1954), Edith Jacobson deals with the same topic. She differentiates between early, magic, pre-Oedipal identifications, which she links to Helen Deutsch's 'as if', from (what are for her) actual Ego identifications associated with representations of the Self and of the Object. The Ego Ideal aims at being one with the mother, and only afterwards at becoming *like* the object. We may notice that Freud, in *The Interpretation of Dreams* (1900), distinguishes between identifications and imitations, in relation to hysteria. He says: 'Thus identification is not simple imitation but *assimilation* on the basis of a similar aetiological pretension' (p. 150).

However, in the cases we are considering, the lack in the Ego due to the faulty introjection and assimilation of the paternal attributes—an unconscious process which involves a relationship full of love, admiration and closeness—is repaired not by an imitation of the father with his attributes (which are narcissistically decathected) but by an attempt to free oneself completely from all filial links. Imitation will concern an 'ideal' phallus such as it is phantasied by the subject. The models, when they exist, are distant and remote abstracts. If they materialize, it will be not in persons who represent idealized father substitutes but rather in persons who have succeeded in avoiding introjection conflicts themselves, and in gratifying themselves with an autonomous magic phallus, or who promise one to their followers, while sparing them the painful process of maturation. The subject belonging to one of the psychic organizations we are investigating will become the disciple of a seer, if not a seer himself.

One of my patients, a fetishist, produced the following

material:

He began his session by speaking of the dog's excreta he had seen in front of my door. He went on to evoke the secretions from his genitals, relating in detail their consistency, their abundance and their smell. He went on talking of his aggressiveness towards his wife, of a painful injection he had given her the day before, and of his sexual difficulties. I noticed that he seemed to be obliged to put into me and into his wife only dirty or painful things. He then remembered a dream in which he had bought a reproduction of an antique for his wife (my house is in an antique dealers' district).

So we find 'falsehood' as an anal (sadistic) penis preserving the patient's genital penis or being its substitute. Therefore we may say that 'falsehood' passes itself off as a phallus, as a penis able to provide narcissistic achievement, but which actually is, in all cases, only an anal phallus. To be sure, at the beginning of the anal phase, the narcissistic cathexis of the excrements made them, in the psychic reality, equivalent to gold. But toilet training will induce the child to decathect and even to despise what had initially seemed to him as infinitely precious. The subsequent phallic stage—where the genital desire is present without the corresponding genital capacities which could satisfy it—will enable him to transfer the cathexis onto the genital penis, which henceforth will be for him the supreme narcissistic value to be preserved. Now, if the anal penis is the prefiguration of the genital penis, once the phallic stage has been reached, it becomes an imitation of the genital penis.

'Falsehood' is built up taking the equation, faeces = penis, literally. The subject will try to re-cathect the anal penis with its formal narcissistic cathexis, yet hiding its pregenital character from himself and others. For, once the phallic stage has actually been reached, the scale of values has been overturned, and a stool can no longer stand for a genital penis. But its advantage over the latter is that it is not unique. The anal phallus has here a pervasive role. It is indefinitely renewable, therefore eternal and invulnerable. Like the Phoenix, the brilliantly coloured mythological bird, it is reborn every day from its ashes. Here we find again the difference between the artificial nightingale and the real one. We may imagine that the mechanism can be changed, whereas the living nightingale, as we know, will die.

Therefore, I think that the admirer of the 'false' work is thus faced with a thing which allows him to preserve (or re-activate) the illusion that his own conflicts linked to introjection may be avoided, without taking away the slightest bit of his potency, and, subsequently, his narcissistic injury may be healed at little cost. Moreover, he preserves the illusion that it is possible to possess a phallus which is both satisfactory for his narcissism and invulnerable to castration. For 'falsehood', if it manages through idealization to mask its specific anal character, nevertheless maintains the benefits of both registers.

In Andersen's tale, he who accepts to be what he is, and who is close to the material world and nature—the poor fisherman, the girl in the kitchen—is not fascinated by the 'false' nightingale as are the music-master, the lord-in-waiting and the courtiers, whose portrait by Andersen is very similar to that of Molière's 'petits marquis'. Indeed, even if I started by saying that our epoch is infatuated by false values, it has no monopoly over this. Attraction to falsehood seems to be a constant feature of the human mind, just as attraction to the perverse solution, with which it coincides in many respects.

I shall conclude by quoting Molière, whose work is dominated by the struggle against 'falsehood': false nobility, false feelings, false creation, false knowledge, pretension to a pseudo-culture, to apparent good manners, etc. Oronte, who is a sophisticated 'petit marquis', reads a sonnet he wrote for a lady. Alceste, the 'misanthrope', is entreated over and over again to give his opinion. After having hesitated awhile, he cannot bear it anymore:

> Do you really *need* to write poetry and if so, why the deuce must you rush into print?... Frankly, the only thing to do is to put it away and forget it. You have formed your style on bad models. The expressions you use are not natural. What's the meaning of "and for a while brings consolation"? or "be followed by frustration"? and "Kinder had been the cruel word"? or "Hope deferred begets blank hopelessness"? This figurative style people pride themselves so much in is false and meretricious. It's just a play upon words, sheer affectation! It isn't a natural way of speaking at all. I find contemporary taste appalling in this respect. Our ancestors, crude and unpolished as they were, did very much better. I prefer to any of the stuff people admire so much nowadays an old ballad such as...
>
>> If King Henry said to me
>> 'Here's Paris, my rich town and fair;
>> All this and more I'll give to thee
>> Gin thou wilt leave thy dear,'
>> I'd up and say to King Henry
>> Keep thou they gold and gear!
>> What care I for thy fair Paris
>> Gin I am with my dear?'
>
> The rimes may be crude and the style old-fashioned but don't you see how much better it is than all this trumpery stuff that's so revolting to one's common sense? Don't you feel this is the voice of true love speaking?
> [He repeats the old ballad.]
> That's just what a man who was really in love would say. [To Philinte who is laughing] Yes Sir, you may laugh, but whatever

your wits and critics may say, I prefer that to the solemn flourishes and superficial polish that everyone makes such a fuss about' (*The Misanthrope and Other Plays*, 1959, Act One, pp. 35-36).

Chapter 8

Reflections on Fetishism

I have already tried to show the links between perversion, anal-sadistic regression, anomie and hubris. The pervert's aim, from my point of view, is to disavow his father's (genital) capacities and to accomplish a (magic) transmutation of reality by delving into the undifferentiated anal-sadistic dimension. Having idealized it, he proclaims its superiority over the father's genital universe. I shall now try to test my hypotheses by applying them to fetishism.

A passage from Abraham's article (1920), 'The Narcissistic Evaluation of Excretory Processes in Dreams and Neurosis', will help me to work out a transition. Abraham diagnoses his patient as a 'neurotic', and we do not have enough evidence to question this. However, the patient's family is fitted for making him a pervert: his mother despised his father and really 'worshipped' her boy's excrements. Such factors make for the maintaining of the child's illusion that he is a more adequate partner for his mother than the father, and that his pregenitality—idealized (worshipped) by his mother—is superior to his father's genitality. Moreover, this patient has phantasies of anal coitus with his mother, and, from the observation of his parents' intercourse, this phantasy also applies to his father. Abraham's study allows us to suppose that these phantasies are *conscious*, i.e., more consonant with perversion than with neurosis. Finally, a fetishistic factor is present, as Abraham points out.

> A neurotic patient, a man who had constantly imagined he was a 'prince', had played at being 'Kaiser' during his early years and had in later childhood revelled in phantasies of dominating the world. This man experienced a peculiar change when he was 11 years old. Up till then he had been entirely fixated on his mother, who had systematically prejudiced him against his father. She had greatly increased his anal eroticism by almost elevating to a cult her preoccupation about his motions. She was constantly concerned about their quality and quantity, and used to give him an enema almost daily. On his side the boy had developed neurotic pains in his stomach in order to compel his mother to continue the enemas.
> When he was 11 years old, he went on a long journey with his parents. One night, when they were staying in a hotel, he

overheard his parents having sexual intercourse. This event made all the more impression on him since for many years at home his parents had had separate bedrooms. He now remembered that this event had seemed unbearable to him, and that he had quite consciously determined to prevent its recurrence. For the remainder of the journey, he managed to arrange things so as to share a room with his father. Since his observation of parental intercourse, he had identified himself with his mother and transferred his phantasies of anal coitus onto his father. Up to this time he had attributed a penis to his mother, the penis being represented by the enema tube. But now he took up a female-passive attitude towards his father. (Abraham's note: In his phantasies, the patient retained the idea of a woman with a penis even in later years. He used to conceal his genital organs between his thighs in order to feel like a woman.) Soon afterwards he was confined to his bed. During this time he went a couple of days without having an evacuation. As a consequence of this, he had a feeling of pressure in the abdomen. That night he dreamed that he had to expel the universe out of his anus.

Abraham compares this dream to some myths about the creation of mankind.

We may infer that the primal scene, disavowed up to that very moment, asserted itself in a tragic manner. He is not the unique and adequate sexual object for his mother. She has indeed a desire for the father's genital penis, a penis which therefore possesses properties lacked by the so excessively valued excrements. All takes place as if, for a moment, the child had tried to acknowledge and accept the dreadful reality which his mother's attitude had previously helped him to reject. The acknowledgement of the father's genital powers obliges the boy to introject them. The homosexual submission to the father constitutes a means of accomplishing this process, which leads to paternal identification. It was in this way that we interpreted Little Hans' plumber phantasy.

The difference in nature between Little Hans' phantasies and this patient's is, however, important: Little Hans' phantasies are the result of an intense symbolic activity, of whose meaning he is not aware. Its significance has to be deciphered. There is nothing of the sort in the case of Abraham's patient. Here, the symbol formation, at the level of his homosexual passive desire, is entirely conscious, as was the phantasy of anal penetration by his mother. Without carrying our reflection any further here, we may suppose that the Superego does not fulfil its role as a barrier against incest, as it does in the case of a neurotic. We may notice that in 'A Child is Being Beaten' (1919) Freud talks about one of his male patients for whom the masochistic idea 'of being beaten by the mother' was present in an undisguised manner.

In the first week of his analysis, Jean-Jaques (my patient of the examination dream) had a dream which was not accompanied by any anxiety: 'I am standing against my mother's body. I touch her buttocks which are beautifully cool and I ejaculate.' The anal-sadistic regression leads the incestuous object to be reduced first to part objects (buttocks, in Jean-Jaques' example). Then, engulfed in the gigantic intestinal grinder, it becomes particles of excrement among other particles. The incestuous act has thus become meaningless; in particular, guilt, which is attached to it in normal conditions, has disappeared. Jean-Jaques casually related that, when he was about 11 years old, he used to exhibit his genitals in front of an old, paralysed and more or less insane grandmother, while knowing that she could neither prevent him from doing so nor denounce him.

As for Abraham's patient, his incestuous wish concerning both of his parents is conscious, though it has regressed to anal-passive form. Abraham's note lets us suppose that the acknowledgement of the paternal genital penis and of the genital sexual complementarity between the parents has not been maintained, since the subject returned to his phantasy of a mother with a penis, the model of which was the rubber pipe-fetish. At the same time, he played at transforming himself into a woman, hiding (and thus keeping) his penis. I suggest the following hypothesis: the trauma of the 'discovery' of the primal scene, after an attempt at working it through which is supported by the phantasy of anal coitus with the father, has been overcome only at the cost of a massive disavowal of reality, as the dream of *an anal creation of the world* shows. The little boy thus manages to disavow the painful sexual truth—that of the genital primal scene, the father's genital penis and the procreative capacities it involves—thanks to a solution which puts an end to his feeling of dereliction. If my hypotheses are well-grounded, fetishism must be closely linked to the whole question. It must constitute a part—no doubt, an important one—of the creation of a new reality in which the father and his attributes are disqualified and in which the genital level of sexuality is disavowed.

I think it necessary that a conception of fetishism should account for all the cases featuring in such a perversion. We must note that clinical observation does not support Freud when, in his article 'On Fetishism' (1927), he states that the fetish spares the fetishist from becoming a homosexual. And, in fact, if the fetish were none other than a substitute for the mother's penis, the subject being unable to bear the sight of the 'castrated' female genitals which arouse in him the fear of castration, this fear should be non-existent for a man whose sexual partner is another man.

If we examine, for instance, Krafft-Ebing's cases in his *Psychopathia Sexualis* (1887), we may indeed ascertain that fetishism does not prevent homosexuality, but that it is often associated with it and also that the subject may even wear the fetish. In his article on 'The Relation of Perversion Formations to the

Development of Reality-Sense' (1932, in *On the Early Development of Mind*, 1956), E. Glover, speaking of this last case, talks of 'narcissistic fetishes'. The fetish is not always placed on a woman's body; neither is it this last piece of lingerie which covers the woman's body before the absence of penis is revealed (Freud, 'On Fetishism', 1927). I knew a man who used to put on riding boots at the request of his boss. The latter would lovingly clean and polish them until they shone, kiss them, and presumably reached orgasm that way.

According to Freud, the edification of the fetish means at once the affirmation and the disavowal of the so-called castration of women. Joyce McDougall (1972), in 'Primal Scene and Sexual Perversion', went further in the resolution of the enigma by stressing that the construction of the fetish is not only linked with the need to disavow the absence of the penis, supporting the castration fears, but is also linked with the need to disavow the maternal orifice which is proof of sexual relations between the parents—proof of the primal scene. In his 'Essai sur le Fétichisme' (1976), Béla Grunberger supported the idea that the fetish is the commemorative monument of intense anal exchanges between mother and son. These two conceptions (of McDougall and Grunberger) have the great advantage of linking the creation of the fetish with the *disavowal of the father's genital penis*. The exclusion of the genital penis and of the genital father is signified and maintained through the very presence of the fetish.

Jean-Jaques had at least two fetishes: his mother-in-law's pyjamas in which he used to masturbate, and the prosthesis of his one-legged friend. If the fetish was nothing but the mother's phallus, then the case of the one-legged man and of his prosthesis would be an actual riddle, for we are confronted here with a twofold paradox: the fetish is linked to a man, and this man is a castrated one!

As a matter of fact, the choice of the prosthesis as a fetish seems to be easy to understand; in times past, any thriving brothel featured a 'wooden-legged woman'. While the anal penis is a prefiguration of the genital one, *a posteriori* it is an imitation of it. At the level of primary processes, orthopaedic instruments or prostheses—which replace, and imitate a missing limb and a defective function—are anal phallic objects substituted for the genital penis, and often set up as fetishes. This leads us directly to the idea according to which the fetish is an imitation of a genital penis, and that imitation, in general, is associated with anality. This leads us back, once more, to the fact that fetishism and perversion are connected with sham, counterfeit, forgery, fraudulence, deceit, cheating, tickery, and so on—in short with the world of semblance.

To return to Jean-Jaques: he remembers having been disturbed, when he was about 4 years old, by a man with a leather jacket. (In French, hooligans are called 'blousons noirs': 'black jackets'. It gives us an inkling of the closeness of delinquency to perversion, and the association of them both with anality and make-believe.) Later on, he had phantasies in which he would jump onto this man's back, put his legs around his neck, and the man would carry him far away. (Here we see an obvious link between homosexuality and fetishism.)

This brings us back to the pervert's fundamental type of problems, the maintenance of the illusion that he has nothing to envy his father, no need for a genital, fertile penis, and can therefore escape from the conflicts ensuing the introjection of the father's virile attributes without needing to identify with his progenitor. He can thus manage to avoid the Oedipus Complex and, what is correlated with it, the threat of castration: his father is not his rival, and he does not want to take away his object—the mother—whom he thinks he already possesses, and who sets him up (or so he thinks) as a privileged partner. He does not try to catch or introject the penis of his father, who, therefore, will not retaliate. Moreover—and this, in my opinion, is essential—he tries to pass off the anal penis, the precursor of the genital one, as equal or superior to the paternal penis whose genital and procreative functions are denigrated or disavowed.

This takes us back to fetishism. I would like to start by putting forward the following hypothesis: the fetish represents the anal phallus in so far as it comes to occupy the place of the genital penis, and excludes it from the sexual scene, and from the psyche in general. It is therefore not only the mother's missing phallus. The excitation the fetishist derives from the fetish (or, rather, the excitation it permits) is necessary to maintain the lure on which his psycho-sexuality is built. The fact that its wearer is a man, woman, or the subject himself, or that it is reduced to an inanimate object—a garment, shoes, underwear or hair—separated from any real support, becomes secondary (although not indifferent, of course) to the need for the fetish to *exist* somewhere in a manner which is indefectibly and perfectly exciting, as a sign of a fundamental change of the psycho-sexual landscape. This is a point to which we will return later on.

In fact, many authors have shown the overdetermined character of the fetish (Gillespie, 1940, 1964; Greenacre, 1953; Parkin, 1963). Parkin's patient, whose fetish was a raincoat, identifies with the anal phallus of the mother when he is squeezed into the fetish, whereas the woman dressed in the raincoat becomes his own penis. On another level, he can also identify with the anal phallus of his father, a strict military man who used to manipulate the testicles of his son, and who, when afflicted with dysentery, would often speak of his own intestinal functions. His mother had died from haemorrhaging colitis. Wulff (1946) links the fetish, the phallus of the mother, to what is supposed to be its origin—the breast—and Winnicott (1953) does the same thing to a certain extent when he compares the transitional object to the fetish. This is also one of the meanings of the fetish according to Sperling (1963), who thinks that it can represent the mother's whole body. For the patient described by Socarides (1960), the fetish was not only the phallus of the mother, but the breast and the abdomen of the pregnant mother.

Indeed, when we attempt to trace the genealogy of these multiple meanings, we cannot but be struck by the fact that authors have increasingly tended to emphasize the pregenital conflicts that fetishism aims to resolve, and no longer castration anxiety alone. Payne (1939) stressed the importance of protection against sadistic impulses toward the object represented by the fetish. Then Gillespie (1940) underscored latent pregenital factors and the anxiety attached to them, reactivated at the sight of female genitals. Like Payne, he stressed the fear concerning the destruction of the object, which is relieved by the fetish. The fetish, an inanimate object, is immutable and permanent; any sadism directed at it remains without response. Greenacre (1968) tried to connect the disturbing effects of phenomena occurring during two phases fundamental for the constitution of the fetish: the first, during the first 18 months of life which lead to faulty development of the body image, and the second, between the ages of 2 and 4, coinciding with the phallic phase, which lead to an 'exaggerated' castration complex.

However, it is due to archaic pregenital distortions that the castration complex is insurmountable without the help of the fetish. As a matter of fact, the sight of female sexual organs deprived of a penis reactivates a tendency toward *primary identification* (with the female partner, a substitute for the mother) linked to the pathology of early development. If it represents the phallus of the mother, and denies the difference between the sexes, the fetish re-establishes the existence of the phallus of the subject himself through visual and olfactory introjection.

For many authors, who have more or less completely abrogated the theory that the fetish represents the maternal phallus and the importance conferred by Freud to the castration complex in fetishism, separation anxiety and the inability to renounce primary identification with the mother are at the heart of the problem in fetishism. For Weissmann (1957), fetishism aims at overcoming separation anxiety through a feeling of complete union with the mother obtained by means of the introjection of the good object (the good breast). The ultimate aim of the fetishist is not to get genital satisfaction, but to feel a state of elation linked to that union with the good object. The fetishistic activity strives to undo an identification with the bad breast in order to establish an identification with the good breast. 'The fetishistic object is not only an object but an identification.' The fetishist acts out his fetishism in his own character and treats his real objects like inanimate fetishes.

This is also the opinion of Sperling (1963), who insists on the omnipotent control exerted by some fetishists on their objects, a control made possible by the use of the fetish which permits the denial or the loss of the pre-Oedipal mother. Sperling observed these mechanisms in fetishistic children. Separation anxiety predominates by far over castration anxiety. This remains the case in adults whose fetishism gratifies the original desire for union with the mother. Socarides (1960), by insisting that the fetish represents a 'child', and that the fetishist wishes to be pregnant, links fetishism to the solution of the same problem: to be the pregnant mother in order to be the child within the mother is to avoid separation from the primary object. Although the stressing of separation anxiety at the expense of castration anxiety accounts for some important clinical observations, it does not recognize the organic link between these two types of anxiety, just as the classic theory does not provide sufficient explanation for the loss of reality in perversion by making it consubstantial with the problem of castration taken in a narrow sense, connecting it with the sight of female genitals (the second phase of the castration complex).

In his 'Contribution to the Study of Fetishism' (1935), Balint had already identified the fetish with faeces, the foetus and a bisexual object. In his paper, 'Fetishism' (1953), R. Bak underlines the pregenital fixation, essential at the anal stage of the fetishist which favours the maintenance of the mother-child unity. The fetish is a symbol of the mother's breast, skin, buttocks, faeces, smell and woman's penis, separately or altogether by means of condensation. It protects just as well from separation as from castration. The fundamental wish of the fetishist is to be one with his mother.

Here we must also quote James Glover's article presented in 1924 at the Eighth Congress of the International Psycho-Analytical Association, entitled 'Notes on an Unusual Form of Perversion'. This paper, written before Freud's study 'On Fetishism' (1927), forestalls the criticisms, complementary views or nuances which were applied many years later to Freud's theory of fetishism, and of which I have just given some examples. James Glover's patient brings into play a complicated ritual which consists of inducing a woman wearing high-heeled shoes to drink alcohol, till her face and general appearance had become loose, and till she had begun to stagger, and her (preferably white) shoes had got soiled and spoiled. Towards the end of the article which includes the patient's story, James Glover writes that the motives of his inducing women into drinking were as follows:

1) To make the withdrawn nipple appear and to punish it.
2) Revenge for anal discipline, which had been especially severe in his childhood, by making the woman untidy and dirty.
3) Revenge for her hypocrisy in deceiving him with the father, by unmasking her sexuality and exposing her as a prostitute.

In doing so, he gratified his strong scoptophilic impulses in various ways, but mainly in reconstituting a scene of parental coitus (1927, p. 18).

We find here a prefiguration of Robert Stoller's views, especially of the emphasis on hostility and revenge in perversions. James Glover adds that, through this ritual, his patient obtained a gratification of his very strong scoptophilic impulses, and that, above all, he re-enacted a scene of intercourse between his parents. The author shows, according to Abraham's classification (published that year), how all instinctual levels are satisfied—always in a sadistic way—as is also the Oedipus Complex in both its forms: the homosexual relationship with the father and the father's castration. Shoe fetishism appeared to be also an alternative to his infantile kleptomaniac tendencies. Behind Oedipal disappointment, we can find the anal conflict, behind the latter a weaning trauma, and further behind, birth trauma. (We are in 1924, the year when Otto Rank's book was published.) James Glover thinks that a strong fixation to an ambivalent oral phase and a strong anal ambivalency play a decisive role here.

Contrary to these theories which, in one way or another, lay more stress on pregenital factors and separation anxiety than on castration anxiety, we find Lacan's and his followers' theory, which carries on to its uttermost conclusions the infantile theory of phallic sexual monism.

> The whole problem of perversions consists in viewing how the child—in his relationship with his mother, a relationship established in the course of the analysis, not because of his dependence on her for his survival but because of her love, that is a dependence on the desire of her desire—identifies with the imaginary object of this desire, which the mother herself symbolizes by the phallus. The phallocentrism produced by this dialectic is the only thing to be taken into account here ('D'une Question Préliminaire à Tout Traitement Possible de la Psychose', 1958).

Lacan refers here to the quarrel about the primary or secondary character of the phallic phase. The imaginary effect of the phallus 'may be felt as a clash only in the name of the prejudice according to which there would exist standards corresponding to instincts.'

It is because the non-acceptance of the theory of sexual phallic monism entails decisive consequences for the theory of perversions (the one on fetishism follows at once) that I have discussed this theory before presenting my own developments on the question. The classical theory seems insufficient to explain fetishism, associating it closely, as it does, to the castration complex understood in a narrow sense, as bearing on the perception of female genitals (second phase of the castration complex). On the other hand, the conceptions which stress separation anxiety at the expense of castration anxiety fail to recognize the organic links between both forms of anxiety. They do this even though they account for important elements encountered in clinical material. I would like to suggest that the very idea of castration has to be enlarged.

I stressed the fact that the Oedipal tragedy is remarkably attenuated for the child ignorant of the fact that the mother's desire has the father's fertile penis as an object. I also stressed that the mother wishes to be genitally gratified, that is, in a way other than by these 'vague and imprecise contacts', which according to Freud the little boy would like to give her, and which by a fortunate accident he is able to bring into play. (Is it not here that we find norms and standards, instinct coinciding perfectly with abilities, more than in the affirmation of a painful chronological lag between the two elements?) Therefore, I propose that we add to the castration complex, as an intrinsic part of it, the painful feeling of inadequacy of the pregenital child unable to satisfy its mother and to give her a child. The castration complex thus understood enables us to link it to what precedes it: separation anxiety. The Oedipus Complex, the father, the desire of the mother for the father's penis, the genital order, then, takes place as factors disrupting the original union between mother and child.

Up to now the ideas developed here are close to those I developed in a paper (1981). But I think that we must introduce here a correction: indeed, if we bring together in such a way separation anxiety and castration anxiety, are we not eluding a decisive aspect of the Oedipal conflict? If castration anxiety and separation anxiety deserve to be associated—and we know, at least from a note in 'Little Hans', that precursors of castration anxiety coincide with different forms of separation anxiety—then the advent of the Oedipus Complex constitutes a breaking in these two forms of anxiety. We know that the setting up of the Superego as heir to the Oedipus Complex ends in keeping the penis and in stopping its sexual functioning as associated with the incestuous wish. So, the dissolution of the Oedipus Complex leads to transforming the libidinal cathexis whose object is the mother: the child's sexual interest directed towards her loses its strength and may even disappear, at least in theory. The tenderness associated with the first object-love is reinforced. Therefore, from the castration complex follows a certain detachment from the mother as the object of sensual love.

In so-called 'normal' cases there is a qualitative 'jump' between the successive precursors of the castration complex and the complex proper. The first are linked to real events in the child's life: birth, weaning, separation from the faeces, whereas castration fear is to be referred to pyschic reality. (However, if we follow Freud, the hypothesis of the sons' castration by their father in the primal hord—*Totem and Taboo*—and the phylogenetic transmission of the event weigh upon this fear, which thus becomes real. But we are not obliged to follow Freud here.) Even if we include in the castration complex the inadequacy feelings of the little Oedipus, as I suggest—an inadequacy linked to physiological reality—then the part of fantasy is here determinant. It can be seen in the Oedipal desire itself and in all the coextensive elements: the identification with the father, as the mother's object, the wish to capture the big fertile penis, the fears of retaliation.

The dissolution of the Oedipus Complex with the implied separation from the mother as a sexual object thus constitutes an actual mutation, as regards the precursors of the castration complex. The precursors successively change the relationship with the mother but they do not involve any renunciation as to her possession. On the contrary, the Oedipal drama ends, theoretically, with the withdrawal from the mother as sexually cathected. Our ideas here are congruent with our conclusions about the rebellion of the pervert against the universal law promulgated by the Oedipus Complex and his 'artful' dealings with reality.

I shall therefore now complete my previous hypothesis, according to which the fetish is an anal phallus which attempts to exclude the genital penis from the sexual stage. I suggest that we consider the fetishist as trying to foil his castration complex by likening it to his previous experiences of separation which had not constrained him to renounce the possession of his mother. The fetish is the deposit of all the part objects lost during the subject's development. As is obvious through the acts of constriction often performed (the corset or the shoe fetishes), the fetish is both content and container. Thus the link between the object and the erotogenic zone is re-established (the nipple in the mouth, the stool in the rectum) and the primal scene is mimed as a pregenital relationship.

The fetish condenses all the elements separating the son from his mother. Genitality represents the major obstacle between the son and his mother because of the differences it includes between the sexes and the generations, that is, reality itself; genitality is thus swept away from the stage. The fetish is like a magic wand. Its presence modifies reality. The theatre where the human drama is performed—with its mourning, deprivations, injuries, renunciations—thus becomes a fairyland where feelings of inferiority, loss, and death exist no more.

From time to time, Parkin's patient sees the woman wrapped in the mackintosh as 'in radiant unspoiled beauty'. This has to be associated with the last vision he had of his dying mother, when he was 5 years old. Holding out her arms towards him, 'she seemed suffused with a spiritual radiance and the aura of her delicate loveliness encompassed him with a heavenly feeling.' In the fetish (of which the author himself outlines the essentially excremental character), this patient could carry through the embalming of the mother's corpse, the ending of the corruption of the flesh. I propose this hypothesis because the practice of embalming, by the Egyptians in particular, exactly produces a fetish. Make-up is applied to the putrefying body, which is then decorated with jewels, dressed up with a golden mask, and made into a god.

Idealization is once more an important ingredient and is inseparable from the building up of a fetish. The French word 'maquiller' (to make up) at the same time means to colour one's face, and to disguise, mask, conceal, transform. 'Make up' and 'maquiller' are close, of course, to the verb 'to make', that is, to create an artificial object as opposed to giving birth. Things which are idealized are coloured, bright, sparkling, glittering. These characteristics are often present in the fetish.

Almost all the authors who have studied fetishism have pointed out a two-fold property of the fetish: it is anal and shiny, often smelly and shiny. For example, E. Glover, in his article on perversions and reality sense (1932), speaks of a fetishist who was excited when he saw a shiny new piano. A damaged piano which had lost its shine was 'taboo', etc. Thus the fetish—anal and idealized—means the entrance into a new dimension. As I have just pointed out, it conjures up all the lost or lacking elements between mother and son which—thanks to it—are united.

In my own clinical observations, the fetishistic activities increase during the periods of interruption in the course of analysis. New meanings of the fetish come to the fore, as in that patient who had the compulsion to put his wife's boot in his mouth whenever either the analyst or his wife were away. As an omnipotent control is carried out on the fetish, the subject can bring it close up to him just as well as he can reject it, thus mastering all kinds of loss.

Puppets, mannequins, waxworks, automatons, dolls, painted scenery, plaster casts, dummies, secret clockworks, mimesis and illusion: all form a part of the fetishist's magic and artful universe. Lying between life and death, animated and mechanic, hybrid creatures and creatures to which hubris gave birth, they all may be likened to fetishes. And, as fetishes, they give us, for a while, the feeling that a world not ruled by our common laws does exist, a marvellous and uncanny world.

Chapter 9

Aestheticism, Creation and Perversion

> Therefore, nothing can be neglected with respect to the infinite presence in the world. There are no poetic objects as opposed to others that are not. Genuine purity has nothing to do with the choice of objects and of means: it is that which courageously faces up to the harshnesses and the impurities of the world, and returns to the light of day having lost nothing of its whiteness. The poet has a right to all words: his only sin would be a lack of love for some fragment of the universe.
> —Jean Rousselot, 'L'Evangile selon Rainer Maria Rilke', in *Les Lettres Nouvelles*, 1952

The relationship between creation and perversion is enigmatic. Indeed, the creative process implies having recourse to sublimation. Now, sublimation makes use of the same instinctual energy as that which is directly released through perverse sexual activity. In both cases, it is pregenital libido. Pregenital instincts are the essential—and probably the sole—raw material of sublimation. Therefore, I shall not dwell upon this matter. I shall merely recall Freud's 'Fragment of an Analysis of a Case of Hysteria' (1905), in which the problem of perversion versus sublimation is clearly set forth:

> Perversions are neither bestial nor degenerate in the emotional sense of the word. They are the development of germs, all of which are contained in the undifferentiated sexual dispositions of the child, and which, by being suppressed or by being diverted to higher, asexual aims—by being sublimated—are destined to provide the energy for a great number of our cultural achievements (p. 50).

Therefore, sublimation does appear in this fragment to be a vicissitude of the pregential instinct, as opposed to direct release in a perverse act. In perversion, the energy available for sublimation would be possibly non-existent, because totally released directly. Moreover, such release being free—at least schematically—one wonders what would drive the pervert to divert part of it into so-called cultural aims. To begin with, and to be able to eliminate this type of patient from my description, I would like to state that, in certain cases, there exists a mere quantitative problem which impedes creation in the pervert.

We can conclude, from a strictly economic point of view, that the perversion-sublimation antagonism would be reduced if we imagined—in the same individual, endowed with an abundant libidinal energy—the possible coexistence of various instinctual vicissitudes and various character areas. There could be a 'perverse' area where pregenital instincts would be released into sexual activity, a 'neurotic' area where they would undergo repression, and a third area where they would be sublimated. As a matter of fact, according to Freud in his *Three Essays* (1905), there are various areas in the personality which make it possible for perversion to coexist with neurosis and also with creation. 'A characterological analysis of a highly gifted individual, and in particular, in one with an artistic disposition, may reveal a mixture, in every proportion of efficiency, perversion and neurosis' (p. 238).

Freud appears to have been thinking of Leonardo da Vinci, whose case had been preoccupying him for some time, as evidenced by his Letter to Fliess dated 9 October 1898. Moreover, it is precisely these three areas that Freud singles out in Leonardo in 'Leonardo da Vinci and a Memory of his Childhood': 'In this way, repression, fixation and sublimation share in the contribution made by the sexual instinct to Leonardo's mental life' (p. 132). Fixation then implies perversion: 'When anyone has *become* a gross and manifest pervert, it would be more correct to say that he had *remained* one, for he exhibits a certain stage of *inhibited development*', Freud said in 'A Case of Hysteria' (p. 50).

Even if we admit that the economic, quantitative factor comes into play and, in certain cases, leaves an area free for creation and sublimation, this does not account for the paradoxical fact that the number of 'perverts' involved in the field of art is probably much greater than the average for the population in general. Examples are superfluous. You certainly have many in mind, from the most creative genius to the insignificant minor artist who nevertheless enjoyed his day of glory and/or left his mark on art history. It can be supposed, therefore, that the pervert inclines in some particular manner to the world of art.

Where psychoanalysis is concerned, it is always most interesting to examine the failures and the stumbling blocks which human activity encounters. I shall concentrate here not on Leonardo's outstanding artistic achievements (though the amount of energy devoted to inventing engines at the expense of his pictorial creation has, possibly, something to do with my subject), but rather on this need to create which gains a hold on so many a pervert, and on the difficulties and failures encountered. In other words, I am going to examine the qualitative factor.

Let me first recall very briefly some elements of the perverse organization which I pointed out previously. At the time of the Oedipus conflict, the neurotic, or normal subject, projects his Ego Ideal onto his father, thus making him his model, his identification aim, in order to become like him, i.e., like the mother's object, in the hope of replacing him at her side. The future pervert—usually encouraged in this by his mother who pampers and admires him and excludes the father—lives with the illusion that, with his pregenital sexuality, his immature and sterile penis, he is an adequate sexual partner for his mother and has nothing to envy in his father. In my opinion, he is forced to project his narcissism onto his pregenital erotogenic zones and part objects; he subjects them to an idealization process in order to preserve his conviction. His Ego Ideal thus remains attached to a pregenital model. Pregenitality, part objects, erotogenic zones, instincts: all must be idealized by the pervert so that he may be able to pretend to himself and to others that his pregenital sexuality is equal, if not superior, to genitality. The staggering blows dealt to his illusion, the existence of genital interests in his fellow human beings, make such idealization utterly compelling, since, at a certain level, the pervert is always threatened with the disclosure of the infantile, pregenital nature of his sexual attributes, objects and Ego. To his often-noted sexual compulsion, I suggest that we add a compulsion to idealize.

In my opinion, it is instincts and part objects from the anal-sadistic stage which will be selectively idealized. Let me say that the pervert will attempt to give himself and others the illusion that anal sexuality (which is accessible to the little boy) is equal and even superior to genital sexuality (accessible to the father), by erasing from the sexual scene all those elements that might act as obstacles to his conviction. It is as if the equation penis = child = faeces, established by Freud (1917), should be taken literally. In reality, in order to have a genital penis and to procreate, it is necessary to grow up, to mature, to wait, whereas faeces are a production common to adult and child, woman and man. The two differences—between the sexes and between generations—are abolished at the anal level. Time is wiped out. The intervention of the time factor, as a phylogenetic transition from one phase of development to the next, was asserted by Freud on several occasions, as early as his letters to Fliess. In correlation, Freud mentions 'organic repression', which he will consider, many years later, as a 'defence against a phase of development that has been surmounted' (*Civilization and its Discontents*, 1929, p. 99). 'This process is repeated on another level when the gods of a superseded period of civilization turn into demons' (p. 99). Moreover, Freud applies this conception to anal eroticism in the same text. In his letter to Einstein, 'Why War?' (1932), he reverts to the idea that changes in civilization are modelled upon organic repression which, once it has taken place, makes

92 Creativity and Perversion

intolerable to us sensations that used to be pleasurable to our forefathers. *'There are organic grounds for the changes in our ethical and aesthetic ideals'* (p. 214).

For my own purpose, I find Freud's comparison between pleasures succumbing to organic repression and the fall of ancient gods very enlightening. It is very easy to understand—and one need only read Sade to be convinced of it—that anal instincts and objects can form the object of a cult. The pervert has not converted his ancient gods into demons. He is more particularly compelled to worship them since his gods are not acknowledged by most of his peers, who have changed their ideals at a certain stage of development. Therefore, he is compelled to worship his gods, to glorify his pregenital instincts, since in this way he magnifies his own Ego. We are dealing here with the disguise of the (anal) Ego.

This is the point where the compulsion to idealize steps in. In my opinion this accounts for the pervert's obvious affinities for art and beauty; the pervert is often an aesthete. The pregenital libido — which, if diverted, may be sublimated — is not always available to the pervert since it is directly released in the perverse act. Moreover, because he has not projected his Ego Ideal onto his father and genitality, he has not introjected his father's genital attributes. The resulting identification gaps constitute a major obstacle to a real sublimation process. Idealization tends more toward aestheticism than creation, and when creation nevertheless develops, it often bears the stamp of aestheticism.

I would like to submit a clinical illustration taken from the material of a patient, which sheds some light on the idealization process as differentiated from a genuine sublimation, with the obvious repercussions this will have on the quality of the pervert's creation. This man had numerous perverse activities. He was an exhibitionist; he also used to fondle women in particular cinemas, usually when they were sitting next to their husband or boyfriend. During one session, he began to speak of his desire to write, after referring to one of my articles which he had just read. He was wondering how to go about realizing that desire when he recalled a forgotten dream;

> I was in a sawmill. There was a huge pile of logs, all alike, and I was supposed to paint them all silver. I had to be very meticulous, carefully covering each of the logs with silver paint. This reminds me that once, as a child, I put some excrement on the logs at the sawmill next to our house. The owner was raving mad. I am thinking, too, of the chocolate I used to have for my afternoon snack, and also of the chocolate cigarettes I used to buy at the tobacconist's, where sweets were also sold.

In my opinion, this example shows the difference between idealization and sublimation. The creation imagined by the patient in his dream (which he associates with his wish to write) consists in covering the chocolate, the logs (the anal penis), with silver paint or paper in order to idealize them, without changing their inner nature. One has only to scratch the surface and the excremental nature of the phallus will reappear under the shiny coating. To make sure that the father (the owner of the saw mill) possesses nothing that his son does not, his genital penis will be transformed into excrement.

One of my female patients led an apparently 'genital' sexual and family life until she was nearly 35 years old. Then she met a pervert who was an art amateur. This led her to collect works of art, visit art exhibitions, became an art patron. It also allowed her latent perversion to appear: she would play with him at being at Auschwitz. (See Chapter 13, Rrose Sélavy's case.) I think that the patient's pregenital instincts could not express themselves except in the aesthetic atmosphere that surrounded her partner and that provided their relationship with an idealizing aura.

The need for the pervert to conceal his instincts, his objects, the pregenital universe in which he lives, ultimately aims at idealizing his own Ego. He becomes one with his worshipped part objects, a transfigured image of his own attributes, thus magnified. He sees himself with complacency in his glorified instincts, just as he used to see himself in his mother's loving eyes in order to find therein the confirmation of his adorable perfection. He must celebrate the gods of pregenitality in order thereby to insure his own divinity.

Let us refer to the interesting young man Freud describes to Abraham in his letter (dated 24 February, 1910, pp. 91-92) mentioning 'the elegance and good taste of his clothes' and his 'idealistic demands'. The same young man had exhibited intensive coprophilic activity. In his article on 'Psychoanalysis of a Case of Foot and Corset Fetishism' (1912), Abraham underlines 'the shoe fetishist's habitual *aesthetic* demands (which) bear witness to the intense need to idealize the object'. While these idealistic demands are particularly obvious in the fetishist, we are under the impression that they are common to the majority of perverts.

In 'Aggression and Sado-Masochism' (1964), Glover refers to the 'apparent efflorescence of sublimations in certain types of homosexuality'; he considers 'the close relationship between the failure of sublimation and the perverse formation' as completely pathognomonic. However, if sublimation is successful, the subject will not fear so much that the infantile nature of his Ego may become apparent under its disguise. Nevertheless, I feel that in general this fear is always present, always active, and that it leads the pervert toward an ever-increasing idealization of his part objects and the perverse act itself. Glover noted that, 'in many cases one finds that perverse activity is more freely exercised where certain aesthetic conditions are fulfilled' ('Sublimation, Substitution and Social Anxiety', 1931, in *On Early Development of Mind*, 1956, pp. 146-47).

He gives the example of 'an invert with whipping fantasies (who) describes how his erotic activities are inhibited unless the whip conforms to certain aesthetic standards, size, shape, tapering, smoothness, color, etc.' (p. 147). We could take this whip to be a fetish. Glover goes on to say:

> Clothing and shoe fetishists show similar reactions. Underwear, for example, has to conform to certain rigid aesthetic laws of pattern, color, line and so on. The rigidity of such standards is reminiscent of the severe canons upheld by some critics or exponents of the fine arts. Indeed, if one did not know what was the actual subject matter of association, it would be very difficult for the hearer to distinguish certain diagnostic discussions of the conditions for perverse sexual gratification from an aesthetic discussion of "good" and "bad" art (p. 147).

Glover resumes this discussion in a 'Note on Idealization' (1938), especially in connection with perversion. He observes that

> ... there are obvious indications of sexual overestimation in the attitude or behaviour of infants towards accessible parts of their own bodies... it suggests a degree of wonderment and adoration... The same reaction can be observed in relation to many inanimate external objects, e.g., dangling pieces of colored glass... Characteristically, these attitudes are more fully expressed in the case of inanimate substitute objects (toys, etc.) than in the case of animate objects (parents, etc.) (p. 293).

In a similar way, the study of perversions shows that: 'Apart from marked sexual over-estimation of part objects and their immediate substitutes, many cases exhibit an attitude of extreme idealization of these objects, however primitive they may be' (p. 293). Glover adds amusingly, referring to the pervert:

> *However devoid of idealization of adult relations he may be, his geese are usually regarded by him as swans...* My experience seems to indicate that these reactions are more common in the case of objects of anal and urethral sexuality. Next to these come those fetishistic idealizations behind which lies a good deal of sadistic interest. In a typical case, *the anal ring was fantasied as a kind of halo suspended in the sky. It was then contemplated, adored and idealized. The qualities attributed to it were mystical and the whole attitude of the patient was religious in type* (p. 294).

Glover shows that not only does idealization extend to 'every variety of part object, food, faeces, urine, sexual zones, etc... [but] at the same time these patients tend to excessive idealization of their natural surroundings, the sun or sunshine, woods, flower gardens, cliffs, valleys and seas' (p. 294). For Glover, 'these primitive idealizations have... a specially close relation to *anal sadism*'

Aestheticism, Creation and Perversion 95

(p. 296). To me, the need to idealize the environment, the scenery, seems to be quite fundamental for the pervert: everything that surrounds the Ego is like a mirror in which it is reflected. This mirror must be refined, and in exquisite taste in order to disguise anality, covering it with a thousand glittering jewels (the pieces of coloured glass referred to by Glover).

In my opinion, Oscar Wilde's writings seem to express particularly well what this aestheticism hides and reveals at one and the same time. A story, 'The Birthday of the Infanta' (in *Stories*, Volume 2, 1888) illustrates the tragedy of a being whose illusions about the magnificence of his Ego collapse when he suddenly sees his image in the mirror of truth: a little Dwarf, who was given a flower by the Infanta, believes she loves him. (The Infanta could represent the mother who deceives her child by making him believe he is an adequate sexual partner for her.) This Dwarf, who lives in the forest, has never seen his own image. Seeking his beloved, he slips into the royal palace and walks through a series of magnificently decorated rooms. He finally reaches the last room:

> Of all the rooms this was the brightest and the most beautiful. The walls were covered with a pink-flowered Lucca damask, pat terned with birds and dotted with dainty blossoms of silver; the furniture was of massive silver, festooned with florid wreaths, and swinging Cupids; in front of the two large fire-places stood great screens broidered with parrots and peacocks, and the floor, which was of sea-green onyx, seemed to stretch far away into the distance. Nor was he alone (p. 300).

You will have guessed that, after the elation derived from his image as reflected by the scenery around him, the Dwarf comes upon his true image, for the first time, in a mirror. When he understands that the horrible gnome facing him is his own reflection, he dies. We may suppose that the Dwarf stands for the child, too small to satisfy his mother, and that his ugliness represents anality unmasked.

In another story, 'The Young King' (1888, *op. cit.*), Oscar Wilde writes:

> And it seems that from the very first moment of his recognition he had shown signs of that strange passion for beauty that was destined to have so great an influence over his life... and as soon as he could escape from the council-board or audience-chamber, he would run down the great staircase, with its lions of gilt bronze and its steps of bright porphyry, and wander from room to room, and from corridor to corridor, *like one who was seeking to find in beauty an anodyne from pain, a sort of restoration from sickness* (italics mine p. 278).

The need for the Ego to preserve illusion at all costs is dramatically expressed in 'The Portrait of Mr W.H.', where Oscar

Wilde tells the story of a literary hoax. The impostor, exposed, commits suicide. The critic who was responsible for the exposure, and thus caused the hero to commit suicide, comes around to agreeing with the theory of the impostor, who pretended to have discovered the identity of the person to whom Shakespeare's sonnets were dedicated. The critic, in turn, commits suicide, after writing a letter to the author beseeching him to believe in the existence of Willie Hughes (Mr W.H.). This is what convinces the author that it really was a fake. He writes 'No one dies for what he knows to be the truth. Men die for what they wish to be true, *for something that an inexpressible fear tells them is not true*' (italics mine).

Oscar Wilde's critical writings can be read at various levels. As a matter of fact, a number of his well-known paradoxes on art should, in my opinion, be taken quite seriously. I am thinking in particular of the one in which he says that it is nature that imitates art. It is a question of inverting the usually acknowledged relationship between art and nature, art and life, art and 'reality', in order to ensure the Ego's perfection. If, as I have suggested, the pervert's environment represents his idealized Ego and provides him with a flattering reflection of himself, art—which is essentially decorative for Wilde—will become the principle of life, the principle of nature, the principle of reality. Thus the Ego's complete conformity with art is ensured, since art is henceforth laid down as the model of life and therefore of the Ego. Thus if the relationship between the object and its reflection is inverted, the Ego, placed in an aesthetically satisfactory setting, is but the reflection of this setting. The beauty of the setting thus projects itself upon the Ego, captures and magnifies it. The perfection of art palliates the defects of nature.

Vivian, the author's spokesman in 'Intentions', offers a criticism of Shakespeare: 'The passages in Shakespeare—and there are many—where the language is *uncouth, vulgar, exaggerated*, fantastic, obscene, even, and rejecting the intervention of beautiful style through which alone should life be suffered to find expression... ' Here life is clearly identified with anality. Art must chase away any trace of anality: 'Art finds her own perfection within, and not outside of, herself... She is a veil, rather than a mirror... Hers are... the great archetypes of which things that have existence are but unfinished copies' ('The Decay of Lying', p. 254).

The ideal and idealistic conception of art corresponds to the fantasy of an Ideal Ego, dissatisfied with its successive incarnations, incapable of recovering its lost perfection, the one it had at the dawn of life. At the same time, it tries to place the subject in the centre of a 'charmed circle' (Oscar Wilde's expression, p. 250). His Ego, basking in the wonderful light that surrounds it, will be thereby transfigured. The fact that art is reduced to its decorative function and that this scenery gets to express itself, so to speak, in the subject's Ego thus idealized, is clearly enunciated in another text of

Aestheticism, Creation and Perversion 97

'Intentions', entitled 'The Critic as Artist'. 'Still, the art that is frankly decorative is the art to live with. It is, of all our visible arts, the one art that creates in us both mood and temperament... the harmony that resides in the delicate proportions of lines and masses *becomes mirrored in the mind*' (italics mine, 'The Critic as Artist', *op. cit.*, p. 332).

The day will come when realism will go down in defeat, when idealism and beauty will triumph. Here, Wilde refers directly to Plato.

> And when that day dawns, or sunset reddens, how joyous we shall all be! Facts will be regarded as discreditable, *Truth will be found mourning over her fetters, and Romance, with her temper of wonder, will return to the land.* The very aspect of the world will change to our startled eyes. Out of the sea will rise Behemoth and Leviathan, and sail round the high-pooped galleys, as they do on the delightful maps of those ages when books on geography were actually readable. Dragons will wander about the wasteplaces, and the Phoenix will soar from her nest of fire into the air. We shall lay our hands upon the basilisk, and see the jewel in the toad's head. Champing his gilded oats, the Hippogriff will stand in our stalls, and over our heads will float the Blue Bird singing of beautiful and impossible things, of things that are lovely and that never happen, of things that are not and that should be (italics mine, 'The Decay of Lying', *op. cit.*, p. 264).

Looming behind this discussion on aesthetics, where idealism is opposed to realism, and, *a fortiori*, to naturalism, we see matters that are vital to the pervert and—we may suppose—to the author himself.

Several tales and stories written by Oscar Wilde ultimately reveal the truth hiding behind the mask — a truth that Oscar Wilde repeatedly attempts to discredit. Thus, 'The Happy Prince' (*Stories* 1888) shows clearly that anality is not changed by the idealization process (which would happen in genuine sublimation), but is merely covered with a coating of glittering jewels: 'High above the city, on a tall column, stood the statue of the Happy Prince. He was gilded all over with thin leaves of fine gold, for eyes he had two bright sapphires, and a large red ruby glowed on his sword-hilt' (p. 347).

Moved by the misery of the city, the Prince asks the Swallow, who wonders why he is not made of '*solid gold*' (p. 349), to carry the ruby from his sword-hilt to some poor people, and then his two sapphire eyes. Charitably, the Prince divests himself of his coating: ' "I am covered with fine gold", said the Prince, "you must take it off, leaf by leaf, and give it to my poor; the living always think that gold can make them happy". Leaf after leaf of the fine gold the Swallow picked off, till the Happy Price looked quite dull and grey' (pp. 352-53).

The fear that anality may be unmasked, and, with it, the illusion upon which psycho-sexuality has erected itself, emerges explosively in *The Picture of Dorian Gray*. You surely are familiar with the plot. A handsome young man possesses a portrait of himself painted by a friend. Whereas his features remain amazingly youthful as the years go by, in spite of his progressive descent into infamy, it is the portrait that alters and ages, until it is repulsive to behold. Here, idealization appears clearly as a means of masking sadism and anality, which, expelled from the person of Dorian Gray, reappear on the portrait, according to the pattern of hallucination. Dorian, indeed, is a collector of works of art: tapestries, embroideries, precious stones, trinkets. 'For these treasures, and everything that he collected in his lovely house, were to be to him means of forgetfulness, modes by which he could escape, for a season, from the fear that seemed to him at times to be almost too great to be borne.' We see clearly, at least in my opinion, that anality is not so much changed by the idealization process as it is merely covered with a coating of glittering jewels, like the Happy Prince, or as in the dream of my patient who conceals the logs or the chocolate under a coating of silver.

I think I have adequately explained what I mean by the pervert's idealization. I shall now attempt to outline a more metapsychological approach to this process. The first question that comes to mind is related to its connections with the anal instincts, the ideas and affects related to them. Given the importance of idealization, I must infer that—contrary to what the formula, 'Neurosis is the negative of perversion', might imply—anal regression is not egosyntonic in perversion, even though anality, in the perverse act proper, escapes from repression. It is as if repressing agencies agreed to avoid repression in the case of ideas or presentations linked with anality only on condition that the latter are 'disguised' by idealization and that the subject's Ego-image is travestied. But what does 'disguised' mean? I am under the impression that these presentations are marked with the sign contrary to that of the original presentations. The shining and the glittering are the opposite of the dull and the uniform (excrement, or the dull grey matter that the Happy Prince is made of). Now, the opposite bears the indelible impression of that which it negates, as shown by Freud in 'Negation' (1925). It is possible to detect anality not only behind the glittering ornament, but also in its very brilliancy.

Freud writes in his article on 'Negation':

> To negate something in a judgement is, at bottom, to say: "This is something which I would prefer to repress." A negative judgement is the intellectual substitute for repression; its "no" is the hallmark of repression, a certificate or origin—like, let us say, "Made in Germany". With the help of the symbol of negation

thinking frees itself from the restrictions of repression and enriches itself with material that is indispensable for its proper functioning... Thus the content of a repressed image or idea can make its way into consciousness, on condition that it is *negated*. Negation is a way of taking cognizance of what is repressed; indeed, it is already a lifting of the repression, though not, of course, an acceptance of what is repressed. We can see how in this the intellectual function is separated from the affective process (pp. 235-36).

I think that idealization could be considered as being a selective process dealing with ideas related to anality, which is comparable to negation, something like: 'No, it is not that, but the contrary', which would enable a partial lifting of repression, and also the admission into the Ego of repressed anal presentations. Idealization implies extreme closeness to what is being masked. It is an unstable and fragile process, very far from a reaction formation. In addition, among other differences, the latter is governed by the Superego, and helps build up our virtues, which is not the case with idealization, the moving force of which is preservation of self-esteem, and has nothing to do with guilt.

I feel that such an approach to idealization brings us close to several points made by Freud in his early works, which are connected with the relation between idealization and perversion. First in *Three Essays on Sexuality* (1905), he writes:

> It is perhaps in connection precisely with the most repulsive perversions that the mental factor must be regarded as playing its largest part in the transformation of the sexual instinct. It is impossible to deny that in their case a piece of mental work has been performed which, in spite of its horrifying result, is an equivalent of an idealization of the instinct (p. 161).

The emphasis laid on this mental work enables us to get a glimpse of the energy modification which we shall discern more clearly in connection with the affect, and which also anticipates the research of mechanisms specific to perversion.

In a Letter to Abraham (14 February 1909), Freud writes:

> The fetish develops as follows: it is the result of a special mode of repression that could be described as a partial repression: one part of the complex is repressed, another part, as a compensation, is *idealized*... In this case, we are dealing with an original olfactory pleasure derived from an ill-smelling foot (which, for this reason, will always be preferred to a clean foot by the pervert). This olfactory pleasure is discarded. In exchange, the foot, a source of pleasure in the past, is established as a fetish. Its smell is no longer a matter of interest.

The partial repression in such a case reminds us of the partial lifting of repression linked with negation.

In his article on 'Repression' (1915), Freud returns to the notion of partial repression as an origin of the fetish, with an accompanying idealization.

Repression acts... in a *highly individual* manner. Each single derivative of the repressed may have its own special vicissitude; a little more or a little less distortion alters the whole outcome. In this connection, we can understand how it is that the objects to which men give most preference, their ideals, proceed from the same perceptions and experiences as the objects which they most abhor, and that they were originally only distinguished from one another through slight modifications. Indeed, as we found in tracing the origin of the fetish, it is possible for the original instinctual representative to be split in two, one part undergoing repression, while the remainder, precisely on account of this intimate connection, undergoes idealization (p. 150).

The common origin of 'the objects to which men give most preference' and 'the objects which they most abhor' accounts, in my opinion, for the lability of the idealization mechanism to which I have just referred, as well as for the ever-near persecution. This is because, at any time, anality threatens to burst through the thin, glittering shell covering it and to reappear in broad daylight, like the hideous corpse of a drowning victim coming back to the surface, a process which is very clearly described at the end of *The Picture of Dorian Gray*.

I would like to end this chapter by quoting a passage which shows that idealization is only a thin film disguising an unchanged material, a mechanism aiming at masking the self. It also shows that there are human beings who do prefer truth to mendacity:

Whilst others fish with craft for great opinion
I with great truth catch mere simplicity;
Whilst some with cunning gild their copper crowns,
With truth and plainness I do wear mine bare.
(Troilus speaking to Cressida)

Chapter 10

Construction in Analysis and Psychic Construction

I have emphasized several times that the problem of perversions, as I consider it, leads us to the more general problem of truth. I recalled that Freud, in 'Analysis Terminable and Interminable' (1937), stated that the psychoanalytical situation was based on the love of truth. So, while wandering away from the question directly associated with perversion, I would like to approach a point relevant to truth within the psychoanalytical situation.

Among the interventions the analyst is led to making during a treatment — and they form part of his interpretative activity — there is one which poses a variety of technical as well as ethical problems. I am thinking of 'construction'. By this word, Freud means, first of all, the analyst's working through, with the help of elements supplied by the patient, the 'information' given, his 'free associations', 'what he shows in the transference', the interpretation of his dreams, 'his slips and parapraxes' (*An Outline of Psychoanalysis*, 1938, p. 177). On the basis of these, the analyst proposes to the analysand a construction concerning forgotten fragments of his past, thus favouring, when it is correct and *carefully* applied, the lifting of the infantile amnesia: 'The more exactly the construction coincides with the details of what has been forgotten, the easier will it be for him to assent: on that particular matter *our* knowledge will then become *his* knowledge as well' (p. 178).

We know that the historical truth of a construction understood in this manner has often been questioned. It is the whole problem of the relationship of event with fantasy which enters here into play. So, it is not this point which I would like to consider. Or, rather, I shall be led to approach it indirectly through another, even more questionable point. I shall examine a kind of construction mentioned by Freud in the article he specially devoted to the topic ('Construction in Analysis', 1937, pp. 255-74).

'What we are in search of', says Freud in that late text, 'is a picture of the patient's forgotten years' (p. 258). The person who is being analysed has to be induced to remember something that has been experienced by him and repressed' (p. 258). As we know, Freud lays stress on the role of the transference relationship which induces a repetition of affects deriving from the repressed material, and expressing themselves inside or outside the psychoanalytical situation. We also recall that Freud ends his account, before approaching the problem of delusions, by stating that, if in principle, a construction is supposed to end in a remembrance, it is not always so. The lifting up of the repressed does not always happen. But, if the construction produces in the patient an assured conviction, it 'achieves the same therapeutic result as a recaptured memory' (p. 266). The whole psychoanalytical theory is against the eventuality of understanding this sentence as involving the effect of suggestion. As early as *Studies on Hysteria* (1895), Freud wrote: 'We learn with astonishment from this that *we are not in a position to force anything on the patient about the things he is ostensibly ignorant of*' (p. 295).

We are in 1937. At first sight, Freud's idea according to which conviction is equivalent to remembrance—as far as its results are concerned—is in contradiction to what he says about interpretation in his article on 'The Unconscious' (1915, pp. 175-76). When the analyst guesses a repressed idea and tells it to the patient, this will be without effect on repression and on the psyche, generally speaking. On the contrary, a new rejection of the repressed idea will occur. The same idea will be registered in two different shapes in two different places of the patient's mental apparatus: a conscious acoustic memory of this idea and its unconscious, repressed memory.

According to Freud, 'Actually there is no lifting of the repression until the conscious idea, after the resistances have been overcome, has entered into connection with the unconscious memory trace.' This summarizes the whole difference between what has been heard and what has been felt, between intellectual knowledge and affective knowledge. However, in my opinion, it is precisely this difference—between what has been heard and what has been felt—that might explain the effect of a construction which carries the patient's conviction without any remembering, the lack of remembering being possibly connected with the immature state of the Ego at the time of the events here involved. Indeed, we may think that this kind of construction is particularly effective in the case of early traumas and of a helpless Ego in a state of distress.

The intended effect of such a construction is to favour the working through of a traumatic situation encountered in the first months of life, when the mental apparatus overwhelmed by excitations, is unable to master or release them. The accumulation of excitations bursts into the very fabric of the psyche, thus creating a hole and remaining there as a foreign body, after having unsettled it from one end to the other. The construction re-establishes the continuity of the web, fills in the hole, and, according to the Freudian metaphor, reconstitutes the missing piece of the 'Chinese puzzle' (*Studies on Hysteria*, 1895), while permitting all the bits of the puzzle, shaken up by the initial shock, to be put back into place.

Now, the construction has an unquestionable therapeutic efficiency in the case of a trauma having occurred at a time when the Ego was unable to send forth the signal of anxiety but reacted by automatic anxiety, and when the Superego was not differentiated enough to help the overwhelmed Ego. If we refer to Freud's work, *Inhibitions, Symptoms and Anxiety* (1926, p. 94), the repressions were then, we may suppose, primal ones: '... It is perhaps the emergence of the Superego which provides the line of demarcation between primal repression and after-pressure... It is highly probable that the immediate precipitating causes of primal repressions are quantitative factors such as an excessive degree of excitation and the breaking through of the protective shield against stimuli.' We may notice that the clinical account in which Freud deals the most with the problems relating to construction—The Wolf-Man—describes a case whose traumatic character is obvious; the dream is itself considered by Freud as a trauma.

You remember the passage where Freud shows that the child must call upon the help of castration fear in order to avoid being overwhelmed by homosexual excitations. The basically economic character of the phenomena thus described by Freud is striking. Homosexuality is not frightening because it constitutes a danger for the penis; it is threatening because it supplies excitations by which the Ego would be overwhelmed. From a certain point of view, we may say that this process is equivalent to an attempt at a psychic working through and to a passage from a merely economic (quantitative) to a qualitative level, more specific to the psychic conflict. Thus, within the transference situation, the construction of an early trauma seems to change the status of the event by granting it the rank of a true psychic process with its complete metapsychological dimensions: economic, of course, but also topographical and dynamic. The traumatic event was only a force; it now acquires a meaning.

However—and I would like to insist upon this—when a construction related to an early trauma 'carries the patient's conviction', its effects (so says Freud) may resemble those of a construction that *is* accompanied by remembered affects bound to their initial presentations. I would like to put forward the idea that the missing piece of the Chinese puzzle will fit into the subject's psychic organization to which it is organically and necessarily linked and which is submitted to an absolute internal logic. The analyst who has succeeded in supplying the missing piece, at the same time, strengthens the entire psychic organization. From now on, the edifice suffers no breaking in its continuity and loses its fragility.

The missing piece is organized in connection with the whole edifice, and the whole edifice has an effect upon the missing piece. It is the recovery of the lost unity which ensures conviction: it is not any effect of suggestion, which would only be felt as a foreign body,

104 *Creativity and Perversion*

a grafted element, so to speak, and not a missing component. The foreign body would sooner or later fall victim to a reaction of rejection. Moreover, is it even necessary to say that imposing ideas heterogeneous to the patient's material and psychic organization is contrary to ethics? Here I am not thinking, of course, of interpretations which are not Ego-syntonic; it is obvious that the progress of the analytical treatment involves such interpretations.

I think a clinical example will allow us to understand what occurs in other cases, even when the construction is not accompanied by memories. Moreover, this case is a typical neurotic one, which will give us the opportunity to make an implicit comparison with the pervert patients I have spoken of till now.

It is obvious that the recollections subsequent to the construction proposed by the analyst allow us to understand that conviction results from the logical and necessary relations between the construction and the whole psychic organization. The patient is a young man of 27 who took my advice for recurrent fears relating to supposedly severe illness affecting his genitals. The aim of the construction I shall speak of is not to allow the working through of a traumatic situation, but to give their full meanings to various events of the Oedipal phase and those closely associated with the Oedipus Complex. Castration then occupies a central place, the Superego (in the Freudian, not the Kleinian meaning of the term) is in the process of formation, and the repressions then at work are after-pressures.

It so happens that the material here involved might lead to the typical construction presented by Freud in his article devoted to this topic:

> Up to your nth year you regarded yourself as the sole and unlimited possessor of your mother; then came another baby which brought you grave disillusionment. Your mother left you for some time, and even after her reappearance she was never again devoted to you exclusively. Your feelings towards your mother became ambivalent, your father gained a new importance to you... and so on. (*op. cit.*, p. 261).

Norbert stretches himself out on the couch. It is springtime and, in spite of the cold weather, the central heating is not on in order to save energy. An electric heater endeavours to warm the chilly temperature of the room. The heat coming from it makes the overhanging chandelier vibrate and clink. Norbert says that this sound reminds him of the three engraved golden bracelets which his mother used to wear round her wrist. These jewels had belonged to her own mother, and were engraved after the Persian manner; Norbert's mother comes from a Middle East family. While his mother was away, Norbert used to wait impatiently for the tinkling of her bracelets that would announce her return. It was a real treat. How happy he was when the light sound came nearer and when at long last the key turned in the lock! The disquiet, sadness and anxiety would vanish.

That day Norbert spoke to me for a long time of his mother's tenderness, of how happy he was to be near her. These memories dated from when he was 4 to 5 years old. The session was the first of the last week before the Easter holidays. At the end of the session, Norbert added that one day he had played with his mother's bracelets and had lost them. He felt mad because he hadn't the slightest idea where he might have put the jewels: a total blank. They were searched for, for days and days, in vain. The session ended at that point. The day after, Norbert went on with his account. 'My mother used to say that she would give one of her bracelets to the wife of each one of us.' Norbert is the eldest of three children. He has two brothers younger than himself by 2 and 4 years, respectively. Now the warm and affectionate atmosphere engendered by the tender closeness of the previous session was to deteriorate progressively. Norbert's reminiscences were to become more and more painful and discordant. The flat was dark, the parents were poor, the buildings he could see through the window were anonymous and made of ugly bricks. Norbert's father drew the meagre pay of an officer. He himself went to school with his belongings in a workman's satchel. The district was a proletarian one. Norbert tried to get over this sadness and ugliness by scrutinizing, one by one, with sedulousness and fervour, the few family belongings he thought beautiful: his father's military cap adorned with gold lace, the silver, the Bohemian glasses that were presents from the grandparents. He would sometimes gaze at these wonders, into which, so he said, his own misery and discontent would disappear. A few days after the disappearance of his mother's three bracelets, an uncle of his came home and drew aside the window curtain: the bracelets were hanging on the window latch.

We could then see the meaning of the disappearance of the bracelets, and their ensuing disquiet as to the 'blank' as well as his fear of having gone mad. Norbert had thus, indeed, symbolically murdered his brother. Had he not told me, several months before, that he had watched out for his mother's return from the nursing home with the new-born child in her arms? Hadn't he been seized by the unsuppressed impulse to throw all his toys out of the window (like the young Goethe) together with several kitchen utensils, a pastry board and a roller, not long after the arrival of his youngest brother, to the point that the 'concierge' who had come out, had said of Norbert: 'This child is mad!'? Norbert had thus symbolically sent the intruder back to where he had come from (the street) as well as the things which—we may imagine—represented the strange parental cooking which had been used to make it. He also probably wanted to clear his mother's belly (the flat) of all its unwanted contents.

We may put forward the hypothesis that Norbert's fascination for golden things, silver and crystal—where we see an aesthetic need, almost *in statu nascendi*—is linked to the violence of his destructive drives against his brothers and parents and, particularly, against his mother who was so tender, so loved and so cruelly unfaithful—all these feelings being reactivated by the analyst's approaching departure. Norbert's hatred, guilt and depression create within him a chaos from which he escapes by gazing at things which he feels are beautiful and which send back to him a reflection of himself and his destroyed objects, a reflection which denies or masks this chaos. It is not the external reality which is actually depressing; it is his internal reality which needs flattering mirrors in order to undo its chaos.

We may suppose that the objects he admires have a precise phallic symbolic meaning. The father's military cap becomes an idealized phallus towards which he turns in an introjective and homosexual impulse in order to fight against the disappointment his mother caused him, and in the hope—according to the positive Oedipus Complex—of acquiring a big penis able to fulfil her and give her a child. The Bohemian glasses and the silver offered by the grandparents likewise have a similar meaning: that of a phallus passing from one generation to another, and implying Norbert's belonging to a lineage. At the same time, the positive cathexis of the grandparents' gifts (as opposed to the negative cathexis of the parents' gifts = babies) possibly represents an attempt at finding a substitute parental couple.

The construction made by the analyst (and partly communicated to Norbert) fits perfectly into his psychic organization. More particularly, it fits into that of his defences such as they appear in the transference within the treatment, and in the behaviour he repeats outside, and of which he speaks to me. So, if the transference relationship has enabled the construction, the latter illuminates in turn many aspects of the transference.

Indeed, Norbert's conflict linked to his fraternal rivalry within the framework of the positive side of his Oedipus Complex, and of his intense love for his mother, is repeated in the transference: my warmth = that of my heater. The tinkle of the chandelier influences the material of the session similarly to the effect of day residues on a dream. The nearing end of the session and my impending departure mobilize again his aggressiveness towards his mother leaving him to give birth, every two years, to a new rival. The object of the aggressive drives is displaced onto a symbolic substitute: the bracelets both represent the brothers and fulfil a function as precious part objects belonging to the mother. The affect (hatred) is turned towards himself and transformed into the fear of being mad. The blank, representing a gap in the psychic life, is equivalent to a castration. We may remember the concierge's (Superego's) words: 'This child is mad!', concerning his symbolic attack on his brothers and the primal scene.

We have here a picture of Norbert's mental activity, his capacities of displacement, condensation, symbolization, etc.—in short, of his ability to employ neurotic mechanisms and of the part played by his preconscious in his mental activity. After recalling the disappearance of the bracelets, a regression takes place in the material. Not only do the affects become unpleasant, but the presentations also are modified, acquiring an anal tinge: darkness, ugliness, poverty make their appearance. Ideas and affects are an indication of the depression following the attacks on the brothers and the mother. We have noticed some marks of an aptitude for sublimation. The construction I proposed to Norbert takes into account what I know of him: the level of conflict, his capacity to face his depression, his symbol formation, and his gifts for sublimation which he expresses now in the scientific field and which, soon after this session, gave rise to interesting developments. Norbert made a discovery fascinatingly related to the conflicts just described. Several times he had a dream in which there were 'niches' ('nichons', a slang word for bosoms), two niches being insufficient for three children. Norbert's discovery is related to the sublimation of his wish to monopolize his mother's breasts.

Norbert is a bio-chemist. He works on a substance which we shall call CLNA. One night he dreams of the formula written on a blackboard, but instead of CLNA, it is written CMMA. He associates the two Ms to two Mammas. Norbert's discovery has certain properties which will enable CLNA to be used against certain severe diseases in children.

In the following sessions and months, Norbert brought several memories associated with that period of his childhood. First of all, the window with the bracelets was the same as the one out of which he had shamelessly ejected the toys and kitchen utensils; it was also the same out of which he had seen his mother returning with the babies. Once he had also completely emptied a whole chest of drawers. Later he remembered a camera for adults that he, Norbert, aged 4, had been given. He was supposed to use it only when he was grown up—it was the promise of the adult genitals he would obtain in the future—and he would gaze at it as at the military cap, the silver plate and the Bohemian glasses. He called the feelings in relation with the depression 'the sky clouding over', and also 'the spot', whereas he called the previous period 'the lost Paradise'. A door opened onto the repetition and the transference of his fraternal rivalry at work. The repression of his hatred against his brothers (who were, at the same time, tenderly loved) had made him incapable of understanding other people's jealousy and envy toward his professional achievements. This inability was the source of a series of disappointments which he was unable to anticipate.

His main resistance in the treatment came out in a particular way, which was difficult to understand and refractory to interpretation till the moment of the construction and the presentation of the material which followed: indeed, he led his analysis at full gallop; after one of my absences he complained of being unable to 'get back on to his horse'. We were running out of breath, he giving very rich and abundant material, complaining of not being able to make headway, with the analyst following, breathless and blaming herself for giving in to the pressing requests for interpretation. It became obvious that he felt as if his brothers were at his heels—they were in fact bright young men. On that account he was ceaselessly obliged to spur himself on, so as not to be outdistanced. He also proved to be excessively sensitive to the rare changes in my timetable and intolerant of my absences, from which there was every likelihood that I would return with my arms full of unwanted and greedy creatures absorbing my care and attention.

I do not want to give the feeling that I overestimate what is, after all, only an ordinary work of construction, greatly facilitated by a gifted patient. Neither do I claim to have covered the whole field of the multiple and complex question involved in the analyst's technical activity. My purpose is to try and show that a construction—when it is adequate, that is, when it represents the missing piece of the Chinese puzzle—occupies a necessary place inside the psychic organization viewed as a whole, such as it manifests itself in the transference, or, rather, in the transference neurosis. I want to show that there is nothing gratuitous in it, but that it asserts itself as a matter of course, and that each of its aspects is bound up with the corresponding aspects of the Ego viewed as a whole, and vice versa. I think that such a point of view allows us to bracket the endless discussion as to whether or not the historical reality or the reconstructed events can be attained. At the same time, such a conception enables us to understand the therapeutic effect (paradoxical, at first sight) of a construction devoid of any ensuing remembrance, and the conviction it carries. This conviction can be explained only if we admit that, then, the patient's Ego is collated, not so much with lost memories—since they cannot be remembered—as with a part of himself he was separated from, and which has become accessible once more.

We may notice that, in English, 'to remember' suggests the word 'member'—whose etymology it shares—a *remembrance* being the action of putting together scattered members or limbs. Indeed, the whole body is that Chinese puzzle which—as a materialization of the psyche—has to be 'remembered', that is, reconstructed. It seems possible to conclude that the 'truth' of the construction—whether or not it leads to remembering—lies in the fact that it finds its natural place in the Ego, that it slots in and that it enlightens the construction of the entire psyche, with which it has a symbolic relationship, in the etymological meaning of the word 'symbol'.

Chapter 11

On the Therapeutic Alliance and 'Pervert' Patients

My objective in this chapter is rather limited, or perhaps unlimited, as you are going to see. I would like to contribute to the understanding of what renders the therapeutic alliance possible or, on the contrary, difficult or even impossible. But, first of all, I would like to indicate that it is not my intention to speak of the ego-psychologists' thoughts on this question. I do not believe in 'autonomous Ego functions' as independent of the drives. Here I do not define my concept of the therapeutic alliance, nor do I discuss its very existence, which is questioned by some analysts. I hope that my whole presentation leads to an implicit definition of this notion and thus confirms the utility of such a concept.

For a definition I shall turn instead to Freud. He speaks of this topic as follows, in 'Analysis Terminable and Interminable' (1937, p. 135):

> As is well known, the analytic situation consists in our allying ourselves with the Ego of the person under treatment... The fact that a co-operation of this kind habitually fails in the case of psychotics affords us a first solid footing for our judgment. The Ego, if we are able to make such a pact with it, must be a normal one. But a normal Ego of this sort is, like normality in general, an ideal fiction. The abnormal Ego, which is unserviceable for our purposes, is unfortunately no fiction. Every normal person, in fact, is only normal in the average. His Ego approximates to that of the psychotic in some part or other and to a greater or lesser extent...

Thus Freud brings forward the terms of 'alliance', 'co-operation' (in German, 'Zusammenarbeiten'), 'pact', in order to speak of the relationship established or, rather, which should be established between analyst and analysand during the treatment.

Nowadays, we have to deal more and more frequently—it has even become banal to say so—with clinical cases presenting various alterations of the Ego which make the therapeutic alliance very difficult to establish. We even come to doubt that the distinction between a psychotic Ego and a neurotic or 'normal' one can account for such difficulties. Speaking of psychoses in *An Outline of*

Psycho-Analysis (1938-1940), Freud writes:

> The problem of psychoses would be simple and perspicuous if the Ego's detachment from reality could be carried through completely. But that seems to happen only rarely or perhaps never. Even in a state so far removed from the reality of the external world as one of hallucinatory confusion, one learns from patients after their recovery that at the time, in some corner of their mind (as they put it), there was a normal person hidden, who, like a detached spectator, watched the hubbub of illness go past him (pp. 201-2).

Freud asks himself if we might assume that this is so in general in 'other psychoses with a less tempestuous course'; he replies positively. He comes to assume the existence, even in psychoses, of a splitting of the Ego, contrary to his ideas about psychoses in his article 'On Fetishism' in 1927. Indeed, while comparing the mechanisms of disavowal and splitting in fetishism with those brought into play by two young men who had not taken 'cognizance of the death' of their 'beloved father', there Freud had written:

> It was only one current in their mental life that had not recognized their father's death; there was another current which took full account of that fact. The attitude which fitted in with the wish and the attitude which fitted in with reality existed side by side. In one of my two cases this split had formed the basis of a moderately severe obsessional neurosis. The patient oscillated in every situation in life between two assumptions: the one, that his father was still alive and was hindering his activities; the other, opposite one, that he was entitled to regard himself as his father's successor (p. 156).

In other words, these two non-psychotic cases contained, at the same time, mechanisms of disavowal *and* splitting of the Ego, which distinguished them from psychosis. Indeed, Freud says: 'I may thus keep to the expectation that in a psychosis the one current—that which fitted in with reality—would have in fact been absent' (p. 156).

This would seem to imply that, at that phase of his investigations—which extended his two articles, 'Neurosis and Psychosis' and 'The Loss of Reality in Neurosis and Psychosis' (both 1924), and even the 'Wolf-Man' (1918)—Freud understands the splitting of the Ego as linked to fetishism or to neurosis and warranting the persistency of the subject's ties to reality. In a psychosis, however, the splitting is absent, and the whole Ego is detached from reality or from a part of it. Therefore we find a momentous evolution in Freud's thought between 1924-1927 (even 1918) and 1938: the mechanisms splitting the psyche both between different agencies (the Ego and the Id) as well as within one and the same agency (the Ego) are at work in the whole field of mental diseases and even in the normal psyche. (This does not mean at all that we needn't try to delineate the specific organization of the main categories of mental disease, i.e. neurosis, psychosis and perversion.) With regard to an asymptotic, so to speak, psychotic organization, the splitting of the Ego is evidently a mechanism preserving the subject's ties with reality and allowing a normal Ego to survive within a psyche immersed in the deepest chaos.

Experience proves that, in certain cases, it is easier to find an ally—at least a temporary one—in this tiny part of the Ego that has escaped from the psychotic disaster than in the Ego of persons apparently anchored to reality, from an ordinary point of view. They have a job, they are sometimes brilliantly successful, socially speaking, and have object relationships which, seen from outside, may seem normal. Yet, all goes on as if the splitting between a more or less normal Ego and a pathological one were wanting, as if the entire Ego had been broken into bits, were cracked, and deformed to such an extent that no unaltered surface were left. The analyst has no possible ally at his disposal. Paradoxically, he has in front of him a man or a woman, sometimes much more 'adjusted' than himself and, at a certain level, more psychotic than the psychotics.

No doubt you have recognized the kind of patient the analyst grapples with, the patient who understands all the analyst says as either a seduction or as an attack but never as an interpretation. Winnicott's followers would speak here, I think, of a lack of an intermediary area. What is obvious, in any case, is the lack of space between analyst and analysand, the lack of depth, of a third dimension. In such a situation there are not three persons—the analyst, and the 'normal' part of the analysand, investigating, and taking care together of the sick part of the analysand. Instead there is a chimera which, in extreme cases, gives the impression of a 'horrible mixture' made up from parts of the analyst and of the analysand, in an inextricable jumble. It may happen that the analyst's mental apparatus is paralysed and unable to function.

Quite obviously, the different psychic organizations giving rise to such effects would have to be distinguished and the structure of the Ego investigated in each case. But the topic is so huge that I shall concentrate only on some working hypotheses which are, for the time being, sketchy. They might apply to a series of patients whom we might think not suitable for classical psychoanalysis, though nowadays they very often come for treatment. Among them I have particularly in mind the perverts.

There is one thing I must specify: by the schematic description given of that 'hand to hand' (tussle) situation, without any intermediary space, I do not have in mind what is usually called 'resistance by the transference', such as may occur in certain cases of hysteria who prefer the relation with the analyst to the understanding of their mental functioning. In these cases the mechanism is, after all, rather easy to understand, even if it is not always easy to deal with. The main point is that these cases do not arouse in the analyst a counter-transferential suffering, contrary to those I am speaking of. I would even like to say that this suffering is probably the very clue to what they have in common.

This counter-transference may be linked to such violent affects that they are able to sweep away, at least for a time, the so-called 'benevolent neutrality' (the other part of the analytical pact). The analyst begins to function in the same way as the analysand. His capacity to interpret is threatened and is even really affected. He has not at his disposal either an observing part of the Ego, differentiated from that part which identifies with the patient and/or which answers the projections which are effected onto it. The counter-transference then loses its value as a clue and as a tool; it becomes a resistance contributing to the immobilization of the process and the strengthening of the pathological (anti-analytical) situation which has become established.

One of the hypotheses which forces itself upon us is that the organization of the patients inducing this kind of reaction seems typified by a deficiency in and even a default of the period of latency —that space which separates the two phases of human sexuality. The excitation, the absence or the weakness of aim-inhibited instincts (that is, of the affectionate current of the libido), the default of ideas concerning a non-sexual mother, run for that hypothesis. At the same time there is the idea of a destructive primal scene and, at least in cases of perversion, a disavowal of a genital primal scene. The relationship between analyst and analysand seems to me to be a copy of the fantasied destruction of both partners in the primal scene.

Two of the cases I have in mind have carried out abortions as members of militant movements. Another had repeated dreams where the mother (and the analyst in the transference) was made sterile. These are banal dreams, you might say. Indeed, what was less so was the lack of guilt in the patients and the excitation with which their interpretation was met.

Here is an example: 'I am mowing a lawn. I throw the grass into a river. This grass pollutes the waters in such a way that it destroys the fauna and the flora forever. Then I see a mass of jelly. Maybe a small calf.' (The grass refers to the walls of my consulting room as well as perhaps to my husband's name.) The patient's desire to make his mother sterile is then interpreted in order to show the analysand that this desire endangered the analytical process itself. The patient entirely agrees with this interpretation. He goes on about the calf as a foetus and his mother's miscarriage. Then he associates with the excitation he feels when he imagines having intercourse with a woman with shaven genitals, a fact which he associates with genitals of little girls and with those of his sister with whom he had very often had sexual games when a child. (I associated then for myself with Attila's famous saying: 'Wherever I go by, the grass will never grow again', asking myself if that presentation of the earth's sterilization was not strengthened by the grass as a symbol of mother-earth's pubic hairs, a secondary sexual character marking her nubility and her fertility).

The same patient also had a dream in which his father-in-law underwent an operation and had his penis removed. In its place there was a smooth surface. We may note that it was not a nightmare and that the account of the dream did not arouse any anxiety, at least in the patient. Here we may see an attack on the begetting capacities of both parents and analyst.

In those patients, destructiveness and mastery are generally obvious and intense. The same patient had told me the following dream several weeks before:

> I am fighting with a man with a red moustache. I did a judo grip. He falls to the ground. I sprinkle benzine over him and I make him blaze. This is my father, who is a red-head. It is also you. I don't know if the analyst is a Jew, but Freud was. And Jews were burnt during the war.

We may note that this dream—which would have been a nightmare in a neurotic—is told without any affect. The only sign of embarrassment is in the way he wards me off using indirect speech when addressing me—quite a flimsy fire-guard. We may also notice that if, for a neurotic, I would have had to think ahead, making associations for myself, here the patient overtook me! This patient is not a paranoiac, I must add, even if he has some persecutory features. During his military service he had experienced an episode of homosexual prostitution. After that, he lived for several years with a man older than himself. He is now married and a father, and is a distinguished professional man.

Once he dreamt that he was with three gangsters in Chicago. He was a gangster's apprentice and associated with his wish to become an analyst. In other words, the three gangsters representing his three weekly sessions, he does not seek in analysis to discover some truth as to his mental functioning; rather he seeks a support for finding a delinquent solution to his conflicts. We see that we are not in search of a therapeutic alliance but of a perverse one.

It is obvious that in such cases the question of the Superego is a fundamental one. The relationship with the Superego can eventually be externalized, but the Superego is disqualified in the process. Two of my pervert patients—those having performed abortions—assert themselves as being strict moralists, but they actually have a strong moral masochism, as described by Freud in 'The Economic Problem of Masochism' (1924).

I tend to consider moral masochism as described by Freud—a resexualization of the relationship between the Superego and the

Ego—as linked rather to perversion than to neurosis. It would be appropriate to differentiate this masochism from the self-punishment or the inhibitions we find in neurotics: this is already obvious in the transference which is not overwhelmed by a sado-masochistic relationship. I must add that these patients' sadism is at least as strong as their masochism and, to my mind, cannot be considered as mere provocation.

A patient whom I had seen a year before undertaking his analysis (and whose smooth fish dream I shall describe later) called me on receiving the letter in which I informed him that sessions were available for him. He asked me if I had increased my fees. To my astonishment, I heard myself telling him that, indeed, my fees had gone up by ten francs per session, compared with the price indicated when we had met. As I put down the receiver, I reflected on what had impelled me to answer his question, and, what is more, to do so over the phone (but the skill of the masochist to manipulate others in order to get sadistically attacked must not be underestimated). I then received a second call: he was indignant, scandalized by this 'unexpected' rise. It is obvious that the only—non-analytical—answer, the one the patient was probably expecting, would have been to reject him.

During his analysis, the patient went to see his father who was severely ill and treated in a foreign country where the currency was much higher than the French franc. For once, he said the encounter with his father went off without a hitch. They did not quarrel. In the night train back, a French customs officer asked one of the patient's fellow-travellers to open his case. The patient became indignant with the civil servant, whom he designated by a particularly energetic epithet. The customs officer asked a colleague to come and help him. They got the patient out of the train, took him to the station (where he underwent several hours of what I shall leave to your imagination) before letting him leave on another train.

Now, if the patient directs a psychodrama in which he is submitted to being beaten, it is in fact his Superego which is being deceived. Instead of the preventive agency it is supposed to be, it has become a means of obtaining pleasure and thus rendered powerless. It is the Superego which is castrated of its function and not the patient; all told, he gets the upper hand. Moreover, it has lost its impersonal, abstract character. Kant's categorical imperative is now dressed up in a preposterous little customs officer's cap. The Ego's relationship with the Superego has acted out into an erotic scene and has degenerated into a punishment for having broken a rule concerning the respect due to a civil servant discharging his duties. I remind you that, in 'The Economic Problem of Masochism' (1924, p. 169), Freud writes:

We know that the wish which so frequently appears in phantasies to be beaten by the father stands very close to the other wish, to have a passive (feminine) sexual relation to him, and is only a regressive distortion of it. If we insert this explanation into the content of moral masochism, its hidden meaning becomes clear to us. Conscience and morality have arisen through the overcoming, the desexualization of the Oedipus Complex; but through moral masochism morality becomes sexualized once more, the Oedipus Complex is revived and the way is opened for a regression from morality to the Oedipus Complex. This is to the advantage neither of morality nor of the person concerned (p. 169).

I would like to put forward the hypothesis that, in the cases where we find this kind of moral masochism, the patient making the analyst play the father's beating part, this situation has to be considered as a presentation of a sado-masochistic primal scene. Moreover, in the same article, Freud speaks of the 'negative therapeutic reaction' (p. 166). Now, if we consider a kind of negative therapeutic reaction as being linked to moral masochism as understood above, we can understand that it is mainly a question, for the patient, of reproducing a primal scene, destined to remain sterile, producing no effects, i.e., no child, in the psychoanalytical situation. Identifications with Christ are not rare in such patients. The one I have just spoken of wanted to be a priest. In one of our sessions he saw a heart on a golden plate. It was his offering—an offering to the analyst, he added. It is significant that, at certain moments, the patient is perfectly aware of the affects he wishes to induce in the analyst. Indeed, this image was repellent to me. And the patient added: 'It's repulsive. Isn't it?'

I shall continue very briefly with a patient who seemed hysterical, at first sight, but presenting perverse features. She also exhibits a marked propensity for mastery and destructiveness which became obvious on the occasions of terrorist actions such as the murders of Aldo Moro or Hans Martin Schleyer. Her masochism, as it developed during analysis, was impressive. At the same time, everything I say, or nearly everything, is snatched away and put into her sado-masochistic system, thus paralysing her analytical treatment. She rejects the interpretations of her projection mechanisms. If she tells me, 'You are this or that', and I express my interpretation by telling her, 'You ascribe this or that to me', she complains: 'You don't accept that I might feel what you *really* are. I am sure that I know you quite well. Furthermore, Mr So-and-So (a well-known colleague) asserts that an analysis is actually brought to an end when the analysand analyses his analyst.' She said to me, one day, with an absolute conviction which left me feeling completely powerless and rendered speechless: '*You* have no idea what difficulty, anxiety and stupidity are.' I think that she was thus attacking my ability to help her, under the cover of an apparent idealization (since she was making me superhuman) while destroying my capacity to function as an analyst.

If I had to summarize what I have just described in overt perverts or in patients displaying a perverse organization within the analysis as hindering the establishment of an actual alliance, I would say that it is the hatred of life, the non-acceptance of the primal scene as liable to give birth to a child, and, consequently, the impossibility of forming a couple with the analyst so as to give birth to a child that would be themselves, re-created. I would like to add that, in such cases, suicide is always lurking in the background.

On the one hand, I know that this idea might be related to Freud's theory of the life and death instinct. On the other hand, I know that it has to do with what some Kleinians call 'good primal scene' or 'analytical baby'. So much the worse, or so much the better! It is my own clinical experience and my way of understanding my patients which have led me there. The idea that an analysis represents a child or a birth exists, indeed, in Freud's article, 'On Beginning the Treatment' (1913, p. 130). Regarding the fact that the analyst is unable to select one or several symptoms in order to help the patient to get rid of them, but that he is only able 'to set in motion a process', he writes:

> But, on the whole, once begun, it goes its own way and does not allow either the direction it takes or the order in which it picks up its points to be prescribed for it. The analyst's power over the symptoms of the disease may thus be compared to male sexual potency. A man can, it is true, beget a whole child, but even the strongest man cannot create in the female organism a head alone or an arm, or a leg; he cannot even prescribe the child's sex. He, too, only sets in motion a highly complicated process, determined by events in the remote past, which ends with the severance of the child from its mother.

We know that Ferenczi considered analysis as a new birth, a metaphor which was revived by Balint. (See also Rank's theory of the trauma of birth and the psychoanalytic situation considered as the revival of the initial trauma. Analysis is, here, literally speaking, a maieutic.)

I would now like to cite some clinical material where the 'alliance' can be seen establishing itself; this is a mutative moment in a treatment whose initial difficulties I now tend to underestimate, though they were very real. The patient is a 35-year-old woman. She is a sociologist and the mother of two young boys. She came because of a chronic depression. She had had a long analysis with an analyst she was in love with, but her condition had not improved. She told me later on that he used to sleep during the sessions, a fact which did not prevent her from going to the sessions with him, with her heart all aflutter. Her story is characterized by the fact that her mother, a married woman, had had her through an adulterous relationship—a matter the patient was to learn only at adolescence, though under the impression of having always known it. Her mother's husband (i.e., her legitimate father) left them when she was 2 years old; she has no memory of him.

The first two years of her analysis were marked by a strong hostility towards me. For example, her hostility was shown, when coming in and going out, in her way of looking me up and down with a contempt all the more difficult to bear as it was impossible to interpret. This hostility also came out in the rejection of all my interpretations which, notwithstanding, I often found accurate. From time to time her inaudible and monotonous voice rose, becoming high-pitched: she made it clear to me how much she loathed (a word which frequently occurred) those who are fanatical theoreticians or ideologists, among whom she counts me in as being a psychoanalysis fanatic. Her first dreams, which she repeated in various ways for a long time, featured various characters (in particular a certain Anne-Lise, who suffered fatal accidents) and who are all fanatics. Associations led her once to Dürrenmat's play: 'The Old Lady's Return', in which a young jilted woman leaves for the USA and, towards the end of her life, comes back as a multimillionaire to her native village in order to take revenge on her former seducer. I placed myself in the transference as her legitimate father, who abandoned her when she was 2 years old and on whom she wanted to take revenge by denigrating and even killing him. This interpretation interested her (her own words) but did not seem to affect her. Besides, she could not remember him and, therefore, does not see how she could possibly bear a grudge against him.

Things jogged along uneasily until a session in which I felt literally reduced to nothing, not so much by the content of what she said as by her insidious tone of voice which made me feel totally valueless. I said nothing but, for several hours, I remained under a profound impression of unworthiness, so much so that my way of listening to my patients was impaired that day. At the following session, she related a dream: 'There was an armchair which I threw into a dustbin. Then I experienced a terrible feeling of despair. I could have kept it and made something of it. But now, all was lost.' Of course, I analysed this material relating it back to the last session during which she had conveyed to me the idea that I was just good for the dustbin, in the same way as she had denied that she could have missed her legitimate father (I am abbreviating the whole interpretation here). Of course, the feelings she had induced within me are also, we may suppose, her own feelings of annihilation when she had been abandoned at the age of 2.

She was a little more interested. But she resumed her denigration as well as her hatred for fanatic theoreticians. This continued until one session during which I was under such an impression of

118 *Creativity and Perversion*

unworthiness, abasement and hopelessness that an idea flashed across my mind: 'I'm gonna knock myself off!' I pulled myself together and said to the patient that she made me think that somebody near her or her mother committed suicide when she was a child. She replied:

> Yes, X (the legitimate father) committed suicide when I was 16. I had never seen him again, and I read this in a newspaper, for he was quite well known. He took his life because a linguistic theory he had discovered had proved to be false. I thought it was disgusting to commit suicide like that, without a thought for his little 4-year-old daughter.

However, do not think that from then on things were any easier. The patient was not flabbergasted by my strange remark. (*I* was by its result.) It would have been a recognition of the effectiveness of *my* theory, and would thus prevent me from committing suicide.

However, a new kind of dream soon appeared. She was offered gifts she did not want. But she was tempted, especially by three soft, warm night-dresses (the three weekly sessions afforded by a mother-substitute). Nevertheless, she refused them. This material was also worked through. She was not quite so glum and I myself felt a little less like that worn out, springless armchair, just about good enough to be dumped. Then, she dreamt of an analyst who was one of her acquaintances and of whom she was not very fond. The latter had invited her to a circumcision. She remembered an actual invitation to such a ceremony by some Jewish friends of hers. She tried to find the Hebrew word she had been told: 'Brit-Milah', 'Brit', she said, 'I don't remember very well what it means. Something like pact.' I suggested: 'Alliance?' 'Oh, yes, that's it. It's the Biblical word. It makes me think of the therapeutic alliance. When I am with friends who are being analysed, they are full of their analysis. I feel excluded.' I replied: 'Excluded from the alliance?'

At the next session, she related the following dream:

> I am at my grandparents', on their balcony; in the sky, I can see extraordinary colours. It's a nuptial flight. I have seen a programme on TV on the reproduction of flowers... I am thinking of the last session. I thought I knew you. I was sure before that I knew exactly what you were like. *Now, I feel I do not know anything about you.* [See also the patient who claimed she knew what I actually was like.]

Several months later, coming back to the circumcision dream (alliance), the patient noticed that it is a ceremony associated with birth.

Here can be seen a space opening up. Starting from a non-destructive primal scene and a fecund one (we must not forget that the patient's own birth was unwanted), it renders possible the identification of the two analytical protagonists with a couple capable of creating a new life together—the analysis itself. At the same time, a splitting appears between an observing Ego allied with the analyst and an Ego which is the object of the observation. Starting from this example (which is not that of perversion but rather of a character neurosis), I would like to stress how much destruction, mastery, hatred for life and of the primal scene are at the heart of the matter and how their working through—when possible—can provide the analysis with a new dimension, the third one indeed, where analyst and analysand can accomplish a work together, a 'Zusammenarbeit'.

I would like to add that the establishment of the alliance is not wrought by a miracle. My last patient often speaks of the session of the alliance dream as 'the session of change'. I will only partly follow her in this instance. Indeed, water passes from the state of liquid to that of gas when it reaches 100°C, but there is no reason to consider the first 99 degrees as negligible.

Chapter 12

Some Reflections on the 'Perverse' Way of Thinking

Thinking: that is the enemy. It is what becomes evident in the clinical account I will submit to your attention. I must add that thinking is to be understood as the ability to think differences, that is, reality itself. It will then be necessary to annihilate the subject's and, in the cure, the analyst's capacity to think.

A dream of the patient whom I am going to speak about seems to bear witness to it:

> I am breaking the walnuts with my bare hands. I feel as if I should not do it. They are fragile, and I am not skilful enough. *I put them into a melting-pot*. I was struck when awoken that walnuts looked exactly like brains. At the same time, the swollen nutshell makes me think of a woman's belly.

The patient had just dreamt a long dream in which the same melting-pot already appeared, full of heteroclite things, including paper and a pen representing a supposed activity of the analyst taking notes about the dreamer, as well as a ruler. All these things were going to melt, like pieces of cheese in a dish of Savoyard fondue, and become an undifferentiated hotch-potch. Or like grilled pieces of meat, all alike, in a dish of Burgundian 'fondue' (the patient's words).

To destroy thinking and brains is, therefore, also to destroy differences and the contents of the female belly—that is, the foetus and possibly life itself. My purpose here is to draw from a clinical account some elements of the psyche which lead to destruction while considering these elements as existing in a latent state within all of us. As such, my description is not just about the present in a narrow sense. In a way, these elements are permanent, and can be activated under special historical circumstances.

Contrary to some of my colleagues, I think, with Freud, that psychoanalysis is an incomparable tool—although not the only one, of course—for helping us to understand 'the riddles of the world in which we live' (1927, 'Post-Script to a Discussion on Lay Analysis', p. 253). It was indeed Freud's hope that psychoanalysis would be a key to the explanation of human phenomena in general (and not only pathological symptoms) which led him to give strong support to lay analysts, as is clearly said in the paper just quoted.

My intention is to try to circumscribe and to understand the effect on thought of faulty Oedipal identifications. I would like to point out that by 'Oedipal identifications' I essentially mean those which have the father in his function as 'barrier against incest' as their object. That means it is more a question of internalization of this paternal function than of identification with the personal characteristics of the actual father.

In a letter (15 February 1924), addressed to the Committee about Ferenczi's 'active therapy' and Rank's 'Trauma of Birth', and concerning Rank's ideas, Freud writes:

> Obstacles, which evoke anxiety, the barriers against incest, are opposed to the phantastic return to the womb: now where do these come from? Their representative is evidently the father, reality, the authority which does not permit incest. Why have these set up the barrier against incest? My explanation was an historical and social one, phylogenetic. I derived the barrier against incest from the primordial history of the human family, and thus saw in the actual father the real obstacle, which erects the barrier against incest anew. Here Rank diverges from me (Jones, *Sigmund Freud—Life and Work, 3*).

We will leave aside the reference to phylogenesis and the allusion to the myth of the primal horde, in order to remember only the equivalence postulated by Freud between 'father' and 'reality'. Without fear of contradiction, we could equally equate 'father', 'reality' and post-Oedipal Superego resulting from the transformation of the cathexis of the parents into an identification with them. The barrier against incest is one of the essential contents of the moral agency. Moreover, we are in February 1924, very near the introduction of the structural theory of the mental apparatus and to the article on 'The Dissolution of the Oedipus Complex'.

In company with other authors, mostly French, I got into the habit of considering reality as intrinsically linked with the double difference between the sexes and the generations. I think now that to speak simply of 'differences' is enough. I believe that my paper will implicitly show that this definition, which is more modern, in no way contradicts Freud. The Oedipal identifications constitute a decisive stage in the Ego development. And the acquisitions and modifications of the way of thinking correspond to the acquisitions and modifications of the Ego. In the same way, the absence of assimilation of these identifications, and the resulting faulty development of the Ego, bring thought disorders with them.

A patient's dream appears to me as illustrating my point:

> A fish is exhibited with its mouth open. You can see the inside of the body which is smooth. We bet that we can throw a pebble into its mouth, and that it will roll right down to the anus and come out. Then the fish's mouth puckers up and changes into a vagina.

122 *Creativity and Perversion*

It retracts. The vagina and the anus are now one and the same thing. Then it becomes something like a snake-penis. Right beside, there is an exhibition about the Jewish people. There stands X towards whom I feel homosexually attracted. From time to time, people have to climb up onto step-ladders. In fact, we are in gas chambers.

I ask the patient what link there is between the fish story and the exhibition. He answers that anything can be done with both of them. The fish changes into a mouth, a penis, a vagina and an anus. Soaps and lamp-shades were made out of the Jews.

The smooth, completely even aspect of the fish's inside should be noticed. It is the image of an object as well as of a world which the impulse runs clean through, where there are no differences (between the parts of the body, which are no longer separated, now changed one into the other like in Hans Bellmer's drawings). It is a universe submitted to the total abolitions of the limits between the objects and even between their molecules, a universe which has become totally malleable ('Anything can be done'). It is a fatherless universe, where the subject confers upon himself the Creator's powers, the subject having abolished all genital procreation in favour of anal production.

The anal character of the setting of the dream ('We are in a gas chamber'), and the modelling activity which is taking place, are obvious. However, it seems necessary for me to insist upon the fact that, simply by means of regression to that stage, the subject succeeds in again finding a way of functioning proper to the pleasure principle, that of seeking satisfaction by the shortest route, and the quickest, without detours or postponements. This is well brought out in the bet that the pebble thrown into the fish's mouth will travel through its body till emerging from its anus, according to the tendency of free energy to circulate without hindrance. What seems specially interesting to me in that dream is that, in a way, mental functioning according to the laws of primary processes, proper to the pleasure principle, is itself so represented. The dream does not only fulfil a wish by methods which are typical; the wish which is dramatized and fulfilled here is that of a mental functioning according to the pleasure principle, that is, of the dream itself. It is striking that this state of the mental apparatus is reached by the representation of a regression to the anal-sadistic universe, as if the subject were finding there an anchorage which could allow him to employ a mode of functioning attained by others (especially psychotics) by means of a deeper regression to the stage of narcissism, where there is no distinction between subject and object, internal and external, and where the frontiers between the agencies are blurred.

My patient, whom I will call Romain, is 30 years old. He reveals a clinical material in which certain elements refer back to this dream, giving a better understanding of it. Reciprocally, this dream deepens our comprehension of the clinical material. In a session, Romain relates that he was in a shop. In front of the cashier, there was a long queue. In order to reach the various counters, he had to cut across the queue. People were doing so, always passing in front of the same man. When Romain wanted, in his turn, to cut across the queue, the man, probably tired, moved forward in such a way that the patient had to go round the whole queue. He was 'white with fury, shattered, full of hatred', he said. He thinks that this hatred must have been visible on his face. He felt he could have killed the man. Romain goes on speaking of his disputes with motorists, of the hatred and the violence which he feels towards me if I make him wait a few minutes or if I let him go two or three minutes before time, according to his watch. He says violently: 'You have no right, this time belongs to me. I want to break into women's bellies, and take out everything they have inside.' Sometimes Romain becomes physically violent. He has also taken part in demonstrations — as a member of an extreme left group — which have ended in clashes with the police. He says: 'I was tremendously struck by an immense and blind desire for violence, a fury ... I threw Molotov cocktails at the pigs. I could have killed them!'

The day after, he spoke of the fury with which he had killed a rat, 'this impertinent creature which allowed itself to live without asking anyone's permission'. I took him back to the previous session, to his transference reactions, and to the birth of a younger brother which had aroused his anger and jealousy. Romain had performed abortions in a militant organization. But I will come back later to this interpretation.

At the next session, Romain related a dream in which he is hanging by his hands from the ninth floor of a building where there is a public nursery. When he did his military service, he had to clean the latrines for six months. In fact, there was something wrong with the pipes, and the filth came back. With a large profusion of details, which, in fact, made me feel disgusted during the session, Romain told of the different things he had to do. In the end, he had found a kind of pleasure in it. He had heard of cases of women suddenly giving birth in toilets, as if the child were a piece of excrement. At the age of 15, he still believed that it was enough to kiss a girl on the mouth to make her pregnant. For several days he had been feeling a swelling in his mouth and he had thought of the possibility of a cancer in his throat. He said: 'Maybe it's hysterical ...' I pointed out to him that, if a child can be produced like a piece of excrement, men can give birth like women, and that, if at 15 he had thought that children were made through the mouth, it probably was because it was painful for him to realize, during his childhood, that his parents had a sexual life that he could not have.

The day after, he said that, after the session, he had been seized by an urgent need to eat a chocolate cake. Until his marriage, he had eaten a chocolate bar every day. His parents kept some chocolate in their bedroom and they shared it between the two of them. I told him that it probably was easy for him to think that the secret of his parents' intimacy was reduced to the act of eating chocolate together: a thing which he could do perfectly well himself as a child. Romain laughed and agreed. Then he began to speak of physiological defects he had come across in his work as a male nurse, defects both congenital and acquired, such as artificial anuses, or bladders from which urine flows through the abdomen. He had always looked after people with that kind of malformation very well. He referred to his wife's delivery, and to the fact that women are made to defecate before going into labour. Abortions: they're bloody, with scraps of tissue, cut into pieces... the foetus, the placenta, the uterus membranes. Romain had aborted his own wife.

At the following session, Romain did not remember anything about the previous one—only that he had laughed. On returning home, he saw men fighting. There was blood. He wanted to stop his car in order to separate them. A cop arrived. He remembered the day when he had been cheated in the three-card trick. He had almost come back to the same spot in order to see if he could find the same men. To be so much at the mercy of other men... He then thought about sex shops, where you drop money into a slot and then part of the wall opens for a minute to show a naked woman miming coitus. (It seems that, in the evening, the cleaners find plenty of sperm in these rooms.)

He wondered what impression what he was saying made on me— an analyst, and, at the same time, a woman. It is a way of hurting me. (It was the first time that Romain had mentioned that his material might break into me and cause damage.) His father, who has a cancer of the stomach, had been submitted to a whole series of examinations. He had tubes pushed into him. The patients in his department, who were submitted to endoscopies, had hanging genitals, flabby testicles. The other male nurses did not like to be present at these examinations. But *he* was very devoted to his work and never tried to get out of them. One of his friends had a peculiar bedside lamp. The two switches were made from the testicles of a small animal his friend had killed when hunting—Jesus on the Cross... They had pierced his side with a lance to see if he was still bleeding. They had pretty well taken advantage of him... Some time ago, in the resuscitation room, there was a woman, full of tubes. Apparently, it was an analyst...

At the end of the next session, Romain related a dream. He was eating porridge from a brown plate. There were little bits of paper in his plate, fallen from the carton. It reminded him of toilet paper. In his car, he had left a bag of cornflakes bought for his 2-year-old daughter. A tramp had obviously slept in his car, which was still filled with the smell of him, the windows misted with his breath. He

The 'Perverse' Way of Thinking 125

had eaten some of the cornflakes. Romain had hesitated to give them to his daughter, and he decided to eat them all himself. Romain, who was born in Rumania, thought of the word 'placinta' which in his mother tongue means both placenta and pancakes. Romain likes to make cakes and pancakes; he wonders if it is not in order to do what women do, and to have children. (He once brought me some cakes he made; he had associated to his dirty fingers; in the end he took back the cakes.) Then he thought of a nail which would have gone through his feet—like Jesus on the Cross, he added. He wondered why I said nothing. Why did I make him suffer so much? However, it did not matter; he would carry on till the end.

One or two sessions later, Romain related that the insulation system he had fitted up—so as not to hear the man and woman in the next flat making love—was no good, because they made love in another part of the flat. (Till then, he had spoken only of the woman.) He dreamt he was walking with the younger of his two sons. There was a wall. He lifted the child up so that he could see beyond. Then he related that, in a session in front of my husband and me. Here the dream ended. Then I asked him what there was behind the wall. He thought for a moment:

> The Paradise... I imagined Paradise to be surrounded by walls... Or perhaps a villa in Bucharest. It belongd to Jewish Bankers. [He gave me their name. In fact, it was that of Rumanian aristocrats whose name resembled the word for mother.] In fact, this wall reminded me of the wall of a concentration camp I had visited.

I had a lot of difficulty in showing Romain that it was the sexual activity of his parents as a couple, and that of the couple formed by my husband and me, that was at stake. He reduced it to something happening in a concentration camp after having idealized it as if Hell were concealed under Paradise. Romain said that, for the first time, he understood that a dream was composed not only of the dream itself, but of the associations as well.

Then, at the following session, he said that he did not understand the meaning of the session. However, the material began to change, and depressive themes began to appear in the dreams. Particularly, they represented his wish to take possession of the analyst's husband's sexual attributes in the shape of a green (Grün) bird, and his sadness at seeing the bird change into a fish and disappear into water (the mother's belly). This image was a rudimentary recognition of the value of the father's penis.

I shall stop my account there in order to examine the main elements of the clinical material I have just set forth. Romain's aggressiveness is essentially revealed by his rage when he meets obstacles in his way: the man in the queue, his younger brother, the rat, the foetuses, the queue itself, the motorists and the analyst who is not immediately available. He then has the desire to remove the contents of the mother's belly. In spite of the apparent Oedipal elements, I would ascribe to them a much more regressive position. The fantasy of emptying the mother's belly is central to Melanie Klein's work and is considered by Béla Grunberger (in 'Narcissus and Anubis') as the essential expression of a primal and fundamental aggression. In Romain's case, it seems to me this fantasy is strictly a part of his desire, fulfilled in his dream, of once more finding the universe that is smooth and even, identified with a maternal belly which is freely accessible, that of a mental functioning without obstacles, with free energy circulating according to the pleasure principle.

If father and reality are equivalent, one could say that this desire corresponds to the most archaic content of the Oedipus Complex, which is at one with the desire to destroy reality itself together with the roughness of which it is composed ('To embrace harsh reality'—Rimbaud). The representation of this levelled universe being one and the same with that of the maternal belly stripped of its contents leads to the wish to return to the intra-uterine life (according to Ferenczi and Rank), matrix of the Oedipus Complex, of which you can find traces in the evolved Oedipus and in the myth itself: the murder of Laïus at the crossroads; the destruction of the obstacle on the way to the mother's genitals. However, this desire by itself, if it is not interwoven with more evolved components—love for the mother, admiration for the father, and identification with him—is intrinsically and fundamentally regressive, and, in some way, is entirely opposed to the classical Oedipus Complex. I shall not here go into the links between this principle and the hypothesis of death instinct; I shall link it only with the pleasure principle.

The performing of abortions, in Romain's case as well as in others which I have encountered, goes beyond the individual history (that is, the murder of the siblings), and reaches a meaning fundamentally bound up with the destruction of reality itself. The internalization of the father as an obstacle and a barrier against incest has not been brought about. It is as well to add that the wish contained in that archaic Oedipus is not to fight against the father but to cause the paternal principle itself to disappear with all its offshoots. Moreover, the wish to return to the womb can appear in the clinical situation under a totally different guise, even as its opposite, as a merging with the mother, which does not entail or which even avoids aggression (as in the case of people with allergies, for example).

A second point seems very obvious to me in this material. It concerns the process leading to a total lack of differentiation which appeared in the dream described at the beginning of this chapter. It is not only a question of merging mouth, anus, vagina, penis, child and adult, man and woman, but also of creating new erotogentic zones in entirely new places (again, as in Hans Bellmer): artificial anuses, bladders opening into the belly, etc. It is a teratogenic world where all permutations and combinations become possible. Fellini had an intuition of this link between freaks and perversion. The pervert does not want to be limited by the laws of creation (which are the Father's Laws) and exults in the existence of the aberrations which occur from time to time. All this reinforces his belief that he can substitute his own (anal) universe for the father's genital universe.

The intended purpose of substances also evades the usual laws. The copraphagia evident in the clinical material—the dream about porridge, the tramp's cornflakes, the compulsion to eat chocolate cakes—seems to me linked in no way to a mourning process, but to the need to change the relation between things and to ingest what is specifically intended to be expelled (cf. Sade). Here we find again the 'Everything can be made out of it' of the dream, as well as with the animal testicles which have become electric switches.

I shall raise one last point which is connected with the primal scene, that is, its obvious reduction to a pregenital activity—to eat chocolate, and above all to have a sado-masochistic relationship. It seems to me it is here that it is interesting to place Romain's intrusive aggressive activities. They are more evolved than those which aim at destroying reality and at making the universe perfectly levelled. They seem to me at the same time to represent the parents' sadistic coitus. Romain's identification with Jesus Christ, his moral masochism (see the article by Benno Rosenberg), perfectly obvious in the transference, seems to me to have the same meaning. In fact, behind the obvious resexualization of the relations between the Superego and the Ego, it is a question of playing indefinitely with the analyst a primal scene—clearly symbolized by the Crucifixion—made up of suffering and attacks whose reciprocity should not be underestimated. Thus the parental intercourse, the genital activity and fertility of the father's penis are denied (cf. Joyce McDougall). The primal scene thus repeated session after session is, by definition, destined to remain sterile, since it is situated outside the parental genital order. And this is not the least of the difficulties of these treatments: the analytical work has to remain fruitless. The baby resulting from the parental intercourse, which is unconsciously acted out in the analytical relationship, is destined to remain in limbo or to be aborted.

You will have certainly noticed yourselves how much every interpretation of the reduction of the primal scene to an infantile sexual activity, although seeming understood, and probably for that very reason, is immediately followed by a frantic attempt to return to an undifferentiated world. Here, I would like to recall what I said in the first chapter about the anal-sadistic stage as constituting a preliminary sketch, a rough draft of genitality. But I also said that later on it becomes an imitation, a parody of the genital world, that is, of the father's world. I said that to try and replace genitality by the stage that normally precedes it is to defy reality. It is an attempt to substitute a world of sham and pretence for reality. 'The Planet of the Apes' takes the place of a human world.

The disorder which ensues, the confusion over values, the abolition of the differences—all must be ascribed to this anal-sadistic regression. It is a question of escaping the paternal order. And this fatherless world, without genital procreation, is a causeless world, too. Here I borrow a simple but powerful idea expressed by Béla Grunberger, who has reiterated it on several occasions and again in his article on 'Narcissus and Anubis' (1982): The cause is to the effect what the father is to the child.

In the universe I am describing, the world has been engulfed in a gigantic grinding machine (the digestive tract) and has been reduced to homogeneous (excremental) particles. Then all is equivalent. The distinction between 'before' and 'after' has disappeared, as, too, of course, has history. Only quantities are taken into account, as in the case of the fetishist who told me: 'I can't see why the Jews complain so much. They suffered six million dead, but the Russians suffered twenty!' One must notice—and it is important for our topic—how these patients' material is related to terrorism, World War II events and sometimes, an active destruction of life (e.g. abortions)

I would like, by the way, to note how certain words, designating modes of thought or mental activity, have connections with what I am trying to describe here. That is to say, they connect with the role of the Oedipal identifications in logical thought, for causality and logic are one and the same thing. On the other side of the coin, anal-sadistic regression is synonymous with 'confusion' in the realm of thought. Similarly derived, we find the noun 'muddle', which also means mental confusion, and the adjective 'muddleheaded'. On the other hand, we find the terms 'conception' and 'conceive', this latter having the double meaning of 'to receive into or form in the womb' and 'to form in the mind' (*Chambers Twentieth Century Dictionary*, 1972).

Every judgement on a situation which does not take into account either the why or the how—which takes an event out of its context, without putting it into perspective—seems to me to share the perverse way of thinking which I am trying to describe. It is a mode of thought which is linear and lacks historical dimension. One understands that these conclusions—if they are, at least in part, correct—have important ramifications in the field of historical method, of information, of the group functioning, of ideology and of propaganda. In France it has been customary for several years to designate by the name of 'amalgam' the mixing and assuming as equivalent acts or ideas which are disparate. Such 'amalgams' register with the functioning of perverse thought as I understand it: for instance, the Nazis speaking of the 'Jewish-English-Bolshevik plutocracy', or the French students shouting: CRS = SS, or the word 'genocide' being applied to situations which do not correspond to the real meaning of this word.

When Noam Chomsky cites 'freedom of thought' as his reason for respecting the rights of those who deny the existence of gas chambers, he does something equivalent. The words are deflected from their meaning as substances are deflected from their intended purposes in perversion. It is the *cause* which fixes an idea. If the cause disappears, ideas, things, words and beings begin to float in the air and 'anything can be done'.

Perverse thought can also find its way into the realm of justice and law. Let us think of one of the expressions children use in the period of latency when quarrelling: 'But, Mummy, *he* started it!' This sentence points to what is left when the Oedipus Complex has been overcome: actions do not have to be considered 'in themselves' but are subordinated to a causality as the child comes, in his turn, to take his place in a lineage. It is precisely from this paternal universe that the pervert seeks to escape in his sexual behaviour as well as in his thought: all is 'possible' (a gay magazine in France is called 'Possible'), pregenitality is equivalent to genitality, etc...

The possibility that perversion reaches the levelled and heavenly world of equivalence, homogenization, and finally of the pleasure principle by means of the anal-sadistic regression seems to account partly for its role as a defence against psychosis. This was pointed out long ago by E. Glover, when he showed the chronological coincidence of some remission is schizophrenia or of pauses in some regressive processes thanks to perverse behaviour suddenly displayed by some patients. But, in my opinion, perversion can be a solid organization which must be then considered as an independent nosological entity.

I would like to conclude this chapter by relating a story and asking a few questions. Since my childhood I have been puzzled by the following story told by a man who was a prisoner of war during the First World War. It was in a special camp in Hanover where there were prisoners of various nationalities. The Russian ones were particularly badly treated and bady fed. A Russian prisoner one day went to a dustbin and, having taken out some fish bones, began to suck them greedily. A German officer came near, watched the scene with horror and disgust, said 'It is not a man, it's a dog!' and transfixed him with his bayonet. I think that my approach to perverse thinking allows an understanding of this scene other than a mere labelling of 'psychotic', which would be a means of easily getting rid of the actual problem. Moreover, one can compare this story with that of photos and films of the Warsaw Ghetto brought back by the Nazis, for whom the pictures purported to show the Jews' bestial characteristics. Yet the pictures ultimately led to the Nazis being accused of having thus brought about dehumanization of human beings ('accuse' and 'cause' have the same root).

However, we know that the mental functioning according to

primary processes and the pleasure principle is still alive within all of us. Perhaps it is even the contradiction existing between technique (strengthening the illusion of an 'even' universe), and bureaucracy developing from it (endowing it with obstacles), which leads this mental functioning to be so easily activated nowadays in the way I have tried to describe. And perhaps this contradiction makes of our world a Tragic Circus, where the temptation to smooth the Mother-Earth's belly by means of an apocalyptic outburst is becoming more and more insistent.

Chapter 13

A Clinical Account: Rrose Sélavy

A young woman comes to see me, asking for an analysis. She has already had two psychotherapies, followed by an analysis—for some months with an analysis from the 'Quatrième groupe'—which appears to have been interrupted on the advice of the analyst. What is Rrose Sélavy complaining of? She has bought a mansion which she is unable to manage or to furnish. Whatever she puts into this house does not make it really beautiful, animated or habitable. She does not know why. She is uneasy about this. And she has also separated from her husband. She is a very beautiful young woman and the mother of three children.

Now she is having a love affair with a man who is also being analyzed. However, this relationship is unsatisfactory, and yet she cannot leave him. It went rather well sexually with her husband whom she left precisely for this man with whom 'it doesn't work'. He is brutal and sadistic. But he is a remarkable man. His friends and acquaintances treat him as something of a genius. She is unable to leave such a man. She lost her father in the war. She was 2 months old when he went away and 9 months old when he was killed. Her mother remarried when she was 2½ years old. Her stepfather was kind to her. Three girls were born of this second marriage. The twins were born first, when she was 3½ years old, and then another sister. Her mother was rather hard on her. Her lover is an art enthusiast. He taught her to appreciate beauty. She often journeys to Paris to visit exhibitions and occasionally organizes one herself since she financially supports a few artists. (I am to learn later that she has a large private income coming from an important family business in the south where she lives, far from Paris.) She underwent an abortion, and her lover became totally uninterested in her during this period (an issue which will recur during this analysis).

Rrose Sélavy appears to me to be the object and not the subject of the story which she relates. She is knocked about by events which overcome her. At 36 or 37 years old she is totally unable to say why she left her husband—why she left a comfortable middle-class life for a liaison which, she says, is unsatisfactory and tumultuous with a 'genius' and an 'artist'. She will not at any moment pronounce the word 'love'. Did she therefore want to fill the empty house and become unsuccessful—the void of her father's presence? Alternatively, does the mismanaged, disharmonious house represent 'the return of the repressed', a symptom of her nostalgia for her father, the scars of which this strange relationship with her lover tried to efface? I ask her if she sometimes thinks of her father. 'No, it is too far back. I never knew him.' Did her mother talk to her of him? 'No.' She will tell me at a much later point in the analysis that, having asked her mother to speak to her about her father, the former replied dryly: 'How do you expect me to remember a man whom I only lived with for one year?' She will interpret her mother's reply at a much later stage in the analysis as expressing not only real indifference towards her dead husband, but as possible desire not to revive painful memories. Whatever the reason, the subject of her father was never raised at home.

Ever since this first meeting with Rrose Sélavy, I felt sympathy for her. As I shall explain, that sympathy will be replaced by feelings of humiliation over a long period of time and will reappear once more at a specific moment in the analysis. This sympathy sprang from my feeling that Rrose was defenseless against the blank produced in her Ego by the absence of her father and that this had pushed her into totally reconsidering her life, whilst never realizing that here was an attempt at an act of mourning which she had never accomplished. I secretly thought that the house which she had not succeeded in furnishing could split and that Rrose was in danger of cracking up. I spoke of these impressions to her, saying that perhaps she had come to me so that I could help her face all that had been aborted in her (in contrast to her lover, who had been completely uninterested in her when she had an abortion). I was intrigued by the status of the relationship with her lover. Was it a real perversion? She said that she did not enjoy it. I did not ask questions about this subject. I decided to take her into analysis.

It is difficult for me to describe the first experiences in this treatment. I took no notes, and no report could be more arduous than one detailing her troubled way of thinking; this fact became apparent from the start. The gap between the way her mind and mine functioned (as also that of the 'ordinary' neurotic) was so great that a faithful account of the sessions could have been possible only through the use of a tape recorder. This meant that I had to translate a phrase of hers into my own language and logical categories. I had little success at this, and I was incapable of memorizing in parallel the strange distortions which dotted her speech. To remember them, I would have had to succeed in identifying myself totally with her mental processes. The fact that we spoke two different languages, more so than had I been treating a schizophasic patient, was obvious to me and caused me real counter-transference suffering. (I shall try to understand why.) She was, for her part, unable to grasp my interpretations, especially their intention.

Her first dream in analysis was the following: I opened the door for her, wearing the expresson of her maid. She associated this with the fact that, on the birth of her sisters, her mother had relegated her to the servants' floor, to make room for the newly born. Then followed several sessions in which she displayed great arrogance, speaking of her acquaintances and of me. I was sitting on my armchair as if I were sitting on the toilet; this occasion to look down on me made her happy, she said. At the same time, she was under the impression that I admired her quite a lot during the sessions: her beautiful arms, her bracelets, the way she spoke so well (indeed, she distilled her words slowly and with application, like so many pearls she was threading one after the other), the way she dressed so beautifully; she was convinced that I envied her the clothes she wore. Once, during this time, I had put on a waistcoat which came from a shop near my home. She reproached me for having copied her, because she had just bought a similar one. The fact that she had bought it after me and that she had not yet worn it at a session did not change her conviction in the least.

I pointed out to her that she wanted to make me live the humiliation she had felt when her mother had dispatched her to the servants' floor by making me into her maid and the unhappy rejected child she had been at that time, attributing to me the feelings of envy which she had felt regarding her sisters and her mother's maternity. Contrary to all expectations she concluded that, because she was 'like that', she should follow her desire to its end and subject everybody to her whims. Her arrogance and her contempt were exasperating. With not the slightest trace of humour, she told me one day that she was 'imperial'. She used the haughty words pronounced with the accent of a tea-drinking lady of the 16th arrondissement of Paris. Her sentences were sprinkled with psychoanalytical terms which she did not understand or whose meanings she deformed, and her material was full of bookish interpretations. She was also wont to use certain English words; for example, she said that her lover had a 'flat' which was rather 'cheap' and that he should buy one that was a little more 'smart'.

When I uncovered the meaning of such-and-such an element in her material, she then regularly asked me what she should do. Upon explaining to her that she wanted to establish a dominant-dominated relationship with me similar to the one established with her lover (she had begun to describe some of their sado-masochistic sexual practices), she lost all patience. Why did I not explain to her the purpose of the analysis? After all, when you buy a car, you also buy the directions for use. Regularly, after each of my interventions or interpretations, she asked: 'What is the purpose of this?' 'What do I have to do?' 'Does this mean that I have to be like this or like that?' She invariably came to the conclusion that because she was 'like this', she had to accept this way of being and to take pleasure

134 *Creativity and Perversion*

from it—be it the sadistic or the masochistic side of her perversion.

During the same period, she spent whole sessions describing to me the underclothes she bought: their colour, the texture of the material (satin, silk or angel-silk), or else the jewels she had acquired on her trips to Paris, especially the shape and lustre of the stones. Other sessions were devoted to the minute description of pictures, or the decoration of her apartment, the shade of the wallpaper, etc. (She had sold her house on the advice of her lover, practically without mentioning it to me.) She also bought a lot of dresses which she expected me to admire. When I remarked on the amount of time she spent buying ornaments for her body—was she not putting beautiful objects *on* herself because she was not able to fill an emptiness *in* herself?—she told me that, during a period in her life, she had spent entire days running to shops in order to buy clothes.

In fact, it all just seemed as if she expected the analysis to confer on her own feelings and behaviour a label of beauty and nobility—as she was doing by covering her body or her house with jewels, materials and works of art. This search for a confirmation of the idealization of the self, in the transference, allowed me to formulate in my mind the following hypothesis: that the change brought about in her life, when she had begun the relationship with her lover and had enacted her 'latent' perversion, had been rendered possible by the fact that the latter was an aesthete who had pushed her into becoming a patron of the arts. The idealization of her objects and her pregenital drives which had then ensued had made her fall into a new dimension—perversion. The split between her bourgeois life, where she made 'l'amour à la papa', and her new life, where her lover led her to play alternately the role of Sir Stephen or that of 'O' (characters from the French erotic book *Histoire d'O*), was due to this idealization which she needed me to confirm. I became sceptical as to her capacities for transformation. There was never a suggestion of changing her object relations. She seemed to ignore totally the existence of any other form of relationship.

She related a childhood memory which appeared to me to condense the elements of the solution she had adopted: Her mother was joking with her own father and with her, the little girl, on a scatological subject. Rrose smeared her head with excrement, amusing her mother whilst at the same time forcing her to give her a bath. By being a dirty brat and a dirtied child, both sadistic and masochistic, she had an anal exchange with her mother, who in turn had one with her father (the maternal grandfather of the patient). This allowed her to skip over all reference to genitality and to the image of Rrose's father. In her perversion she relived this anal game with her mother and the avoidance of the genital dimension of psycho-sexuality. The (at least apparent) absence of a projection of her Ego Ideal onto a genital primal scene and onto genitality seemed to me indicative of a bad prognosis. Of course, her need for idealizing her pregenital objects, her perverse acts and her perverse Ego, and seeing this idealization confirmed, made apparent a split. This split occurred between, on the one hand, the affirmation that only the pregenital dimension of the psyche existed, and on the other hand, a repressed and strongly counter-cathected idea which was trying to push its way upward towards consciousness: that genitality, and all that is assignable to it, is superior to pregenitality. This splitting can be detected in the necessity to idealize. I have spoken of the compulsion to idealize (which explains the pervert's frequent affinities with the aesthetic), regardless of whether or not sublimation of pregenital drives follows in a specific sphere.

Rrose's Superego manifested itself in a strange way. She never seemed to question her perverse activities on the guilt level, nor her tendency to reduce her objects to the state of part objects and to fecalize them (which I shall talk about later on). On the other hand, she paid a lot of attention to manners. For example, she spent a whole session asking herself if, in spite of the heat in my office, she was going to take off her suit jacket, thinking that 'it was not the done thing'.

I have already spoken of my feelings of humiliation. These were tied to this side-tracking of the use of the analysis enforced upon me by my patient. For her it was neither a question of understanding, nor of changing, but of adding a narcissistic zest to her perverse behaviour—a zest which the analysis represented for her sole benefit, since she devalued me, complaining that I was not famous enough, whilst she held the analysis itself in high esteem. My impression was that of wasting a precious product which could otherwise have been used and appreciated by somebody else.

In addition—and I do not know if this is evident from my narrative—Rrose was remarkably stubborn. An attempt to interpret her childhood problems of feeding—namely, the projection of her aggressiveness onto the breast, turning it bad—was met with a wall of incomprehension. The idea of attributing her own hostile wishes to the object (the breast) appeared to her as absurd as the sight of a Martian landing in the analyst's office. Several times she repeated what I had told her, as if trying to let it sink in; she then concluded that, if there is aggressive feeling with regard to the breast, it is because all that is ingested is ejected. I pointed out that there are many stages between the moment a child suckles and the act of expelling what is ingested, remarking too that she had just told me about her greediness. She stuck to her point of view; in other words, she reduced the whole process to her violent wish for incorporation followed by expulsion, repeating endlessly that everything swallowed is expelled. At the same time, she was showing me her incapacity for psychic working through, which coincides with the short-circuiting of the metabolism of the object processes. It was at about this time that I had the fantasy of writing a meta-psychological

136 *Creativity and Perversion*

study on stupidity; inspired by her case, such a study would be a counter-transferential compromise between my feelings of irritation and my desire to find a psychic etiology for her stubbornness.

I would like to go back a bit. The first months of her analysis were the most trying. I was grappling with a haunting fantasy. Indeed, I imagined her as a concentration camp guard. The blend of arrogance, stubbornness, sado-masochism and her capacity to adopt the opinion of others without criticism: all these seemed to me to make a very adequate combination for an S.S. soldier. By capacity to adopt the opinion of others, I mean her tendency to enact her perverse component under the influence of a person who grants it a narcissistic flavour, thus giving her an aura of idealization. Certain collective movements, whereby a whole human group idealizes cruelty, play the role which aesthetics play for Rrose Sélavy. This fantasy made me question whether or not I would continue with the treatment. Could I continue dealing with a patient who awoke in me such thoughts, accompanied by their corresponding affects? When she told me one day that, if her children died, she would manage to feel no sorrow, I was numbed and my fantasy became more vivid. Paradoxically, I felt relieved when she told me that she and her lover were 'playing at Auschwitz'.

My fantasies concerning her were the real echo of her own. Later on, in the transference, she expressed in various ways the reduction she operated on me in order to transform me into a part object. She imagined me in bed, in a night-dress, buttering slices of toast and amusing my husband 'like a dog amuses his master'. I interpreted this fantasy as relating to her wish to have had a father capable of reducing the power of her mother. She received this interpretation with a certain scepticism: can a child, less than 2½ years old, feel that she misses her father? When her mother remarried she had had a father. She came back the following day, wondering if I was a good analyst. Perhaps I was wrong in my interpretations. It was around this time that she questioned her mother about her father and that she asked her for her wedding ring. Her aim to reduce me to a part object appeared again, in a dual relationship this time, just before the Christmas holidays. When I returned from holiday, she, in her turn, had to leave for three weeks, which meant a separation of five weeks. She came on a Friday—the day before her last session, a Saturday, and also the day the banks are closed—telling me she had forgotten to withdraw money to pay me. I asked her what she thought about it. She answered: 'Oh, for me money runs from a spring.' I then said to her: 'Your spring does not flow to where I live', referring to a material connected with oral frustration that had been interpreted previously.

The next day she came back with the following dream, which showed that my intervention had touched her unconscious, but not where I would have expected. 'I am lying on the ground. There is a spring not far from me, and my leg, which has some red ribbon around it, is in this spring. It is there to be kept cool as if it were in a fridge.' It appeared that she had transformed me into her leg (allowing her to use me as a part of herself, to 'pull my leg') and that her forgetfulness about payment was destined to keep in touch with me during her absence (by keeping me in cool storage). I am also a Christmas present, tied with red ribbon. This transformation of the object into a fetish aims at abolishing all pain due to our separation. I think it is clear that the control exercised on the object in this manner reduces it to the state of excrement. However, as the material shows, this control is also protection against a dangerous object—as, for instance, her image of me as a dog relating to its master. Rrose Sélavy often begins the sessions by commenting on very fine details of my clothes: 'the dress which you are wearing is a pale mauve. It must be woollen cheesecloth. The flowers on the edge are a little brighter than your shoes. Your lipstick is a little dark. I would like to make you up in another way. I bought a cream for my mother.'

I feel myself being caught in a web. Rrose Sélavy adds: 'I like describing people, tracing their outline like a stain on a tablecloth...' I then ask her: 'If you did not reduce your mother, me and other people in general to the state of being stains on a tablecloth, would you be frightened that they would escape you by virtue of their autonomous existence and then that you would lose them?' (Usually I give rather short explanations. The length of some of the interpretations I used to give Rrose Sélavy is probably an inadequate counter-transference response to her lack of capacity to understand, to internalize and to work through.) Rrose retorts yet again: 'But if I am like that, I have to accept it. One has to be what one is...' I ask her if she is certain of being only that and if she does not think she is 'like that' because she is frightened of being otherwise. Rrose does not seem to understand: 'My lover says that you have to be what you are.' I give up.

In another session just after this one, she tells me: 'My lover says I must come and see him without panties and wearing boots. I don't want to. I've got to understand why I don't want to.' Rrose rarely has an orgasm with her lover; when she does, though, she thinks she is closer to accepting herself as she is, because this means that she accepts being beaten and finding pleasure in it. He, she says, is egoistic. He enjoys himself without bothering about her. On a cassette he has recorded for her what he expects of her. She too has recorded all her own wishes. 'Why?' 'So that he can get that into his head' (sic). However, a few sessions later, she tells me that Pierre, a friend, told her that she treated him and Mary, his wife, as if they were things. This sentence meant nothing to her. It was double Dutch. She understands better now.

Julia, her daughter, is soon to have her fifteenth birthday.

Rrose will not come to her sessions as there are great preparations to be made. (Her sessions are grouped at the end of the week because of the distance separating her house in the south of France from Paris.) She telephones me and asks me if I will give her extra sessions on other days of the week. I give her two appointments, Tuesday at 1:15 p.m. and on Wednesday morning. On Tuesday she does not come. As usual, I leave at 2:00 p.m. I receive a phone call, informing me that a person had turned up at 2:15 p.m. My employee told her that the appointment was for 1:15, but it seems that she was furious and insisted that I had made a mistake. It so happens that I am certain of having specified 1:15 p.m. I was not alone in the room when she rang and the time of her appointment was fixed. The following day, when she arrives, she is irritated and tells me that her journey was very expensive, etc., and that I am the one to have made the mistake. She then tells me that on her return journey from the last session a man in the train had told her the story of his life. He had just broken off with his mistress whom he loves, etc. At a certain point he had asked her if she was thirsty. She had said she was and he went and bought her a Coke. She began to cry. Her lover never pays attention to her, never bothers to think whether she is thirsty or not. Why does she have to be with such a man? This is the first time that she shows so great an awareness of her own feelings. I then explain to her that there is something in her which is very afraid of changing this type of relationship in which she suffers and makes others suffer. When I make appointments for the extra sessions she had asked for, when I give her a Coke to quench her thirst, she forces frustration on herself and re-establishes a quarrelsome relationship with me. She has got to see me as a bad person and to fight with me. She leaves, calm and smiling.

She comes back after Julia's birthday and tells me of a memory dating back to when she was 8 years old. She was in a boarding school in Switzerland. Those children who still wet themselves were beaten by the lady director, who was called Aunt Malvina. She herself was clean, but one day she wet her pants and in turn was beaten. Was this already her masochism perhaps? She had a dream. She was lying on a lounge chair, a sort of bed like the one she had in Switzerland. She had a military blanket. She was neglected and sick in the head. Buses, cars, planes and red helicopters were taking off into the air. Men, like Folon's figures, were driving these machines. They beat their arms, their great immeasurable arms, and made friendly signs to her. She admires the fact that they can rise into the sky like that.
A: 'Folon's figures?'
R: 'Yes. With black arms and no faces... Black arms like the mourning bands I wore when I was little, not for my father of course, it was later, for others...'
A: 'You were sick in the head. What does that mean?'

Rrose launches into a long description of the work which she had to undergo to receive 200 people at Julia's birthday reception. She was all alone. Her husband did not want to come. He told her he had made a new life. He hates his in-laws. She told him her parents would not be there. But there was nothing to do about it. He detests this kind of reception. Julia's father was not there. And her lover did not want to come either. What will people think of the life she leads? At the beginning, her lover had said that he was going to be a father for her children. But he hates them in fact. The day before the party she telephoned him at 3:00 a.m. She told him she hated him and called him a 'pain in the ass'. She was like a mad woman. She was delirious. She had taken a Mogadon. Usually it did not have that effect. But this time she was like someone let loose.

I then told her that her constant complaint about her daughter's lack of a father expressed her own pain at not having a father. But she is afraid of feeling this pain and of hoping that these men of another age—the figures of Folon who, like her father, have no face—will come to her. She must disguise everything dealing with her father's death (the military blanket) because the emergence of feelings connected with him raises in her the fear of becoming mad. It is the end of the session. Rrose Sélavy says nothing and leaves smiling.

It should be noted that the idealization is no longer connected to Rrose's body (she is neglected); and instead, it projects onto celestial engines. At the same time, this is the first mention of madness in the material of the patient. (Fol-on, sickness of the head: 'fol' and 'folle' mean 'mad' in French.) She returns the following day and straight off she protests my interpretation of the previous session. She is afraid that I am wrong. Perhaps I am a bad analyst—apart from which, a good analyst can also be wrong. This dream is related to her stay in Switzerland. Well, evidently 'this does not exclude that'. I then suggest that perhaps she found a solution to the pain related to her father in Switzerland, in her relationship with Aunt Malvina.

The patient describes the dream she has just had. A man who had been her lover and who left her suddenly, in spite of the fact that he was a warm person, is there with his wife; he offers books in a fatherly manner to Rrose's son. Despite her denials at the beginning of the session, Rrose seems to have accepted my interpretation and sets up an Oedipal scene in this dream: the couple, her ex-lover and his wife, and the present (a book, i.e. knowledge) given by the father to the child who represents her. The engines which rise into the air in her dream of madness represent the penis of the father which is admired, at last, and for which she had substituted Aunt Malvina's whip.

Rrose continues her story. She had gone to see the movie, 'A Special Day', and talks about the scenario with a coherence and a clarity which are unusual for her. The love between this woman and the homosexual, who are the only people not to flock to Hitler's arrival in town, has visibly moved her. Is she beginning to imagine a relationship outside the psycho-sexual dimension so obviously tied to Hitlerism?

The following session is entirely devoted to an account of a dream which she has not yet told and which took place between the dream of madness and the two sessions I have just outlined. Rrose is in a very long, low, dark room with a window at each end. Here and there are partitions of a sort, but at the same time it is just one single room. Her lover, who is sleeping on a pallet, takes up part of the space. Her lover's brother and Rrose, the brother's girlfriend (whose Christian name is the same as the patient's), are also present. Rrose, the girlfriend, is dressed in a masculine manner, as usual. She compliments the patient on her silk clothes, which she finds 'feminine'. Her lover's brother moves into the space where the patient stands. In his hand he holds a 'frying pan in which an omelette and two very appetizing tomatoes with their bottom sides up are frying'. They are perhaps breasts, she adds. In reality her lover's brother is a good cook. It is as if the kitchen were in the middle of the room. The long, dark room has something unhealthy about it. At the beginning of her marriage she had rented a villa by the sea. She had difficulties with contraception. She had a coil inserted. This hurt her. She cried. She had to have it removed. By the way, she forgot that a former lover of hers, who has just got married, was in her dream. He was there with his wife. Rrose does not know how to cook. This is a bone of contention with her lover. Her mother does not know how to cook either. She never learned from her. There was a great fuss on Sundays, because it was the servants' day off. Her mother used to make an omelette which she spoiled. Augustine, the housekeeper, knew how to make wonderful tomato omelettes. Rrose too tried to make them but without success. The juice of the tomatoes mixed with the eggs. Perhaps it is because of this that the tomatoes which 'are frying bottom sides up' in the pan are separate.

I think to myself that we have returned to the world of confusion. The long, low, dark and unhealthy room with its windows at both ends reminds me of Rrose's conception of the alimentary canal (which came out in the episode concerning Rrose's problems with food reported above): a tube with two openings, for entrance and exit, a homogeneous tube through which the object passes without differentiating any stage. It is also an anus where Rrose and her lover are again cornered (the pallet) and an image of her 'unhealthy' vagina, her painful and fruitless sexual life. It is the man who nourishes (and not the woman). The tomatoes are at one and the same time 'asses' and breasts. Rrose, by projecting her masculinity onto her namesake, sets herself up as being courted by a woman, etc. Result: confusion of zones, confusion of sexes, confusion of functions. Whilst I am reflecting on this return to undifferentiation, Rrose says: 'What a hotchpotch, or what an omelette!'

As I have already said, I am of the opinion that this indifferentiation is inherent to the sadistic-anal phase, where all objects, erotogenic zones, ideals, etc. are pulverized by the alimentary canal and homogenized into identical particles, the faeces. I have had the opportunity to set out to show that this regression is inherent to perversion, whatever form it may take, and not only to sadomasochism. My theory is founded on the equation, penis = faeces = child, which in perversion is to be taken literally. Faeces belong to both men and women, children and adults, whereas one has to be a man to own a genital procreative penis, one has to be a woman to bring a child into the world, and in either case one has to have reached the status of adulthood. In other words, her considering the penis and the child as equivalent to the faeces results in erasing the double difference between the sexes and the generations—the basis of reality and of all differences. Thus, the genital order and the genital penis of the father disappear from the psychic scene.

However, there is attempted differentiation in the would-be partitions inside the long room and in the separation between the tomatoes and the omelette. This last point allows me to state that the most simple daily acts can be inhibited by regressing to the anal-sadistic dimension and to the lack of differentiation which is inherent to it. Thus, Rrose is incapable of making an omelette without reducing it to a hotchpotch. The ability to think of cutting and cooking the tomatoes separately to extract their juice, and then mixing them with the beaten eggs to make the omelette, would suppose that Rrose had not fallen into a universe where the specific properties of objects can mix only by destroying themselves in order to form an amalgam similar to various digested foods as they form the faecal mass. It would have been necessary for Rrose's mother to be an adequate identification object. She did not teach her how to cook ('the mixture', genital sexuality).

I do not mean that sadistic-anal regression proper to perversion has always the same end result. For every pervert, of course, there are other factors which intervene, giving a whole range of possibilities. It can be suggested that the clothes which appear in the dream are an indication of a new attempt at idealizing the perverse self and the anality which is linked to it, whilst the couple whom Rrose had forgotten to mention represent an Oedipal vestige. Rrose told me about her mother who did not know how to cook. Her mother, she says, is a managing woman who pushes men around. 'My father was certainly weak and my stepfather is too. My mother has an old lover who is supposed to look like my father. Perhaps she got on with him after all and does not want to talk about it...'

One problem which arises is the emergence, whether permanent or temporary, of the perverse mechanisms of anal-sadistic regression and idealization of this psycho-sexual dimension and the accompanying exclusion of the father, his genital penis and the genital universe in general. Another problem is to determine the function of this perversion in relation to psychosis. Is it simply a question of avoiding the psychic suffering connected with the father's death, replacing it by a sadistic relationship with the mother (the managing woman, the lover) in which she alternatively plays the role of the mother with the whip and the whipped child, the father being excluded? Or is it that, in the manner of a perverse boy, she tries to maintain the illusion of being the mother's sole object of love, by rating the little girl's pregenitality and infantile sexuality higher than the genitality and the genital penis of the father, helped in this by her father's death? As Rrose would say, this perhaps does not exclude that!

The following week, the first session is marked by a strong emergence of perversion, similar to the last session of the week I have just described. Rrose arrives, very spruce. She is dressed in a fuschia-coloured dress with spangled matching shoes somewhat in the 'disco' fashion. An image sprang to mind: the doll Olympia from Hoffman's Tales. She said as she lay down: 'Every time I lie on the couch, well, almost every time—in any case, today—I wonder if I am proper, just as I should be, and if I conform.'

> A: Conform to what?
> R: My mother was a very strict woman. She had a strict code of morals. Not sexy. When she went out at night she used to wear a tight, glittering evening dress. [This recollection of her mother in a sparkling dress has already appeared in the material.] But not sexy. She was sublimely beautiful. A film star. A goddess. She put herself on a pedestal. A type of Greta Garbo. Divine. She hates vulgarity. She is like me. I am like her a lot in that. As I lie down, I wonder whether the hem of my dress is at the right height. Things have happened this week. This worries me, telling you about them. You are not going to agree perhaps. I surrendered myself entirely to my lover, like O or Justine [she has recently seen a pornographic film based on Sade's Justine] or like nuns searching for the absolute "Lord, Thy will be done." I enjoyed it.

(All her grand phrases are evidently borrowed and are not part of Rrose's vocabulary. She often adorns her speech with a mosaic of quotations. One day, whilst looking at herself in the mirror, she told me she saw 'a ravaged, pathetic, lost and translucent face—like a shell tossed by the sea and carried by the waves to the shore.' Apart from these literary reminiscences, a lot of her phrases are repetitions of her lover's language.)

At this moment I light one of the sticks of incense I have in my office. The counter-transferential character of this gesture appears to me immediately. Rrose then speaks:

R: You have just lit a cigarette. That is a sign that you are happy. It's an Egyptian cigarette. Perhaps you are taking drugs... Well, I don't think so, not with the life you lead, the works you are leaving behind you...(sic). I'm glad I was angry with my father because he died.
A: Angry with your father?
R: Yes, in the last sessions. The hatred which I feel for my lover or my children (sic) is connected to what I feel for my father.
A: Is that all you got out of the last sessions? Hatred, and not suffering?
R: Me, suffer? I never let that enter my life; I wall it out immediately. [She says this proudly] ...After my sessions I realized that I had given Julia's reception on the 40th anniversary of my father's death. When I saw my mother did not want to talk about my father, I thought she despised him. I put him and the memories that went with him to the very back of my mind. I am the black sheep of the family. Physically, I'm not like the others... I wonder what I'm going to tell my lover about this session. Is it good, is it bad?
A: Then you have to talk to him about it? So as not to keep it between the two of us? [We can see here how difficult it is for Rrose to give up her perverse relationship and, instead of it, to face the painful mourning of her dead father.]
R: No, but I can't keep myself from thinking what I will tell him.

In the following session, but nevertheless with a certain reserve, Rrose goes into more detail concerning her sexual relationship with her lover. Sometimes her lover asks her to force him to do certain things, sometimes she submits herself to his will.

A: Sometimes you are his object, sometimes he is your object? [Once again I am using the word 'object' of the previous sessions.]
R: Yes. I don't see how there can be anything else for it... Perhaps I should finish my analysis... Perhaps I am cured... All these fantasies... It is as if I had found a new shining object in the sand. [The 'perverse solution' as an idealized ordure.]

In the following session Rrose announces: 'I didn't finish telling my dream the other day when I lay down on a lounge chair in Switzerland with plane engines landing and men with black mourning bands.' (She had not in any way inferred that the dream was not finished.)

R: I am with my lover, inside a house. We are talking about our trip to the United States. Then I go out. I meet my pottery and weaving teacher who says something to me. I go to the toilet. I no longer remember if I met the teacher on my way to or from the toilet. I go into the toilet. It is absolutely sumptuous. Very refined. It is like the powder room in England. I adore the English toilets. They are luxurious. Toilets remind me of my mother's bathroom. Such elegance... [Rrose uses a mannered, affected and airy tone.] The one in my dream was turquoise and white. The window was covered with several coats of paint to give a soft, mellow light. A deep carpet covered the floor. There were soft towels... There was a flamboyant red-headed English girl who reminded me of the woman in the beauty salon where I go. She deals with my legs. She depilates them. The toilet, with its refinement, brings to my mind the shop called Divine Beauty where I buy soaps and beauty products. That's also connected to my mother. I have said that she was divine. There was an insect dying or in its death throes on the floor—it was a scorpion or dung beetle. The pottery teacher... I've stopped weaving. The United States is the New World...

A: You have separated the two parts of your dream by several sessions... Perhaps it is because you have just found the solution represented by the second part of your dream in relation to what the first part expresses: nostalgia for your father and fear that this nostalgia could drive you crazy. The New World is the world of your lover, your mother and the water closet which you are trying to embellish in an attempt to hide that it is shit...

I think that the pottery and weaving teacher—an attempt at sublimation?—represents me. So does the English girl who takes care of depilating her legs—making them smooth, eliminating the hairs, the anality. This time I help her to idealize herself and to mask the excremental world with a surface of shining paint. In the previous session she had reprimanded me sharply because I had taken her up on a word she had pronounced. Surely I knew French as well as she. She would have understood, of course, had she been speaking in English...

Rrose is puzzled, then angry.

R: I don't understand anything you are saying. At first my lover explained to me that love was masterful control. His analysis confirmed this (sic). Moreover I don't see how there can be anything else in love. Sexual reviews show only this: sado-masochism, mastery, homosexuality, exhibitionism. Well, perhaps there is no control in exhibitionism, but what else can it be?

A: Other than a shitty relationship? [We had spoken of toilet-training quite a long time ago.]

R: [Amazed, and speaking loudly] Of course, and what's more, not only in the figurative sense. It's true. It comes into our fantasies. To shit and to make one's partner shit.

It could be that Rrose calls 'fantasies' what are in fact real actingsout. Rrose goes on: 'In any case, everything is coercion. Love is, writing is, and weaving too. It is coercion. I am writing a diary of my analysis. I said nothing more. It was the end of the session. Rrose left me with a nasty look.

A short time later, Rrose broke up with her lover, having had the following dream: She is lying on the analytical couch. She is wearing boots with 'coil-like' heels. In reality, her lover told her to get some made for her. Her feet hurt. I take off her boots. We chat in a friendly manner and I massage her feet. She is wearing cheap tights which she bought near my home. Perhaps it was in 'La Ville de Nancy'. She thinks they are quite good. Perhaps she has had enough of restraint? In fact the break with the lover lasted only a few months. The first dream which Rrose has upon resuming her relationship with her lover is the following: She has a sexual relationship with him. There is blood everywhere. She is embarrassed to tell him this, but his penis is very like some kind of dog's shit that litters the pavements.

Chapter 14

A Metapsychological Study of Perversions

In this concluding chapter, I have tried to gather together the tenets of a conceptualization concerning the loss of reality in perversion compared with the loss of reality in neurosis and psychosis. Here I would like to approach perversions from a metapsychological standpoint. But, before taking the liberty of presenting my own ideas, I think it necessary to recall those of Freud on perverse mechanisms. He says: 'Neurosis is the negative of perversion. This aphorism renders justice neither to the complex, rich and diverse working-through of neurosis, nor to the originality of the mechanisms specific to perversion. Let us recall that in the 'Three Essays' (1905) Freud goes as far as to speak of 'positive perversions' and 'negative perversions', to designate perversions and neuroses, respectively. Still in the 'Three Essays', speaking of neuroses, he even says that the 'study of "positive" perversions provides [their] exact counterpart' (p. 167).

The study 'On Fetishism' (1927) is nothing less than a mutation. It led Freud to point out—as being linked with the construction of the fetish—two mechanisms which differ from the neurotic defence mechanisms proper, whose model is repression. In the latter the maintenance in, or the thrusting back, into the unconscious—whose sphere is that of isolated psychic groups composed of ideas or presentations associated with instincts—is performed without any alteration of the Ego. As for the affect, we know it is suppressed, converted (in hysteria), separated from the idea, displaced, forming a false connection with another idea (in obsessional neurosis) or discharged in the form of anxiety. As early as 'Draft K' (1 January, 1896, 1950) Freud supposed that delusion is linked to an alteration of the Ego and to its distortion, an idea to which he comes back in his article, 'Further Remarks on the Neuro-Psychoses of Defence' (1896). In his first article on 'The Neuro-Psychoses of Defence' (1894), he already contrasted neurotic mechanisms with psychotic ones. In psychosis,

> The Ego *rejects* [my italics] the incompatible idea together with the affect and behaves as if the idea had never occurred to the Ego at all. *But from the moment at which this has been successfully*

> *done the subject is in a psychosis...* The Ego breaks away from the incompatible idea; but the latter is inseparably connected with a piece of reality so that, insofar as the Ego achieves this result, it, too, has detached itself wholly or in part from reality (p. 59).

We may notice that the examples given by Freud, of what are to be considered as prefigurations of the mechanism called *disavowal*, are linked with the rejection of ideas or presentations referring to object loss: a jilted fiancée awaiting her intended for years on end dressed in her most beautiful clothes; a mother who, after her child's death, unwearyingly rocks a piece of wood in her arms.

We know that, in 'The Wolf-Man' (1918), disavowal and splitting, without being named, are described and ascribed to the castration complex.

> In the end there were to be found in him two contrary currents, side by side, of which one abominated the idea while the other was prepared to accept it and console itself with femininity as a compensation. But beyond any doubt a third current, the oldest and deepest, which did not even as yet raise the question of the reality of castration, was still capable of coming into activity (p. 85).

If it is usual to consider 'The Wolf-Man' as the first writing where disavowal is referred to the castration complex, we may notice that a very clear prefiguration of this is to be found as early as the article 'On the Infantile Sexual Theories' (1908). The little boy, on seeing his sister's genitals, already has a strong enough prejudice 'to falsify his perception'. In fact, the link between *disavowal* and the castration complex is strongly emphasized in the years preceding the article on fetishism (in 'The Infantile Genital Organization', 1923, pp. 143-44), in 'The Economic Problem of Masochism' (1924, p. 165), and in 'Some Psychical Consequences of the Anatomical Distinction between the Sexes' (1925, pp. 252-53).

The article 'Neurosis and Psychosis' (1924), in which Freud applies his new structural theory of the mental apparatus to the comparative study of neurosis and psychosis, ends with direct hints at splitting, on the one hand, and disavowal, on the other:

> It will be possible for the Ego to avoid a rupture in any direction by deforming itself, by submitting to encroachments on its own unity and even perhaps by effecting a cleavage or division of itself. In this way the inconsistencies, eccentricities and follies of men would appear in a similar light to their sexual perversions, through the acceptance of which they spare themselves repressions.

> In conclusion, there remains to be considered the question of what the mechanism analogous to repression can be, by means of which the Ego detaches itself from the external world. This cannot, I think, be answered without fresh investigations; but such a

mechanism, it would seem, must, like repression, comprise a withdrawal of the cathexis sent out by the Ego (pp. 152-53).

The article 'The Loss of Reality in Neurosis and Psychosis' (1924) brings us back to disavowal as referring to object-loss. Returning to Elisabeth von R., a case history published in the *Studies on Hysteria* (1895), Freud reminds us that the girl's hysterical pains had been triggered off by the repression (and the ensuing return of the repressed) of the thought which had come into her mind while she was standing at her sister's death-bed: 'Now he (the sister's husband) is free and can marry me.' Freud says: 'The *psychotic* reaction would have been to disavow her sister's death.' Further, in the same article, Freud writes: 'In neurosis a piece of reality is avoided by a sort of flight, whereas in psychosis it is remodelled... or expressed in... another way: neurosis does not disavow the reality, it only ignores it; psychosis disavows it and tries to replace it' (pp. 185-86).

The article on 'Fetishism' (1927) is indeed in line with Freud's attempts to differentiate the relation to reality in psychosis compared with that in neurosis, and to discover one or several mechanisms which would be for psychosis what repression is for neurosis. It is obvious from Freud's writings that disavowal in psychoses sometimes applies to an object loss replaced by the formation of a delusion (which is the case in hallucinatory confusion), and it sometimes comprises much larger pieces of reality ('The Loss of Reality in Neurosis and Psychosis', 1924). This is in line with Freud's conceptions of psychosis, as he developed them in 'On Narcissism: An Introduction' (1914) and in 'A Metapsychological Supplement to the Theory of Dreams' (1917). In each case, satisfactory hallucinations do not simply come and replace the disavowed incompatible idea. The psychotic regression and the attempt at recovery involve a much larger loss of reality, irrespective of what initiated the disease. If, before the article 'On Fetishism', the limits between neuroses and perversions were blurred, one of the problems this article presents us with is the following: can and must the disavowal of reality which takes place in psychosis be linked with the disavowal of the lack of a penis in women? And, if not, what is the difference?

For now, it is the distinction between perverse and psychotic mechanisms which seems to be blurred. For Freud, the fetish is a substitute for the mother's penis, which the child has not been able to renounce. 'The boy', Freud says, '*refused to take cognizance of the fact of his having perceived* [my italics] that a woman does not possess a penis.' If there do exist castrated beings, such as women, then castration is possible; the threat can be carried out and the child's possession of a penis is in danger 'and against that there rose in rebellion the portion of his narcissism which Nature has, as a precaution, attached to that particular organ'. It is with surprise that we see Freud describing the defensive process the child is initiating:

> The oldest word in our psychoanalytic terminology, "repression", already relates to this pathological process. If we wanted to differentiate more sharply between the vicissitude of the *idea* as distinct from that of *affect*, and reserve the word "Verdrängung" (repression) for the affect, then the correct German word for the vicissitude of the idea would be "Verleugnung" (disavowal) (pp. 152-53).

Indeed, we know that all Freud's writings on repression, and especially the metapsychological article devoted to its study (1915), assign different destinies to the two instinctual representatives, destinies which are clearly defined: only the idea can be repressed. As for the affect, it can never become unconscious. This turn-about deserves to be emphasized. Maybe it is an indication as to a subsequent way of approaching the question of disavowal. In any case, it shows us Freud's own difficulty in solving the problem. Freud goes on to say that, as a matter of fact, the perception has remained, and 'that a very energetic action has been undertaken to maintain the disavowal' (p. 154). The child has simultaneously maintained and given up his belief in the mother's penis. The fetish has been appointed its substitute and, in the same breath, 'the horror of castration has set up a memorial to itself in the creation of this substitute' (p. 154). We understand that the fetish serves to repress and counter-cathect (must we say, after Freud?) the 'affect' associated with the perception of female genitals. Now, the fetish condenses at one and the same time the disavowal of castration and the horror of castration. Freud then comes to his two articles of 1924: 'Neurosis and Psychosis' and 'The Loss of Reality in Neurosis and Psychosis'. He thinks he ventured too far in supposing that in a neurosis the Ego, in the service of reality, suppresses a piece of the Id, whereas in a psychosis the Ego lets itself be induced by the Id to detach itself from a piece of reality. Two young men had lost their father as children, and both of them had failed to take cognizance of this death. But neither of them had developed a psychosis. The mechanism involved here is a disavowal applied to a piece of reality just as in fetishism is disavowed 'the unwelcome fact of women's castration' (p. 156).

It is at this point that Freud, for the first time, clearly associates splitting with disavowal: 'It was only one current in their mental life that had not recognized their father's death; there was another current which took full account of that fact. The attitude which fitted in with reality existed "side by side".' Here, we are presented with a splitting between two attitudes of the mind, a splitting which fractures the Ego; but, to the degree that the part of the Ego clinging to reality still exists, it prevents the subject from becoming psychotic.

'I may thus keep to the expectation that in a psychosis the one current—that which fitted in with reality—would have in 'fact been absent' (p. 156). (Freud was to give up that idea in *An Outline of Psychoanalysis*: even in psychoses there exists a splitting of the Ego.) Therefore we are in the presence of the same association of splitting with disavowal as in fetishism: the fetish simultaneously confirms and disavows women's castration.

The article 'Fetishism' (in spite of its lack of precision) therefore includes the first description as being closely linked with it. This coupling of the two mechanisms is from now on part and parcel of the theory of perversions. The importance of the discovery of this defence—as an intra-systemic mechanism, affecting the same agency, the Ego—can never be overestimated. This taking into account of a possible cleft in the Ego—causing part of it to function in a psychotic way while allowing the Ego to keep in touch with reality—opens up large perspectives on mental functioning in general and on the possibility of the existence of a psychotic part in non-psychotic personalities (and vice versa).

In 'The Splitting of the Ego in the Process of Defence' (1938-1940), Freud supposes that a child

> is under the sway of a powerful instinctual demand which it is accustomed to satisfy and... it is suddenly frightened by an experience which teaches it that the continuance of this satisfaction will result in an almost intolerable real danger. [This particular child] will reply to the conflict with two contrary reactions... On one hand, with the help of certain mechanisms he rejects reality and refuses to accept any prohibition; on the other hand, in the same breath, he recognizes the danger of reality, takes over the fear of danger as a pathological symptom and tries subsequently to divest himself of the fear. It must be confessed that it is a very ingenious solution of the difficulty. [But, as everything has to be paid for,] the success is achieved at the price of a rift in the Ego... The two contrary reactions to the conflict persist as the centre point of a splitting of the Ego.

The example Freud gives of this 'ingenious solution' is precisely a case of perversion. A boy between the age of 3 and 4 is seduced by an older girl and given the opportunity to observe her genitals. He begins to practise masturbation. A threat of castration is then proffered by a governess. The perception of the little girl's genitals acquires now the meaning that the threat may be put into effect. In the case of a 'normal' or neurotic person the masturbation activity, connected with incestuous fantasies, ceases. The child renounces the instinctual satisfaction in order to preserve his penis, internalizes the incest prohibition, and establishes the Superego. The young boy in Freud's example found another way out: he created a fetish which, according to Freud, is a substitute for the mother's missing penis.

This allows him to disavow the reality of castration. Allow me to leave aside the meaning Freud attributes to the fetish, but let me emphasize that perversion—fetishism in this case—constitutes a means of eluding the fatal character of the Oedipus Complex. It appears as a rebellion against that universal law. Speaking of this process in the same article, Freud says: 'This way of dealing with reality... almost deserves to be described as artful.' (In German, Freud speaks of 'Kniffige Behandlung der Realität'.)

I would now like to show how my own investigations permit me to point out the elements of the pervert's 'ingenious solution', of his 'artful' way of dealing with reality. I shall come to conclusions which are different from Freud's but, I think, complementary in certain respects. For this purpose I must reassemble in a few plain statements various elements whose core has already been defined by me in two or three previous papers. These elements describe my understanding of the perverse solution. The future pervert is helped by a seductive mother to maintain the illusion that he is the only object of her desire, to the father's prejudice: indeed, the latter's capacities and genital attributes are disqualified. In order to perpetuate this illusion, the child is obliged to set up a new universe where all the differences originating conflicts and psychic pain will be abolished.

This universe which claims to have nothing to borrow from the Father-Creator's (genital) world is that of anal-sadistic regression. In order to preserve the conviction of the superiority of the anal universe over the paternal universe, all the elements composing this neo-creation will be submitted to a process of idealization. I shall examine the statements included in this formula. I shall leave aside the problem of the seduction by the mother, only recalling that it is pointed out by most contemporary authors, and that it had already been emphasized by Freud himself in the 'Three Essays', and in 'Leonardo' as an aetiological factor in perversions.

In the same vein, let me rather quote a passage from 'Negation' (1925, pp. 237-38), where Freud wants to describe the acquisition of the capacity to distinguish between what is subjective, and what is objective:

> The antithesis between subjective and objective does not exist from the first. It comes only into being from the fact that thinking possesses the capacity to bring before the mind once more something that has once been perceived, by reproducing it as a presentation without the external object having still to be there. The first and immediate aim, therefore, of reality testing is, not to *find* an object in real perception which corresponds to the one presented, but to *refind* such an object, to convince oneself that it is still there... It is evident that a precondition for the setting up of reality testing is that objects shall have been lost which once brought real satisfaction.

Of course, the mechanisms described here are very primitive, but they let us understand that the maintenance of the illusion of a full possession of the mother may be an obstacle for the access to reality.

I have greatly emphasized elsewhere the fact that the dimension of illusion introduced by the mother into the child's psyche led to the flattening out of time. I have described the shorter path chosen by the Ego Ideal of the future pervert as opposed to the longer path of one who has chosen his father as a model. His mother has made him believe, as I have stressed, that he doesn't need to grow up and identify with his father in order to take his place. The obstacle on the way to maturation will be eluded, foiled or considered as non-existent. His mother is there not to help him face them but to avoid them.

In order to grasp better what is at stake here, I would like to turn to Freud's ideas as expressed in the Letters to Fliess about giving up erotogenic zones. The idea first appears in the Letter dated 6 December 1896. This process of giving up would not have taken place in perversions. In the Letter dated 12 December 1897, where Freud announces to Fliess his discovery of the development of the libido, he speaks of an *organic* element taking part in the mechanism of repression, and which would be the giving up of erotogenic zones. This process would not have taken place in perversions. Human civilization would be associated with verticalization and the disaffection of 'olfactory gratifications'. The memories of the stimulation of the given up sexual erotogenic zones provoke

> an internal sensation similar to the disgust felt in the case of an object. To say it more coarsely, the memory now gives off the same stink as an actual object. Just as we turn away, with disgust, our sensory organ (head and nose) from the stinking objects, our preconscious and conscious understandings turn away from the memory.

Speaking of the 'organic repression', later on, in *Civilization and its Discontents* (1929, p. 99), Freud considers it as a 'defence against a phase of development that has been surmounted... This process is repeated on another level when the gods of a superseded period of civilization turn into demons.' If that process of decathexis of the erotogenic zones does not happen, the child becomes a pervert. It is striking that Freud, in his very first intuition, should have so strongly linked perversion to anality in numerous writings.

I have already had occasion to insist on the pervert's compulsion to idealize. Thanks to idealization, he tries to disguise from others and from himself the anal character of his impulses, of his objects and of his Ego. This compulsion accounts for the pervert's affinities with beauty and the world of art: the pervert is often an aesthete. It is interesting to observe that Freud, in his very first writings, associated perversions and idealization as he linked perversions and anality. First, in 'Three Essays on the Theory of Sexuality' (1905), he writes:

> It is perhaps in connection precisely with the most repulsive perversions that the mental factor must be regarded as playing its largest part in the transformation of the sexual instinct. It is impossible to deny that in their case a piece of mental work has been performed which, in spite of its horrifying result, is an equivalent of an idealization of the instinct (p. 161).

We can find therein a stressing of the performance of a work which permits us to glimpse an energetic modification which we shall discern more clearly in connection with the affect, and which also anticipates the research of mechanisms specific to perversion.

A Letter from Freud to Abraham (dated 14 February 1909) reads as follows:

> The fetish develops as follows: it is the result of a special mode of repression that could be described as a partial repression: one part of the complex is repressed; another part, as a compensation, is *idealized*... In this case, we are dealing with an original olfactory pleasure derived from an ill-smelling foot (which, for this reason, will always be preferred to a clean foot by the pervert). This olfactory pleasure is discarded. In exchange, the foot, a source of pleasure in the past, is established as a fetish. Its smell is no longer a matter of interest.

In his article on 'Repression' (1915), Freud returns to the notion of partial repression as an origin of the fetish, with an accompanying idealization.

> Repression acts... in a *highly individual* manner. Each single derivative of the repressed may have its own special vicissitude; a little more or a little less distortion alters the whole outcome. In this connection, we can understand how it is that the objects to which men give most preference, their ideals, proceed from the same perceptions and experiences as the objects which they most abhor, and that they were originally only distinguished from one another through slight modifications. Indeed as we found in tracing the origin of the fetish, it is possible for the original instinctual representative to be split in two, one part undergoing repression, while the remainder, precisely on account of this intimate connection, undergoes idealization (p. 150).

The common origin of 'the objects to which men give most preference' and 'the objects which they most abhor' accounts, in my opinion, for the obvious lability of the idealization mechanism, as well as for the ever-near persecution. For, at any time, anality threatens to burst the thin, glittering shell that covers it and to reappear in broad daylight, like the hideous corpse of a drowning victim coming back to the surface.

The subject who eludes all identification with the genital father—who renders values, objects, and sources of pleasure homogeneous by transforming them into particles of excrement—must have the annihilating intuition of the anal nature of his Ego. Idealization must, first of all, disguise the Ego itself and the objects in which it is reflected. This leads me to think that disavowal, in perversion, covers a much larger psycho-sexual area than the perception of female genitals and the lack of penis which is supposed to be their characteristic. The disavowal bears on genitality as a whole, on the genital primal scene (cf. J. McDougall, 1972, 'Primal Scene and the Scenario of the Pervert'), on the father's genital penis and its procreative powers, on the mother's vagina and on genital complementarity between the sexes in general. This disavowal is common to perversions. It is around this that perversion is organized.

If idealization comes to mask anality, at the same time, it is what unveils it. Indeed, if anality had been successfully repressed and counter-cathected or perfectly sublimated, or if the anal-sadistic regression had been entirely ego-syntonic, idealization would have constituted a useless mechanism. So in perversion, anality is neither really accepted by the Ego, nor really repressed; it is accepted or repressed to different degrees, according to the subjects. This leads me to the idea according to which idealization plays the role of a kind of negation, referring to the representation the subject has of himself and of his objects. Idealization would be a way of saying '*No*' to the anal character of the ideas and presentations about to re-emerge, and, at the same time, of adding something such as: 'It's not that; it's the contrary.' It is not a reaction formation as is shown by its lability and its tie with self-esteem and not with guilt. If negation is associated with a part lifting of repression, as Freud says in his article on this topic, idealization would be, for its own part, associated with that kind of part repression which Freud speaks of to Abraham, referring it to the construction of the fetish.

It seems to me that this 'part repression' Freud spoke of could coincide with the part lifting of repression peculiar to negation. Thus would we remain in the field of a splitting between the Ego and the Id (which takes place in neurosis). But here, in perversion, the agency of repression would admit into the Ego some repressed contents referring to anality after having 'disguised' them, that is, idealized them. I mean that these contents have not been split, as Freud seems to suppose in his article on 'Repression', one part being repressed while the other is idealized. It is a certain quantity of these contents that crosses the barrier of repression and enters the Ego, thanks to the mask of idealization. But idealization has also another function now in regard to disavowal. Indeed, if the idea did not exist somewhere in the pervert's mind that the father's universe is the standard by which all values are measured, then he would not need to disguise the anal universe (with its anal Ego, anal penis, etc...) which he tried to substitute for the genital dimension of psycho-sexuality. Anality would then reappear without any modification. It is this last hypothesis which would be congruent with Freud's assessment: 'Neurosis is the negative of perversion.'

Therefore, in my opinion, idealization holds a fundamental place in perversions. It indicates the existence of a 'peculiar means of repression' bearing on anality. The ideas associated with it are admitted by the repressing forces provided they have been idealized. Idealization tries to give anal values as superior to genital ones, which are the object of disavowal. It is, at the same time, the pointer to a splitting of the Ego, for it bears evidence in favour of a superiority which could not exist without its correlative fundamental disputability.

In perversion, idealization—as a result of the projection of the Ego Ideal, the heir of narcissism, on to pregenitality (the shorter path)—includes the whole dimension of illusion, on which the pervert has built his psycho-sexuality. As such an Ego Ideal aims at whisking away the reality of the difference between the sexes and the generations, it can only be considered as deceit, at a certain level. The mother who contributed to its setting up is an object of hatred (although in most cases this feeling undergoes numerous transformations). So, in perversion, idealization is always very close to persecution. Freud writes in his article on 'Repression': 'The objects to which men give most preference, their ideals, proceed from the same perceptions and experiences as the objects they most abhor.' In my opinion, this is always true of the instincts and objects idealized by the pervert, insofar as this idealization comes from a fundamental lure which may only be desperately maintained.

If we follow the destiny of anality in the pervert, we may see that—after having been cathected in a positive way, as it is and has to be in normal development—it did not subsequently undergo the usual transformations (repression, sublimation, character modifications, integration under genital primacy). The ancient gods have not changed into demons. But to change what is usually destined to become a demon into something 'divine' does not reduce to the mere persistency of the worship of the ancient gods. It consists in the strengthening of this worship precisely because and to the extent to which faith has been unsettled. Thus the incense arising from the altars erected to the ancient gods poorly conceals its sulphurous smell.

This projection of the Ego Ideal on to pregenitality (anality) and on to pregenital models has to be maintained in a compulsive way. For it is based on the disavowal of genitality and of the father's genital powers which are entirely decathected of narcissistic libido. As I have said, this disavowal inevitably coexists with the recognition of the genital dimension of psycho-sexuality. We may consider idealization as a forced way to make instincts, values and love for the objects of the anal phase all Ego-syntonic. When this syntony is unsettled, they may become persecutions: Sade became more or less paranoid and Sacher-Masoch, in his final delusion, strangled his beloved cats, the prototypes of the Venus in Furs.

We can imagine that, in certain cases, neurotic aspects of the pervert Ego try to reverse the mechanisms of idealization and succeed in cracking, then in cleaving the veneer masking anality. The papier mâché universe of the pervert may be unsettled: its false pillars (the anal penis) are in danger of collapsing, its stucco capitals (his treacherous mode of reasoning) are about to tumble down. These tremors are at once a terrible threat and a more or less strong temptation—that of giving up the domain of mendacity to reach that of truth. We have seen that Freud tried to differentiate psychotic mechanisms from neurotic ones (mainly repression) in his very first writings. A conception of psychosis is spotlighted from the start. The defence is considered not only as being directed against sexuality but also against the external world, with the rejection into the outside world of the incompatible idea. In the case of hallucinatory confusion, the idea unsettled by reality is underlined. In the case of paranoia, the reproaches are rejected into the external world.

What would then be the difference between disavowal in the case of perversion in comparison with psychoses? It seems to me that the disavowal of the genital order is inseparable, in the pervert, from anal-sadistic regression. The (part) withdrawal of sexual and narcissistic cathexis, the loss of 'interest' for the genital psychosexual dimension, is carried back by the pervert on to the anal universe. I have emphasized the fact that we find here the creation of a 'new world'. Nevertheless, it could not be likened to the autocratic creation of reality by the psychotic as decribed by Freud in his article on 'Neurosis and Psychosis' (1924):

> Not only is the acceptance of new perceptions refused, but the internal world, too, which, as a copy of the external world, has up till now represented it, loses its significance (its cathexis). The Ego creates, autocratically, a new external and internal world; and there can be no doubt of two facts—that this new world is constructed in accordance with the Id's wishful impulses, and that the motive of this dissociation from the external world is some very serious frustration by reality of a wish—a frustration which seems intolerable.

The pervert's success, his 'artful' way of dealing with reality, consists in the creation of a world which borrows its materials from some elements of his internal world which really exist within himself. They exist inside all of us, for we have all been through the anal phase, even if it has been differently and individually integrated.

We have already seen that the anal universe can be considered as a preliminary sketch of the genital universe. Thus the anal universe is a sunken continent, a fabulous Atlantis which the pervert magically conjures up. This 'new world', though it is 'constructed in accordance with the Id's wishful impulses', rests, at the same time, upon a certain kind of reality—that of a phase of development usually left behind but whose sediments subsist in each of us. It all takes place as if the pervert had found a 'trick' to escape the neurotic's sufferings without breaking off his links with reality to the same extent and in the same way as the psychotic. The gap between the genital and the anal world is filled not by delusion or by means of hallucination but by idealization. I am referring here to Freud, who says in 'Neurosis and Psychosis' (1924): 'In regard to the genesis of delusions, a fair number of analyses have taught us that the delusion is found applied like a path over the place where originally a rent had appeared in the Ego's relation to the external world' (p. 151). Idealization has the same function as delusion: that of reconstructing the links with reality. In his article 'On Narcissism: An Introduction' (1914), Freud describes a first pathological phase in psychosis (here in paraphrenia) which consists in a withdrawal of libido in the Ego. In perversion this phase corresponds to the anal-sadistic regression.

The narcissistic withdrawal (part withdrawal of narcissistic interests and significance) from genitality does not end in megalomania; this is despite the fact that there is an actual narcissistic withdrawal from the father, as playing the part of the Ego Ideal, and a move to the anal Ego. But the greater part of narcissistic cathexis is saturated by the work of idealization. This spares the pervert the second phase of psychosis (delusional megalomania) and the second phase of the neurotic process, i.e., anxiety. Indeed, it governs, at least in part, the vicissitudes of affects. Affects associated with the valorization, exaltation and overestimation of objects, Ego and impulses are displaced from genitality to anality.

As a summary we may now propose the following statements: At the Ego level, there exists a splitting between the *disavowal* and the *recognition* of reality.

Disavowal bears on a basic element of human reality: the double difference between the sexes and the generations. A withdrawal of object libido as well as narcissistic libido occurs for the benefit of the anal-sadistic universe.

The *recognition* of reality, i.e., of the double difference between the sexes and the generations involving that of the father's genital prerogatives and that of the complementarity between the parents, is shown by the work of *idealization* of anal elements aiming essentially at the preservation of self-esteem through an acceptable image of the self. This idealization is the necessary condition for the admission, in the Ego, of repressed anal contents. Anality remains, in fact, subject to a part-repression, as long as it influences the anal character of the Ego. The disguise conferred upon anality through idealization enables it to cross the barrier of repression. Therefore, in perversion, anal-sadistic regression is not merely accepted by the Ego. That is a point which has to be emphasized.

The *affect* (associated with narcissistic cathexis) is displaced from one side to the other of the dividing line of the split Ego—and is not repressed, as was stated by Freud in his article on fetishism.

Repressed ideas (we are now in the Id) are those which affect the anal character of the Ego, insofar as it has not been disguised by idealization.

It would be possible to advance the following hypotheses: The derivatives of the repressed, associated with the primal scene, are eventually submitted to a secondary repression similar to that which occurs in neurosis. Moreover, as far as they succeed in linking up with elements of the Ego, they become a matter of disavowal.

In short, we have here mechanisms of repression as well as of disavowal, with idealization playing a dialectical role vis-à-vis both of these mechanisms. In the *Outline of Psychoanalysis* (1938-1940), after having described the splitting of the Ego in psychosis and in fetishism, Freud compares it to the old mechanism of splitting between the Ego and the Id, that is, the repression specific to neurosis. I find it interesting that there Freud inclines towards bringing together, without confusing them, the mechanisms of division. I think that the two forms of splitting—the horizontal and the vertical—do not exclude each other; on the contrary, they coexist in perversion.

THE STATE OF PSYCHIC APPARATUS IN PERVERSIONS
— A Proposed Schema —

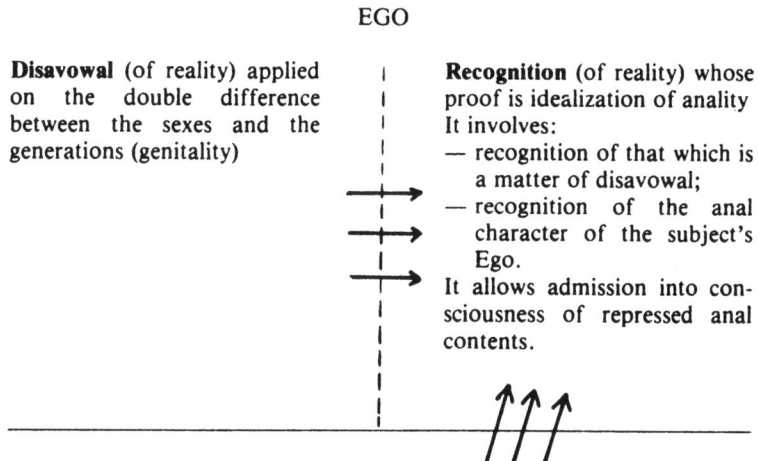

EGO

Disavowal (of reality) applied on the double difference between the sexes and the generations (genitality)

Recognition (of reality) whose proof is idealization of anality
It involves:
— recognition of that which is a matter of disavowal;
— recognition of the anal character of the subject's Ego.
It allows admission into consciousness of repressed anal contents.

Repression

Repressed Ideas
— those which refer to the anal image of the Ego;
— those which refer to the genital primal scene.

ID

(Note: The arrows show the thrust of the split elements as well as the repressed elements and the dialectical function of idealization vis-à-vis these two groups of elements.)

NOTES ON SOURCES

Chapter 1
This chapter, 'Perversion and the Universal Law', is based on the author's Inaugural Lecture as Freud Professor at University College, London, 1 November 1982.
Translations from de Sade's *The 120 Days of Sodom* are from the Random House edition; translations from his other works have been arranged by the author.

Chapter 6
This chapter, 'Narcissism and Group Psychology', deals with a topic which the author has developed in a similar way in the book, *L'Ideal du Moi*, published in English as *The Ego Ideal* by Free Association Books, in press.

Chapter 8
The Lacan quotation is translated by the author.

Chapter 9
The Rousselot quotation is translated by the author.

BIBLIOGRAPHY

Abraham, H.C. and Freud, E.L., eds. (1965) *A Psychoanalytical Dialogue. The Letters of Sigmund Freud and Karl Abraham—1907-1926.* New York: Basic Books.
Abraham, K. (1910) 'Psycho-Analysis of a Case of Foot and Corset Fetishism', in *Selected Papers on Psycho-Analysis.* London: The Hogarth Press, pp. 125-36
—— (1920) 'The Narcissistic Evaluation of Excretory Processes in Dreams and Neurosis', in *Selected Papers on Psycho-Analysis.* London: The Hogarth Press, pp. 318-22.
Anzieu, D. (1971) 'L'illusion groupale', *Nouvelle Revue de Psychanalyse,* 4: 73-93
Bak, R. (1953) 'Fetishism', *Journal of the American Psychoanalytic Association, 1*: 285-98.
Balint, M. (1935) 'Contribution to the Study of Fetishism', *The International Journal of Psycho-Analysis, 16*: 481-83.
Bellmer, H. (1934) 'La poupée', in *Obliques.* Paris: Borderie, 1975, pp. 58-65.
—— (1957) 'Petite anatomie de l'inconscient physique ou l'anatomie de l'image', in *Obliques.* Paris: Borderie, 1975, pp. 115-25.
—— (1965) 'Post-scriptum à Oracles et spectacles d'Unica Zürn' in *Obliques.* Paris: Borderie, 1975, pp. 109-10.
Bible (1944) *King James' Bible.* Cambridge: University Press.
Brun, J. (1975) 'Désir et réalité dans l'oeuvre de Hans Bellmer', in *Obliques.* Paris: Borderie, pp. 7-12.
Camus, A. (1945) *Caligula, suivi de Le malentendu.* Paris: Gallimard, 1958, pp. 15-150.
—— (1965) *Caligula*, transl. by Stuart Gilbert. Harmondsworth: Penguin.
—— (1967) *Albert Camus — Théâtre, Récits, Nouvelles*, textes éstablis et annotés par R. Quillot. Paris: Gallimard.
Chasseguet-Smirgel, J. (1968) 'le rossignol de l'Empereur de Chine—Essai psychanalytique sur le "faux" ', in *Pour une psychanalyse de l'art et de la créativité.* Paris: Payot, 1971, pp. 183-216.
—— (1973) 'Essai sur l'Idéal du Moi: Contribution à l'étude de la "maladie d'idéalité" ', *Revue Francaise de Psychanalyse, 37*: 709-927 (to be published in English by Free Association Books).
—— (1978) 'Reflexions on the Connexions between Perversion and Sadism', *The International Journal of Psycho-Analysis, 59*: 27-35.
—— (1981) 'Loss of Reality in Perversions', *Journal of the American Psycho-Analytic Association, 29*: 511-34.
Chambers' Twentieth Century Dictionary (1972) Edinburgh: Chambers.
Deutsch, A. (Grand Rabbi) (1976) *Manuel d'instruction religieuse israélite.* Paris: Fondation Sefer.
Deutsch, H. (1942) 'Some Forms of Emotional Disturbance and their Relationship to Schizophrenia', *The Psychoanalytic Quarterly, 11*: 301-21.

―――― (1955) 'The Impostor—Contribution to the Ego-Psychology of a Type of Psychopath', *The Psychoanalytic Quarterly, 24*: 383-505.
Dostoievski, F. (1873) *Les démons*. Paris: Fernand Hazan, 1963.
Eliade, M. (1956) *Forgerons et alchimistes*. Paris: Flammarion, 1977.
―――― (1962) *Mephistophélès et l'Androgyne*. Paris: Gallimard.
Ferenczi, S. (1924) *Thalassa: A Theory of Genitality*. Albany, New York: The Psychoanalytic Quarterly, 1938.
Freud S. *Complete Psychological Works*, Standard Edition, 23 volumes. London: The Hogarth Press and The Institute of Psycho-Analysis, 1951 (referred to in text as *S.E.*).
―――― (1894) 'The Neuro-Psychoses of Defence', in *S.E., 3*: 45-61.
―――― (1895) *Studies on Hysteria, S.E., 2*.
―――― (1896) 'Further Remarks on the Neuro-Psychoses of Defence', in *S.E., 3*: 162-88.
―――― (1900) *The Interpretation of Dreams, S.E., 4/5*.
―――― (1905) 'Fragment of an Analysis of a Case of Hysteria' (Dora), in *S.E., 7*: 7-122
―――― (1905) *Three Essays on the Theory of Sexuality*, in *S.E., 7*: 135-243.
―――― (1907) 'Obsessive Actions and Religious Practices', in *S.E. 9*: 117-27.
―――― (1908) 'Creative Writers and Day-Dreaming', in *S.E. 9*: 143-53.
―――― (1908) 'On the Sexual Theories of Children', in S.E., 9: 209-260.
―――― (1909) 'Analysis of a Phobia in a Five-year-old Boy' (Little Hans), in *S.E., 10*: 5-149
―――― (1910) 'Leonardo da Vinci and a Memory of his Childhood', in *S.E., 11*: 63-137.
―――― (1911) 'The Two Principles of Mental Functioning', in *S.E., 12*: 218-26.
―――― (1912-1913) *Totem and Taboo*, in *S.E., 13*:1-161.
―――― (1913) 'On Beginning the Treatment (Further Recommendations on the Technique of Psycho-Analysis I)', in *S.E., 12*: 121-44.
―――― (1914) 'On Narcissism: An Introduction', in *S.E., 14*: 73-104.
―――― (1915) 'Instincts and their Vicissitudes', in *S.E., 14*:117-40
―――― (1915) 'Repression', in *S.E., 14*: 146-58.
―――― (1915) 'The Unconscious', in *S.E., 14*: 166-216.
―――― (1917) 'A Metapsychological Supplement to the Theory of Dreams', in *S.E., 14*: 222-35.
―――― (1917) 'On Transformation of Instincts as Exemplified in Anal Eroticism', in *S.E., 17*: 127-33.
―――― (1918) 'From the History of an Infantile Neurosis' (The Wolf-Man), in *S.E., 17*: 7-122.
―――― (1919) 'A Child is Being Beaten. A Contribution to the Study of the Origin of Sexual Perversions', in *S.E., 17*: 179-204.
―――― (1920) *Beyond the Pleasure Principle,* in *S.E., 18*: 7-64.
―――― (1921) *Group Psychology and the Analysis of the Ego*, in *S.E., 18*: 69-143.
―――― (1923) *The Ego and the Id*, in *S.E., 19*: 12-66.
―――― (1924) 'Neurosis and Psychosis' in *S.E., 19*: 149-53.
―――― (1924) 'The Economic Problem of Masochism', in *S.E., 19*: 159-70.
―――― (1924) 'The Dissolution of the Oedipus Complex', in *S.E., 19*: 173-79.
―――― (1924) 'The Loss of Reality in Neurosis and Psychosis', in *S.E., 19*:

183-87.
───── (1925) 'Negation', in *S.E., 19*: 235-39.
───── (1925) 'Some Psychical Consequences of the Anatomical Distinction between the Sexes', in *S.E., 19*: 248-60.
───── (1926) *Inhibitions, Symptoms and Anxiety*, in *S.E., 20*: 87-174.
───── (1927) 'Fetishism', in *S.E., 21*: 152-57.
───── (1927) 'Post-Script to a Discussion on Lay Analysis', in *S.E., 20*: 251-58.
Freud, S. (1929) *Civilization and its Discontents*, in *S.E., 21:* 64-145.
───── (1932) 'Why War,' (Letter to Einstein), in *S.E., 22*: 203-15.
───── (1933) 'The Dissection of the Personality', in *S.E., 22*: 57-80, In *New Introductory Lectures on Psychoanalysis, S.E., 22:* 5-184.
───── (1933) 'Femininity', in *S.E., 22*: 147-78, in *New Introductory Lectures on Psychoanalysis, S.E., 22:* 5-184.
───── (1937) 'Analysis Terminable and Interminable', in *S.E., 23*: 216-53.
───── (1937) 'Construction in Analysis', in *S.E., 23*: 255-74.
───── (1938-1940) *An Outline of Psycho-Analysis*, in *S.E., 23*: 144-207.
───── (1938-1940) 'Splitting of the Ego in the Process of Defence', in *S.E., 23*: 275-78.
───── (1950 [1892-1899]), 'Extracts from the Fliess Papers', in *S.E., 1*: 175-282.
───── (1950 [1895]) *Project for a Scientific Psychology*, in *S.E., 1*: 283-387.
Gillespie, W.H. (1940) 'A Contribution to the Study of Fetishism', *The International Journal of Psycho-Analysis, 33*: 397-402.
───── (1964) 'The Psychoanalytical Theory of Sexual Deviations with Special Reference to Fetishism', in *The Pathology and Treatment of Sexual Deviations*. London: Oxford University Press, pp. 123-45.
Glover, E. (1931) 'Sublimation, Substitution and Social Anxiety', in *On the Early Development of Mind*. London: Imago Publishing, 1956, pp. 130-60.
───── (1932) 'the Relation of Perversion-Formations to the Development of Reality-Sense', in *On the Early Development of Mind*. London: Imago Publishing, 1956, pp. 216-34.
───── (1938) 'A Note on Idealization', in *On the Early Development of Mind*. London: Imago Publishing, 1956, pp. 290-96.
───── (1964) 'Aggression and Sado-Masochism', in *Pathology and Treatment of Sexual Deviations*. London: Oxford University Press, pp. 146-72.
Glover, J. (1927) 'Notes on an Unusual Form of Perversion', *The International Journal of Psycho-Analysis, 8*: 10-24.
Greenacre, P. (1953), 'Certain Relationships between Fetishism and Faulty Development of the Body Image', *The Psychoanalytic Study of the Child, 8*. London: The Hogarth Press, pp.78-98.
───── (1958) 'The Impostor', *The Psychoanalytic Quarterly, 17*: 359-81.
─────(1968) 'Perversions: General Considerations Regarding their Genetic and Dynamic Background', *The Psychoanalytic Study of the Child, 23*. London: The Hogarth Press, pp. 47-62.
Grunberger, B. (1956) 'A Psycho-Dynamic Study of Masochism', in *Perversions*, ed. By S. Lorand and M. Balint. New York: Random House, 1958.
───── (1959) 'Etude sur la relation objectale anale', *Le narcissisme*. Paris: Payot, 1971, pp. 171-96. Translation: 'Study of Anal

Object-Relations', in *Narcissism*. New York: International Universities Press, 1979, pp. 143-65.

─── (1966) 'Le narcissisme et l'Oedipe', in *Le narcissisme*. Paris: Payot, 1971, pp. 331-48. Translation: 'Narcissism and the Oedipus Complex', in *Narcissism*. New York: International Universities Press, 1979, pp. 265-81.

─── (1976) 'Essai sur le Fétichisme', *Revue Francaise de Psychanalyse*, 40: 235-64.

Ionesco, E. (1965) 'La lacune', in *Le Nouvel Observateur*, 28 January 1965, n° 11, pp. 22-23.

Jacobson, E. (1954) 'The Self and the Object World: Vicissitudes of their Infantile Cathexes and their Influence on Ideational and Affective Development', *Psychoanalytic Study of the Child*, 9. London: The Hogarth Press, pp. 75-127.

Jelinski, C. (1966) *Les dessins de Hans Bellmer.* Paris: Denoël et Hans Bellmer, Nouvelle édition Denoël, 1973.

Jones, E. (1933) 'The Phallic Phase', *International Journal of Psycho-Analysis*, 14: 1-33.

─── (1934-1957) *Sigmund Freud, Life and Work*, 3 volumes. London: The Hogarth Press.

Josephus, Flavius (AD 70) *Histoire ancienne des Juifs*. Paris: Lidis, 1968.

Khan, M. (1979) *Alienation in Perversions*. London: The Hogarth Press.

Krafft-Ebing, R. (1887) *Psychopathia Sexualis*. Paris: Payot, 1969.

Lacan, J. (1966) *Ecrits*. Paris: Seuil.

McDougall, J. (1972) 'Primal Scene and Sexual Perversion', *International Journal of Psycho-Analysis*, 53: 371-84.

Molière (1666) *The Misanthrope and Other Plays*, transl. by John Wood. Harmondsworth, Middlesex: Penguin Books, 1959.

Novey, S. (1955) 'Some Philosophical Speculations about Genital Character', *The International Journal of Psycho-Analysis*, 36: 88-94.

Parkin, A. (1963) 'On Fetishism', *The International Journal of Psycho-Analysis*, 44: 352-61.

Payne, S. (1939) 'Some Observations on the Ego Development of the Fetishist', *The International Journal of Psycho-Analysis*, 20: 352-61.

Reich, A. (1953) 'Narcissistic Object Choice in Women', Psychoanalytic Contributions. New York: International Universities Press, 1973, pp. 179-208.

─── (1954) 'Early Identifications as Archaic Elements in the Superego', *Psychoanalytic Contributions*. New York: International Universities Press, 1973, pp. 209-35.

─── (1960) 'Pathologic Forms of Self-Esteem Regulations', *Psychoanalytic Contributions*. New York: International Universities Press, 1973, pp. 288-311.

Sade, D.A.F. (1967) *Marquis de Sade — Oeuvres Complètes*. Paris: Cercle du Livre Précieux.

Sade, The Marquis de (1966) *The 120 Days of Sodom and Other Writings*. New York: Random House.

Sandler, J. (1960) 'On the Concept of Superego', *Psychoanalytic Study of the Child*, 15. New York: International Universities Press, pp. 128-62.

Schmideberg, M. (1956) 'Delictious Acts as Perversions and Fetishes', *International Journal of Psycho-Analysis*, 37: pp. 422-24.

Shakespeare, W. (1604) *Othello*.

―――― (1609) *Troïlus and Cressida*, ed. by Aurélien Digeon. Paris: Aubier-Flammarion, 1969.
Socarides, C. (1960) 'Development of a Fetishistic Perversion', *Journal of the American Psychoanalytic Association, 8*: 281-311.
Sperling, M. (1963) 'Fetishism in Children', *The Psychoanalytic Quarterly, 32*: 374-92.
Suetonius. 'Caligula', *Suetonius, 1*, in *Suetonius,* 2 vols., transl. by J.C. Rolfe. London: Heinemann, 1964.
Weissmann, P. (1957) 'Some Aspects of Sexual Activity in a Fetishist', *The Psychoanalytic Quarterly, 26*: 494-507.
Wells, H.G. (1896) 'The Island of Dr Moreau', in *Seven Famous Novels by H.G. Wells.* New York: A.A. Knopf, 1934.
Wilde, O. (1888) *Stories,* ed. by G.F. Maine. London and Glasgow: Collins, 1952.
―――― (1889), *Poems and Essays,* ed. by G.F. Maine. London and Glasgow: Collins, 1952.
―――― (1890) *The Picture of Dorian Gray,* ed. by G.F.Maine. London and Glasgow: Collins, 1952; also in *The Works of Oscar Wilde.* London: Spring, 1963.
Winnicott, D.W. (1953) 'Transitional Objects and Transitional Phenomena', *The International Journal of Psycho-Analysis, 34*:89-97.
Woolf, M. (1945) 'Prohibitions against Simultaneous Consumption of Milk and Flesh in Orthodox Jewish Law', *The International Journal of Psycho-Analysis, 26*: 169-76.
Wulff, M. (1946) 'Fetishism and Object-Choice in Early Childhood', *The Psychoanalytic Quarterly, 15*: 450-71.

INDEX

Subheadings are arranged in the order they first appear in the text.
As in the Bibliography, publications by the same author are arranged by date of publication; the index includes only those publications whose contents are directly quoted in the text.
This index has been prepared by A. S. Thorley.

A

Abraham, K. 'Psychoanalysis of a Case of Foot and Corset Fetishism' (1912) 93; 'The Narcissistic Evaluation of Excretory Processes in Dreams and Neurosis' (1920) 78-80
acting out: by Jean-Jacques 34; creations may be a form of 71; method used to fulfil fantasies of greatness (H. Deutsch) 72
Adlerian theory, Freud's rejection 46
aestheticism: in perversion 92-8; a shoe fetishist's habitual demands (K. Abraham) 93; hides and reveals its origins (writings of O. Wilde) 95-100
affect, disposal of, in anxiety, hysteria and obsessional neurosis 146
alimentary canal *see* digestive tract
alliance, therapeutic 109-19
anagrams, Hans Bellmer 21-2
anal eroticism increased by mother's concern (Abraham's case) 78-9
anality *see also* anal eroticism, anal phallus, regression, sadism: masked by idealization (writings of O. Wilde) 96-100; partially repressed in perversion 152-5, 158
anal phallus, creations of 68-9; symbolized in 'The Baron of Arizona' 71; indefinitely renewable, like the Phoenix 75; imitation of a genital penis 81-2; represented by a fetish 82, 87
anal-sadism, portrayed in a film, 'The Corpse Incinerator' 55-6
anal-sadistic universe *see also* regression; perversion 2-6
anal sexuality, equal or superior to genital sexuality in perversion 91
analysis *see* psychoanalysis
Andersen, Hans Christian, 'The Nightingale' 66-8, 76
animals *see also* horses, rhinoceroses, wolves: phallic characteristics of 38; anxiety-inducing 46, 49-50; in comparison between 'Little Hans' and the 'Wolf-Man' 49-50; instinctive knowledge of 51-2
anomos, meanings of 9
anus-island, Doctor Moreau 18-20
anxiety, castration, *see also* castration complex: social, conscience 57-8; castration and separation 83-6

Anzieu, D. on the 'group illusion' 60, 63
apocalyptic outbursts, means of smoothing world problems 130
art and perversion 90
'as if' subjects (H. Deutsch) 71-2, 74
Astarte, worship of 7, 10
atheism, The Marquis de Sade 5-6
Auschwitz, 'the anus of the world' 55-6

B

'Baron of Arizona, The', Samuel Fuller (film story of a swindler) 71
Bellmer, Hans, 'The Doll' 13, 20-2; *Anatomy of the Image* 21; teratogenic world where all permutations and combinations possible 122, 126-7
Biblical prohibitions 6-8, 11
biological factor, prolonged period of helplessness in the human young 2, 53-4
black mass 10

C

cabarets, transvestite 1
Caligula 13-18; life story 13-14; as a monster 14-18
Camus, A. *Caligula* 16-18
case studies (named subjects) *see* Jean-Jacques, Norbert, Romain *and* Rrose Sélavy
castration complex: case of perversion (Freud) 25-6; Little Hans 35, 43; restriction of term by authoress 43; Wolf-Man 44-6, 48-50, 147; motive in dissolution of the Oedipus Complex 52-3; motive in setting up of Superego 56; and fetishism 83-5
'Chinese puzzle', Freudian metaphor for the reconstitution of the infantile mental apparatus 102-3, 108
'cloacal theory', Wolf-Man 44-5
coitus, children's sadistic view 35-6
conscience: coupled with the 'starry vault above' (I. Kant) 23, 57; social anxiety 57-8; development of 69
constructions (Freud) 101-4, 106-8
conviction, equivalent to remembrance (Freud) 102
'Corpse Incinerator, The' (film) 55-6, 64

168 Creativity and Perversion

counter-transference 112; in authoress (Rrose Sèlavy) 132, 135-7
creations: factitious, made by those failing to project their Ego Ideal onto their father 69-71; considered as acting out 71; of mankind (K. Abraham) 79; and sublimation 89-90
curiosity, children's 36-7

D

delinquency and perversion 71, 81-2
dependency of the child, long period of 2, 53-4
Deutsch, H. 'Some Forms of Emotional Disturbance and their Relationship to Schizophrenia' (1942) 71-2; 'The Imposter – Contribution to Ego-Psychology of a Type of Psychopath' (1955) 72
development, psychosexual see also time lag, 50-4
Devil, The, Lucifer, Satan 10
Devil religion 9-10
digestion, fragmentation of food to produce a homogeneous mass, the faecal bolus 55-6
digestive tract: comparison with Caligula's wish to modify reality 14; Sadian setting for Doctor Moreau 18-20; gigantic grinding machine 128; alimentary canal (Rrose Sèlavy) 140-1
Dionysiac rites 11
disavowal 147-9; in perversion 150-1, 154-9
'Doctor Moreau, The Island of', H. G. Wells 13, 18-20, 22-3
'Doll, The', Hans Bellmer 20-2
Dostoievski, F., *The Devils* (1873) 1
dreams: anal creation of the world (Abraham's comparison) 79; showing difference between idealization and sublimation 92-3; traumatic (The Wolf Man) 103; relation between a discovery and conflicts revealed in analysis (Norbert) 107; illustrating destructiveness and mastery 112-13; changing during treatment 117-18; symbolising destruction of thought 120; representing a regression to the anal-sadistic universe 121-2; deepening comprehension of clinical material, case of Romain 122-5, 127; Rrose Sèlavy 132-3, 136-40, 143-4

E

egalitarianism in groups 58-60
Ego: splitting as response to conflict 25-6, 110; in examination dreams 31-2; overwhelmed by excitations 46-7; differentiation from the Id 53, 159; reunited with the Ego Ideal in groups 58, 60-3; perfection insured in perversion by inverting the usual relationship between art and nature 96; effects of therapeutic construction 102-3, 108; in psychosis 109-11; analyst's observing part 111-12; proposed schema of the state of psychic apparatus in perversions 159
Ego Ideal: as conceived by Freud 26-9; devalorised in case of Jean-Jacques 34; in examination dreams 31-3; differences from the Superego 56-7; in neurotic and normal projected onto father 91; attachment to a pregenital model 91, 152, 155-6
embalming and fetishism 87-8
equality: Caligula's gift 17; egalitarianism in groups 58-60
ethics and reality, tie between them 12, 23
examination dreams: Freud's account and interpretation 29-32; interpretations by authoress 30, 34; case who had failed the examination, later passing a 'special examination' 32-3; Jean-Jacques, link with avoidance of Oedipal conflict 33-4

F

'false', falsehood: differentiated from 'true' 66; study of 66-76; identified with the inanimate (H. C. Andersen) 68; built up by taking the equation 'faeces = penis' literally 75
family romance 72-3
fantasies induced in the authoress by Rrose Sèlavy 135-6
father: dethronement by Hans Bellmer's doll 20-1; identification with 27; disqualified by pervert 29, 151; primal, the group ideal 58; equated with reality 121, 126
father-complex (Freud) 59-60
father's penis, Little Hans fears and wishes both to obtain and remove it 37-40, 42
fear, as a pathological symptom 25
Ferenczi, S., basic human wish to return to the womb 27
fetish: a comb (in 'The Corpse Incinerator') 55; rubber pipe (Abraham's case) 79-80; mother-in-law's pyjamas and a friend's prosthesis (Jean-Jacques) 81; riding boots (authoress) 81; raincoat (A. Parkin's case) 82, 87; represents the anal phallus 82, 87; aids control of the castration complex 83; anal and shiny 88; its idealization 88; aesthetic demands (Abraham) 93; development of 99-100, 153
fetishism: means of avoiding the fatal character of the Oedipus Complex 26; further note on 'Little Hans' (Freud) 43; and homosexuality 80-2; and perversion connected with the world of semblance 81; aims at the resolution of pregenital conflicts 83-4; and separation anxiety 83-4; a magic and artful universe 88; mechanisms of disavowal and splitting (Freud) 110, 150
fixation, implies perversion 90
Freud, S: 'The Neuro-Psychosis of Defence' (1894) 146-7; *Studies on Hysteria* (1895) 102; *The Interpretation of Dreams* (1900) 24, 30-2; 'Fragment of an Analysis of a Case of Hysteria' (1905) 89; *Three Essays*

on the Theory of Sexuality (1905) 35, 90, 99, 153; 'Creative Writers and Day-Dreaming' (1908) 26-7, 28-9; 'On the Sexual Theories of Children' (1908) 35-6; 'Analysis of a Phobia in a Five-year-old Boy' (Little Hans) (1909) 37; 'Leonardo da Vinci and a Memory of his Childhood' (1910) 90; 'On Beginning the Treatment' (1913) 116; 'Repression' (1915) 100; *Beyond the Pleasure Principle* (1920) 52; *Group Psychology and the Analysis of the Ego* (1921) 58-9; further note on 'Little Hans' (1923) 43; *The Ego and the Id* (1923) 69; 'The Economic Problems of Masochism' (1924) 114-15; 'Neurosis and Psychosis' (1924) 156; 'Negation' (1925) 98-9, 151; *Inhibitions, Symptoms and Anxiety* (1926) 103; 'Fetishism' (1927) 110; *Civilization and its Discontents* (1929) 91, 152; 'Construction in Analysis' (1937) 101; 'Analysis Terminable and Interminable' (1937) 109; 'Splitting of the Ego in the Process of Defence' (1938-1940) 25, 150; *An Outline of Psycho-Analysis* (1938-40) 109-10

G

Genesis, based on principles of distinction, separation and differentiation 8-9
genetic manipulations 23
Glover, E. 'A Note on Idealization' (1938) 94; *On the Early Development of Mind* (1956) 93-4
Glover, J.: 'Notes on an Unusual Form of Perversion' (1927) 84
gods, ancient *see also* Astarte 7, 10 *and* Devil religion 9-10; turn into demons 91-2, 152; strengthening of the worship in perversion 155
Gospel of Thomas, belief in the creation of a new kind of reality 11
Greenacre, P. 'The Impostor' (1958) 72-3
groups: dissolution of the Superego 58; esprit de corps arising from sibling rivalry 59; analogous to dreams 60
guilt: lack of, in perversion 112; absent in Rrose Sélavy 135

H

Hans, Little: analysis of a phobia in a five-year-old boy (Freud) 37; plumber fantasy 38-9, 79; phobia focussed on positive side of Oedipus Complex 44; comparison with Wolf-Man 46; castration and separation anxieties 86
'Happy Prince, The', O. Wilde 97-8
herd instinct (Freud) 59
homosexuality: playing a part in identification with and introjection of father's virility (Little Hans) 39; intensity of instincts (Wolf-Man) 46, 48-9; submission to father

(illustrative case) 79; and fetishism 80-2
horse(s): Caligula's 15; 'Little Hans' fear of being bitten 37-8, 42
hubris 9-10; Caligula's 14-17, 20; Doctor Moreau's 20, 23
hybrid beings, Doctor Moreau 19-20
hydridization 9; spirit of 15
hysteria: affect, suppressed and converted 146, 148; case history (Freud) 148

I

Id, proposed schema of the state of psychic apparatus in perversions 159
idealization: illustrated in Andersen's Nightingale 69; and the building of a fetish 88; tends more toward aestheticism than creation 92; in perversion 92-100; of pregenital objects (Rrose Sélavy) 134-5; of anality 151-9
identification: paternal, method of achieving it 39; failures of 70-1; distinguished from imitation 73-4
ideologies 56, 61-5, 128
imago, maternal phallic 44, 47, 49
imitation, magic identification 73-4
Impostors: studies of: H. Deutsch 72; P. Greenacre 72-3; with a symbolic phallus (Abraham) 73
impotence, infantile 2
incest (fantasies, love, wishes): prohibitions against 2, 6-8, 11; Sade's destruction of reality 3; associated with narcissism 26-9, 53; involvement of the penis (Freud) 35; barrier against 121
inferiority, sense of 52
instinct: conflict with the prohibitions of reality 25; to know and see 36-7; theory, Eros 52
instinctive knowledge 51-2
'intermediary space' between analysand and analyst, lack of 111
interpretations, in analysis 101-2, 104, 108, 117; rejected 115; Romain's dream 123; in case of Rrose Sélavy 133, 135-9, 144
Ionesco, E. 'Something is Missing' (play) 32; totalitarian temptation 56, 64

J

Jean-Jacques, illustrative case used by authoress 33-4, 79-82
Juliette, Story of, Marquis de Sade 3, 5
Justine, The New, Marquis de Sade 4-6, 10

K

knowledge, confusion with magic 22

L

leaders of groups 59-61, 64; mediator between the group and ideological illusion 61-2, 64
Leonardo da Vinci (Freud) 47, 90
Libido theory 27-8
Lind, Jenny, 'The Swedish Nightingale' 68
Lucifer, *see also* The Devil 10, 13; three characters 13-23

M

magic circumventing reality 22
manipulation in masochism 114
masochism: softening of Superego 39; moral 113-15
masturbation, persistent: Freud's case of fetishism 26; associated with sado-masochistic fantasies (authoress' case, Jean-Jacques) 33
metamorphoses: The Marquis de Sade 4; Hans Bellmer 21-2
metempsychosis, Buddhism ('The Corpse Incinerator') 55
mimicry, a disturbance of the sublimation process 72
missing piece of the Chinese puzzle (Freudian metaphor for a therapeutic construction) 102-3, 108
mixture, forbidden: hubris and hybrid 6-12
Molière, struggle against falsehood 76
Montherlant, Henri de, 'The Son of Nobody' 70
moral motives, source of 53
mother: responsibility in child development 28; seduction by 28-9; imago of phallic 44, 47, 49; roles in Little Hans and the Wolf-Man 47; almighty, represented by the group 60; Mother-Goddess in Nazism 62; seduction maintains pervert's idea that he is the object of her desire 151-2
murder: Sadian assertions 4-5; in film 'The Corpse Incinerator' 55; sanctioned by the group 62-3

N

Narcissism: and Perversion 24-34; and its associations 26-9, 53; and Group Psychology 55-65
Nature: the melting pot 4-5; imitates art (O. Wilde's paradox) 96
Nazism 1, 22, 56, 62
necrophilia 55-6
Negation, hallmark of repression (Freud) 98-100, 151
neurosis: infantile (Wolf-Man) focussed on the negative side of the Oedipus Complex 44; sense of inferiority 52; 'biological factor' – a major part in causation 53; and repression 90; loss of reality 146, 148

'Nightingale, The', Hans Christian Andersen 66-8, 76
nomos, meanings of 9
Norbert, case given by the authoress illustrating constructions 104-8
nouns, function of 9

O

object relationship 28
obsessional neurosis, pathology of 8-9, 146
Oedipus: ill-defined link with the sexual impulse 35; dissolution of 37, 46, 52-3, 86-7; Little Hans' wishes 40, 42, 44, 49; negative (inverted) 'The Wolf-Man' 44-5, 48, 50-1; phylogenetically inherited schemata 50-1; avoidance of, in perversion 82, 151; satisfied in a sadistic way (J. Glover) 85
Oedipus Complex 2, 26-9; motive in setting up the Superego 56-7
120 Days . . . , The . . ., Marquis de Sade 3, 6, 8, 10

P

'paranoiac core', universal 45
passivity, fear of 45
penis = child = faeces, equation taken literally 75, 91, 141
'perverse core', universal 1, 56
perversion *see also* anality, idealization: confusion between sexes and generations, peculiar to 1-2; and the anal-sadistic universe 2-6; equivalent of Devil religion 9; represents a reconstitution of Chaos 11; three Luciferian characters 13-23; pregenitality equal or superior to genitality 29; comparisons with neurosis 29, 34, 38, 40; rejection of 'dilatory time' 34; 'prototype' of those preferring falsehood 66; penis = child = faeces 75, 91, 141; projection of Ego Ideal onto archaic pregenital images 70; aim of 78; and delinquency 81-2; disavowal of father's genital penis 81-2; complicated ritual described by J. Glover 84-5; versus sublimation 89-90; inclines to the world of art 90; anal sexuality equal or superior to genital sexuality 91; 'geese usually regarded as swans' (E. Glover) 94; environment represents the idealized Ego with a flattering reflection 96; disavowal of the primal scene 112; lack of guilt 112; defence against psychosis 129; elements of the pervert's 'ingenious solution' 151; superiority of the anal over the genital world 151; proposed schema of the state of psychic apparatus 159
phallic monism: reconsideration of theory 35, 46, 52, 61; Little Hans 37, 40; Lacan's theory 85
phallus, anal *see* anal phallus, father's penis
phylogenesis, inherited schemata 50-1

Picture of Dorian Gray, The, O. Wilde 98, 100
'Planet of the Apes' 12, 128
plasticity of living form, Doctor Moreau 19
play, child's 28-9, 48;
play, children's anal games (Rrose Sélavy) 134
pleasure principle 22, 28, 52; alive in all of us 130
pregenitality: desires and satisfactions 2; in perversion 29; idealized by mother (K. Abraham's case) 78; conflicts resolved by fetishism 83; idealized by the pervert 91
primal horde: scientific myth of 50; group as a revival of 58
primal scene: differentiation between neuroses and perversion 43; the Wolf-Man 44; analogy with the instinctive knowledge of animals 51; Abraham's case 78-9; mimed as a pregenital relationship 87; disavowal in perversion 112, 154; reduced to a pregenital activity (Romain) 127
proselytism, need of groups 64
psychoanalysis: relationship between analysand and analyst 109-19; represented as the birth of a child 116; lay analysts 120; use in understanding 'the riddles of the world' 120; a clinical account – Rrose Sélavy 131-45
psychosis: Ego's detachment from reality 109-11; loss of reality 146-8
puberty, genital primacy 35

R

reality: bedrock of 2; destruction of 3, 126; new kinds of 11-12, 15, 22; Caligula's attitudes 14, 17; violation of, Hans Bellmer's doll 22; principle 22, 24-5, 28; recognition of obstacles and temporality 34; ability to think differences 120; equated with father 121, 126; loss of in perversion compared with neurosis and psychosis 146-8; testing is the refinding of something once perceived 151; recognition of 157-9
regression: to anal-sadism 2-6, 156-7; in groups 60, 63; in Romain 121-8; Rrose Sélavy 141-2
religion, substitute for a longing for the father (Freud) 69
repression: of homosexual attitude (Wolf-Man) 46; forgotten material recovered by analysis 101-3; 'return of the repressed' (Rrose Sélavy) 132; development of Freud's ideas 149; organic, giving up of erotogenic zones 152; partial in perversion 153-4; proposed schema of repressed ideas 159
resistance by the transference 111-12
rhinoceroses (Ionesco, E.) nearly anybody may become a member of an extremist organisation 56, 64
Romain, illustrative case (authoress) 121-7
Rrose Sélavy, account of her analysis 131-45

S

sacrilege 4
Sade, The Marquis de 1-6, 10; comparison with mysticism of a necrophile ('The Corpse Incinerator') 55; anal instincts and objects form the object of a cult 92; became more or less paranoid 156
sadism *see also* anality 2-6, 11-12, 17-18, 125-6
sado-masochistic phantasies (Little Hans) 39
Sandler, J. 'On the Concept of Superego' (1960) 62
scoptophilia (J. Glover's case) 84-5
seduction: by mother 28-9; of Wolf-Man by sister 47-8, 51
seething a kid in his mother's milk 6-7
sexes and generations, confusion between 2-3
sexual intercourse (Sade, Marquis de) 2-3
'student revolution' (1968 – 'All of us will go to heaven') 61-2
sublimation versus perversion 89-90, 93-4
Suetonius, I., Caligula 13-15
suggestion in psychoanalysis 101-4
Superego: discredited in case of Jean-Jacques 34; masochistic mechanism of softening it 39; heir of the Oedipus Complex and the castration complex 56; comparisons with the Ego Ideal 56-7; identical with the Ego Ideal (Freud) 57, 69; dissolution with union of the Ego with the Ego Ideal 58, 60-2; rare capacity to resist group pressure 64-5; emergence of 103-4; Rrose Sélavy's 135

T

Talleyrand, 'Shit in a silk stocking' (Napoleon) 71
thinking: seeing differences equated with reality 120-1; perverse way of 120-30
time lag in sexual development 2, 53-4, 61, 86
transference: role of the relationship 101-3; influence of constructions 106-8; resistance by 111-12; as used by Rrose Sélavy 134-5
'true': differentiated from 'false' 66; identified with the living (H. C. Andersen) 68
truth: *see also* reality; or falsehood 24-5; in psychoanalysis 101-2, 108

U

uniformity of individuals in groups 58-60
universe: anal-sadistic 2-6, 17-18; creation anew 13, 157
upheavals, social and political 1-2

V

vagina: Little Hans' fantasies 40-3; Wolf-Man's knowledge of 44-5, 50; 'ignorance of' and 'innate knowledge' 52

W

Wells, H. G., 'The Island of Doctor Moreau' 18-20

Wilde, O. *Stories* (1888) 95, 97
wolf, fear of being devoured by one (Russian Wolf-Man) 45-6
Wolf-Man 44-54; the dream itself a trauma 103; disavowal referred to the castration complex 147